SOUL'S LONGING SERIES

The DESIRE

SATISFYING THE HEART

JAMES M. HOUSTON

Victor®

The Bible Teacher's Teacher

COOK COMMUNICATIONS MINISTRIES
Colorado Springs, Colorado • Paris, Ontario
KINGSWAY COMMUNICATIONS LTD
Eastbourne, England

Victor® is an imprint of
Cook Communications Ministries, Colorado Springs, CO 80918
Cook Communications, Paris, Ontario
Kingsway Communications, Eastbourne, England

THE SOUL'S LONGING: THE DESIRE
© 1990, 1996, 2007 by James Houston

This book was previously published by Regent College Publishing under the title
The Heart's Desire: Satisfying the Hunger of the Soul, ISBN 1-57383-209-X.

First Printing, 2007
Printed in (Country)
1 2 3 4 5 6 7 8 9 10 Printing/Year 11 10 09 08 07

ISBN 978-0-7814-4424-8

Dedicated to our grandchildren:

Jennifer,
Nicholas and Julian,
Allison and Stephen,
Jonathan and Natalie,
Amanda and Justin,

that in their generation they will express their desires
faithfully and truly before God.

CONTENTS

PREFACE

It has been said that we live not so much through our achievements as through our desires. The successes we achieve do not last, but we desire what is immortal. Sadly, in order to survive, most people have to concentrate on making a living and are unable to think about the heart's desires. Western affluence and a spoiled society seem to be the causes of this. Yet now in the West we do seem to have paused, and many have begun to question whether we are making the right choices for ourselves. Suddenly, many people are interested in "spirituality"; they want to experience something real, not just talk about "authenticity." Moreover, as change in our culture happens faster than ever before, we need to find a longer-term point of view. The faster we move, the more we need to be on the right road.

Desire is the throbbing pulse of human life. What we long for determines the scope of our experiences, the depth of our insights, the standards by which we judge, and the responsibility with which we choose our values. It matters a great deal whether we long for things that go beyond the material, that are transcendental.

In the former Soviet Union, the *glasnost* of the early 1990s opened up new opportunities and a new freedom for the human spirit. We in the West need to seize similar opportunities. Perhaps if we try to find out what our hearts truly desire, we will come to yearn for things that satisfy us better. This book is an invitation to reflect on those deepest and most fundamental desires.

I believe that human beings are not merely a useless passion—which was how Jean-Paul Sartre saw us—burning ourselves up as we struggle to find meaning in our isolation. Indeed, the struggles for political and sexual freedom in the course of the twentieth century have brought disappointing results. More and more people feel that we have come to the end of one age and are at the beginning of another. The change is as great as that from the Middle Ages to the modern world. We do not know what lies ahead, and the prospects are daunting.

For the past forty years I have been blessed with the opportunity of sharing the intimate feelings of many young people. My students have been my teachers, as I have learned from them the essential qualities of honesty, a desire for truth, and the possibilities of personal transformation. Their love and affection have made it possible for me to have great hope for the future.

My circle of friends in the "fellowship of the hazelnut" has also helped me with practical and spiritual support. I owe much to Mary Manson, who has been my research assistant and typed the manuscript. My friends at Lion Publishing have encouraged me all along and have made the final draft of the book more presentable. Finally, I am most deeply indebted to my dear wife, Rita, who made possible the gift of a loving family and grandchildren, and who has put up with my many months of taking time alone in my study to write this book.

Part One

Chasing the Wind—
The Distortion of
Desire Today

April is the cruelest month, breeding
Lilacs out of the dead land, mixing
Memory and desire.

—T. S. Eliot, *The Wasteland*[1]

1

THE SECRETS OF OUR EXISTENCE

I magine the countryside when winter turns to spring. The bleak picture made up of white, brown, and gray changes as the fresh green shoots poke through the earth and the buds open in delicate whorls of yellow. You long for the new season, its warmth and its abundance.

The surge of hope that marks the onset of spring reflects our deep inner longings. For too long, we have been living in the wintry environment of "modernity." Ever since the so-called Enlightenment of the eighteenth century, we have been taught to observe the material world around us, draw logical conclusions, and accept only what is "reasonable." This approach has brought about technological marvels, but has also cut us off from something vital.

Just as the spring eventually transforms the bleak Russian winters, so *glasnost* brought a social thaw to the peoples of Eastern Europe. They realized that Marxism never knew the human heart. The people who once shivered in its icy grip now enjoy a new quality of life.

In the West, too, there is a change in the air. While we have been grateful for our democratic political system, has that not also been abused? We cannot afford to be smug about democracy in the West—our way of life today is marked by greed, selfishness, and isolationism. Perhaps we need to have our own *glasnost*. People feel disillusioned with modernity, some calling themselves "postmodernists."

LIVING WITH COTTON CANDY

I still vividly remember spending six pleasant months in the southern United States where everyone was very "nice." After a spell on a campus in New York, where life is tough, aggressive, and hard-hitting, it came as a welcome surprise when every stranger greeted me with a smiling "how y'all"! But I soon discovered that it was cotton candy courtesy. To make cotton candy, you take a teaspoonful of pink sugar, put it into a revolving drum, then extract a sackful of cotton candy. It squashes to nothing in your hands, and leaves you with only a pink stain for your efforts.

When I recently tried this idea out on a southern "belle" now divorced and living very unhappily elsewhere, she told me how true this had been in her own family. Her parents were concerned only with appearances. They bought the things that "showed"—the smart colonial-style house (just like in the TV program *Dallas*), the new cars in the driveway, the periodic changes of furniture, and of course their daughter's appearance. "But," admitted Jane, "my folks never knew me, who I really was, how my heart ached, nor gave me the intimacy I longed to have. So I started romantic affairs far too young, had an abortion, and now in middle life my marriage has broken down, I live alone, and I am unable to trust any man. More than anything else I have become thoroughly disillusioned with all the

Hollywood style of living that I was brought up to believe in." All this goes to show that you can't put much trust in cotton candy.

In that southern university, where I taught for six months, a student had gone berserk shortly before, killing over thirty young people in a mad shooting spree. Yet never once did anyone refer to the incident while I was there. It was too ghastly to talk about in a "candy" community. Jane, however, had lived long enough away from home to see through the illusions of her upbringing. As she confessed, "I now have a more complete realization of how far removed I've been from any real happiness in my whole life. Only now have I been given that most precious gift of trust which I lost so long ago, and which I was certain I could never again give to anyone." She was sitting in on my classes in a series of lectures that became the core of this book. Her experience, and that of many others, made me determined to share these thoughts with a wider audience. I have become convinced that we need to grapple with life as a whole. There is no place for viewing life unrealistically as cotton-candy entertainment.

CONSUMERS AND COMMODITIES

It has become a cultural cliché of our time that we are a "consumer society." We in the West, a tenth of the world's population, actually consume more than two-thirds of the world's resources—consumers indeed! So many of us have grown up with the belief that more is better and that big is best. Now we are beginning to see that big corporations can also become big losers, that cutbacks may be the new order, and a culture of beer, brawn, and bed does not give a nation much economic uplift, still less any kind of a spiritual life.

A cartoon depicted a tramp on a city garden bench with the caption "What was your downfall? Wine, women, or a PhD?" Nowadays education and professional training are no longer guarantees for a successful career. For one therapist dealing with teenagers' suicides, it is all part of the Modern Fairy Tale:

> Amy, aged 15, had always got straight As in school, and her parents were extremely upset when she got a B on her report card. "If I fail in what I do," she told her parents, "I fail in what I am."[2]

The message was part of Amy's suicide note. Because Amy never experienced love without any strings or conditions attached, she never found out who she really was. Part of the American Fairy Tale is the myth that what we produce is more important than who we are—our personal uniqueness. It is closely bound up with that other myth, that more possessions mean more happiness.

This all implies that people do not matter in themselves—as unique individuals who can give and receive love. The meaning of life is said to lie in commerce and manufacture, not in the hearts and souls of persons. Reverence for people and their unique qualities has been destroyed by the marketplace and the advertising world, and friendship, joy, love, intimacy, and loyalty have become mere commodities, bought and sold in the currency of prestigious cars, expensive perfumes, status symbols, and sports tickets. Thus marketing and consuming interfere with every area of our private and public lives, every level of conscious behavior, until we are tempted to view ourselves and other people as commodities.

Sex without love leads to a highly developed exploitation of the bodies of women and men alike. A clinical, voyeuristic approach to sex leaves little place for trust and faithfulness—the full relationship of one human being with another.

In the job market many people are finding that their talents and labor have become counters in the games played by business organizations. So we talk of our "marketability" or of our "production value," not of our intrinsic worth as persons. Human life is reduced to a mere object.

No wonder, then, that there is such a deluge of pornography, physical violence, and rape; no wonder that we are all under stress from the domination, manipulation, retaliation, demands, and contempt that are so common in our dehumanized society. The drug culture is only one aspect of the emotional addictions that confront us all.

THE SOUL'S REACTION

Like so many leaders of this "productive" way of life, the father of the poet Emily Dickinson was not ashamed to defend it:

> Let us prepare for a life of rational happiness. I do not expect, neither do I deserve a life of pleasure as some call it—I anticipate pleasure from engaging with my whole soul in business.[3]

But his daughter's reaction was quite different. She opened doors that led far beyond her lyrical poetry, to express her own soul's great yearning:

> Take all away from me, but leave me Ecstasy,
> And I am richer then than all my Fellow Men
> Ill it becometh me to dwell so wealthily
> When at my very Door
> Are those possessing more,
> In abject poverty.[4]

This parodied her father's religious-economic language. As a merchant, he checked the ledger of human emotions and attempted to fix a price on the soul's desire. Emily Dickinson, however, preferred freedom of desire, however high the cost, to poverty of soul.

There has long been conflict between those who value the soul and others who consider human beings as "things" or commodities, or see people as mere animals, clever perhaps, but doomed to die like the other animals.

One of the great achievements of the Greeks was to honor the human soul because it belonged to more than a material reality, to see the soul as immortal, and to hold a high view of human nature and dignity. The soul was also described as the core of a person.

In Hebrew thought, the root meaning of the word for "soul," *nephesh,* refers to breath and the ability to breathe.[5] It was associated with the throat, hunger, thirst, and the need to draw breath in order to keep alive. The word was then extended to refer metaphorically to other desires and expressions of the will. The soul became the seat of the emotions and the whole of the human personality, even the spiritual nature, which is the source both of our eternal longings and the restlessness of the human heart.

A feeling of restlessness is one of the main ways in which desire can dominate our lives. Even if we choose to hide our desires, they may still influence our personalities very deeply. We are therefore cheating ourselves if we do not take our souls, the source of our deepest desires, seriously. This is what lies behind Jesus' challenge: "What shall it profit a man if he gain the whole world and lose his own soul?" (Matt. 16:26).

A further point is that losing a sense of transcendence and mystery has made our lives trivial. T. S. Eliot talks about "stirring out our lives with coffee spoons" and refers to "our only monument, lost golf balls." However, the same poet says: "Humankind cannot bear very much reality."

That is why society so often tries to evade or distort the desires of the heart. Much unhappiness and disappointment comes from our failure to tell the difference between truth and the illusion which avoids facing up to reality. Superficial and trivial ways of living deny our human dignity and undermine integrity and truthfulness.

At one time moral life depended on the church. Now, in our secular society, artists, playwrights, philosophers, and poets are our guides. This is what Hegel meant by the "secularization of spirituality." The playwright Henrik Ibsen, for example, suggests that "respectable" modes of behavior are often based on sham and pretense. In his play *The Wild Duck,* the central character is a weak deceiver who knows that he is dependent on illusions if he is to get through life at all. Instead of examining the deepest desires of his heart, he clings to a small, cozy way of life, buttressed by self-esteem and petty pride and content with his illusions. This self-deception inevitably leads to tragedy.[6]

THE HEART AS THE REAL SELF

We protect ourselves from too much reality, but we also advise other people not to expose their hearts too much. When I was a student at Oxford, I lived with a Russian don who was always asking searching questions. When people heard about it they would say, "Oh, if you survive his interrogations, you must have an opaque soul," meaning that I shouldn't give too much away.

We often say things like: "But I didn't have the heart to tell him or her such-and-such." In other words, the heart is involved as well as the soul. Like the soul, the heart expresses the core of our personality. Yet more than the soul, the heart is used to express the real self, that core of human love and affection, where we must be honest with ourselves about our intimate relationships and desires. Intuitive reasoning comes from the heart, as in Pascal's famous statement: "The heart has its reasons that reason knows not of." In other words, beyond logic and rational deduction, we must also take account of the "sixth sense" of intuition. Pascal condemned the cold logic of his contemporary Descartes as only fit for a "geometric man," because spiritual realities cannot be described by mathematical theorems. As we might say today, it was all "head knowledge" involving none of the heart's experience.

Throughout the history of philosophy, the realm of human feelings, centered on the heart, has been more or less mistrusted. This imbalance can be traced back to Plato, who considered the heart less important than the mind. Ever since then, we have tended to look down on the emotions as "messy" or "confusing," not to be taken too seriously by intelligent people. It is precisely this separation of emotions and thought that has played down the importance of the heart in our daily lives. For it is the heart that unites mind, will, and emotion in an integrated way of living, allowing us to think, desire, and feel as a whole person. Without this unity we will try to seek knowledge without emotion, or emphasize emotions without reflective thought. Both attitudes give a false picture of reality. As this book will show, our emotions need to be complemented by thought. Rationalism that is unfeeling and sentimentalism that is unreflective both distort the truth.[7]

This has been my personal experience throughout my career. I have spent all my working life listening to others, first as a teacher in secular education for twenty-three years, and then as a teacher-counselor in theology for the last twenty-two. Listening to the desires of people's hearts is a more intimate form of education than simply giving lectures, and this book is based on my reflections on these inner revelations. Out of this experience has come my conviction that we cheat ourselves if we are either too rational or too emotional. In neither case can we get close to one another in real friendship or develop an authentic faith in God.

Society expects us to be self-sufficient, to manage on our own, and to solve our own problems in silence, if not in style. We are under pressure to make sure we have the energy and the talent to provide for our material needs, and for our lifestyle to impress those around us. It is not decent to talk about inner aches and pains, and what we propose to do about them—far less the despair that modern life can bring.

This book seeks to explore the nature of the human heart. It uncovers the ruses that we use to deceive ourselves. And it shows that once we accept that God created us to seek him, that our real longings are for things eternal, we can find the path to true fulfillment. It is a process that is rather like having quarreled with a good friend or family member; when we try to make peace, we open up and talk about the problem, making ourselves vulnerable in the process. When it is all over—risky as it seemed—the way is open for renewed understanding and acceptance. Even more wonderful, we dare to build on this new start and dream fresh dreams of our future relationship. That is what I invite you to do with me: to rediscover your heart, to expose false desires that are really addictions and idols, and to find out how to set things right. Becoming "real" is a great relief and an exciting prospect, for we can look forward to a different way of living, an alternative to the unreality that suffocates us. Perhaps, then, we have become sick of the world's cotton candy unreality, and are ready for a more substantial spiritual life.

REDISCOVERING THE HEART

> Above all else, guard your heart
> For it is the wellspring of life.[8]

In his wise advice the writer of Proverbs recognizes that the heart is the core of a person's life. It is the center of those qualities that make us human, rather than animals relying on instinct. Forget the heart, exaggerate the bodily senses, and animals we become! But the human heart is the origin of each individual's personality.

The metaphor of "the heart," which occurs over 850 times in the Hebrew Bible, is a universal symbol which bears many layers of meaning in many languages.[9] Each year on Valentine's Day huge red hearts on cards and presents remind us that the heart is the symbol of love. It may have become linked to a rather vapid sentimentality. Nevertheless, people recognize that at the center of all our relationships lies something more than either intellect or emotion, where we relate to ourselves and to each other. No wonder then, that Christians have found that God speaks to our hearts. The Bible tells us how God had a heart for people before we ever had a heart for him, and he continually reaches out to restore our relationship with him.

Perhaps our culture has neglected the heart in favor of the mind because we tend to lump all our emotions together, whether they are caused by purely bodily feelings or the most profound experiences of love, joy, or contrition. The variety of human emotion is so great that it is disastrous to lump everything together under the heading of "being emotional." The result is that being "heartless" can mean all kinds of things.

People can be reckless, irresponsible, and even lecherous like the character Tom Jones in Fielding's novel, yet they may have a heart that we can respond to. But the heartlessness of Shakespeare's Richard III or a Don Giovanni, like Cain before them, is very different. Such characters are efficient but brutal, driven by pride and the ambition to get their own way. The heartlessness where emotions wither and die because of pride and selfishness is a terrible and deadly disease of the soul. Another kind of heartlessness is the result of being embittered and cynical. Exerting tyranny, either on an emotional level or intellectually, can also stifle the openness of heart we need to have. Or our emotions may be defective and our lives unfeeling. The state of the heart is the test of all these fatal conditions.

In clearing up confusion about the heart and the part emotions play in our lives, we need also to recognize the role of the will. It was defined in Jewish thought as the driving force of the personality, which desires, accepts, and agrees; the will of God is paramount in the Old Testament. The Greek understanding of the will turned it into the drive to live, often regardless of the interests of others or, indeed, of our own well-being. The will can be evil, and there are illegitimate desires, for example the irresponsible use of our sexuality, that are not part of wise living. We must reflect on our desires if they are not to be damaging to ourselves and others; lust is a selfish passion. It is God's will that we change our selfish desires into other, more fruitful and harmonious ways of living, through repentance and a change of heart. While the will of human beings is a force to be reckoned with, it needs control and reflection to be used for good, in harmony with the will of God. So the sage observes:

> In his heart a man plans his course,
> but the LORD determines his steps.[10]

The heart, the real self, is not to be identified with intellect, emotion, or will. Instead, all three are held in balance. To be "at home in the heart" is to be truthful to one's self, to be sensitive to the promptings of conscience, and to be in tune with one's essential nature. Thus the powers of body, emotions, mind, and will are all united in the heart. Clearly, it also focuses on the innermost part of the human personality, the meeting place between people and God.

LEARNING BY HEART

There is something rather satisfying about knowing things so well that you can call them to mind instantly. Children quickly learn multiplication tables; for the rest of their lives they know with complete confidence that seven times seven makes forty-nine and twelve twelves make a hundred and forty-four. Through the tedium of rote learning that information becomes part of us: we know it by heart.

In medieval Christian thought, the idea of learning by heart was something that went far deeper than mathematical tables. It meant the reorientation of one's life by what Benedict called *hágá*, bringing the thoughts of the mind into the heart, so that one's whole person stood in the presence of God. A Russian monk of the nineteenth century, Theophan the Recluse, gives weight to a similar idea:

> The principal thing is to stand before God with the intellect in the heart, and to go on standing before him unceasingly day and night, until the end of life.[11]

Standing before God—not necessarily to ask for things or even to speak in words—means entering into a personal relationship with him, "face to face" as it were. To "stand in the heart," then, is a relationship that springs from the deep center of our personality, where we can be directly in God's presence and open to divine love. The distinction between intellect, emotions, and will is no longer needed. What is sought is an attitude of continual prayer, making our communion with God not just an occasional exercise, but a quality of our whole being.

However, following the teaching of Augustine of Hippo, medieval Christians did not speak so much of intellect, emotion, and will, but instead of intellect, emotion, and "memory."

The idea of "memory" has lost its vitality in our culture. This is not the loss of memory some people experience in old age, or the tendency to absentmindedness that is common enough at any age. Rather, it is a triple loss: a loss of the sense of the past; a loss of symbolism; and a loss of humility. "Memory is necessary for all the operations of Reason," wrote Pascal.[12]

We need a sense of the past in order to appreciate not only our cultural heritage, but also our cultural continuity. The whole succession of humanity may be considered as one and the same person who continues to exist and learn.

Each generation learns anew in the light of what past generations have left them. Henry Ford, innovator in a brash technological age, was optimistic about the possibilities for technical progress and proclaimed proudly that "history is bunk." The mass culture that followed happily ignored history. But now that people are beginning to admit that technology has not fulfilled all our longings, we can see that Ford was mistaken.

Christians should be particularly wary of any dismissal of the past, because it is God's nature to reveal himself in historic acts.[13] We learn from the Old Testament writings that this personal God, Yahweh, frequently reminded the forgetful Israelites that he was the God of the founders of their nation—Abraham, Isaac, and Jacob. It was he who enabled Moses to lead them out of slavery in Egypt. In the New Testament we learn that it is the work of Jesus Christ "in history" that is vital to the message of Christianity.

"History is a pattern of timeless moments." In this pattern of our experience, God reveals himself in the course of human affairs. This perspective upon reality is, of course, contradicted by another long-prevailing worldview that the cosmos itself is the only "reality," that history and life itself are not real but only "appearances," part of the dream of the cosmos. But to live in the presence of God, and to see history as evidence of his presence, is to restore the gift of memory.

Nowadays, however, we have tended to lose our memories of God's dealings in the past. Our insight has become so restricted to the secular world that we run into the danger of becoming culturally cut off from the flow of history. The attendant risk is that we are dying as persons, with no feeling for the past and its experiences of the presence of God. The heritage of spiritual leaders such as Augustine, Bernard of Clairvaux, Francis of Assisi, Teresa of Avila, John of the Cross, John Calvin, and many others has been greatly undervalued. We have also forgotten the contributions of great artists in their worship of God—Bach, Beethoven, and Mozart, Albrecht Dürer, and Rubens. But "learning by heart" implies the enriching of contemporary life through an association with the great minds and hearts of the past. By this process, minds and hearts speak to each other. This, indeed, is an aspect of what Christians call the "communion of saints."

For Augustine, the memory was also the storehouse of personal experiences of God, such as those that flow out of his autobiographical *Confessions*. So he asked of God:

> Where shall I find Thee? If I find Thee not without memory, then am I unmindful of Thee? And how shall I find Thee, if I do not remember Thee?[14]

In other words, how can I know what I am looking for, unless memory of the past helps me, unless I have in some way already known the object of my search? Augustine then asks how the memory of God's love and the experience of following him is retained within our hearts. Is it like memorizing mathematical tables? Is it like the way someone giving a speech learns his lines? None of these analogies are suitable. Can it then be similar to our remembrance of joy? Augustine finds this more encouraging. For we can remember joy even when we are sad. In the same way, having once experienced God's love, we always know it, even when we are in great distress. Memory is a rich storehouse of the heart that offers many other analogies of our relationship with God.

The second aspect of "learning by heart" is learning to respond to symbols, both visual images and ideas which point toward what is unseen and beyond our knowledge. The Greek word *symballein*, from which our word is derived, means "to bring together" or "to come together." A symbol is like a bridge linking two sides of a chasm, as it brings together two otherwise separate ideas. But like the way we look at history, our interpretation of symbols is determined by our worldview. The pagan world interpreted the world and its influence on human beings in terms of many gods, so there were rain gods, gods of war, and so on. Modern science uses signs to correspond to physical matter. In such cases the language of signs is informative, perhaps persuasive, but it is scarcely spiritual, for symbols, which allow for more than one level of meaning, are richer than signs. But if our symbols reflect on a transcendent God, beyond the material world, then they become the language of spiritual life. And if such religious symbols become cut off by disbelief or by careless usage from the reality they are intended to express, then we have what T. S. Eliot has called "broken images."

Consider the symbol we have centered upon in this chapter, the symbol of the heart. I have deliberately called it a symbol rather than a concept or a sign, because it expresses the wholeness of our life, both material and transcendental, and as such is irreplaceable. When someone has shared his or her heart, we have been told a crucial secret of that person's existence. It is also the point where that person can be in communication with God. Merely to speak of the physiological heart, or indeed to describe it as "muscle," has no such symbolic status. Rather, the "heart" is the source of the secrets of our existence. So Brentano prayed:

> Lord, have mercy on me,
>
> that my heart may blossom anew.

And Rilke admitted,

> Uncountable existence flows out of my own heart.[15]

As long as human beings have hearts, neither symbol can mean as much. The heart is the source of all the attitudes that go to make up a person.

If we trust and love God, then we show by symbolically acclaiming him as "Lord" that adoration is the appropriate response to his divine person. By his very nature he is worthy of our worship and service. In the ways in which he reveals his nature to us we can also use the symbols of "the Good Shepherd," "Teacher," "Master," or more metaphorically, "the Way," "the Truth," "the Life." We see him as "the suffering Savior," "the Victor," "the Resurrection," "the true and faithful Witness." Each of these symbols draws from us a particular response to our Lord. They are living realities, mysteries experienced by our soul.

The quality of our existence is also judged by our symbols, for if our soul is dead, then our symbols lose their meaning. What can symbols of immortality mean to those who have no faith beyond the here and now? Without immediacy and intimacy with God, what can the symbols of "the water of life," "bread and wine," "the table of the Lord" convey? Learning by heart means then that we must live lives that make sense of the symbols we use to describe our relationship with God. Otherwise they soon become "head knowledge" instead of "heart knowledge" and wilt away into irrelevance and mere custom.

How different is this richness from the poverty of today's secular signs! They are largely functional: stop signs, traffic lights, advertising billboards, and notices of one-way streets. In contrast, if you go into any of the ancient cathedrals of France, you will find, as Victor Hugo observed, that "in the Middle Ages men had no great thought that they did not write down in stone."[16] The cathedral was the people's book, before ever the printing press was invented. Some cathedrals selected certain themes, as Laon is the cathedral of learning, Amiens of the prophets, or Notre Dame de Paris of the Virgin Mary. But Chartres is the cathedral of God's love for the world, shown in the parables and ministry of Jesus. Conviction and faith pervade the cathedral, itself "like a mighty ship on its long voyage through the history of the church."[17] Its symbols make sense of the world and history.

Within the life of the medieval cathedral all human arts and skills were combined, in speech, music, and the living drama of the liturgy and sacraments, to weld together a community of faith and love, drawing its hope from the future fulfillment of present symbols. It seems nostalgic today to speak of living such a richly symbolic life, for we have made faith so much more a matter of "head knowledge." That is why we must learn to open our hearts again to more inarticulate desires.

The third aspect of "learning by heart" is humility. Whereas the love that most profoundly satisfies the heart is in fact a *divine* virtue, given us by God himself, humility is a *human* virtue, for it is our attitude toward God's love. So humility means being more open to God's transcendence, as a child is, in innocent trust.

All the great saints have seen humility as a precondition of genuine life, that is, life from the heart. Humility is essentially being open to other people and, above all, open to God's ways and thoughts. Its opposite is pride, which blinds and falsifies us, creating that other dread foe of the spiritual life, lust, whose desires are dictated by pride and self-interest. The humble respond instead to spiritual values, and seek to please God. They recognize their creaturely status by rejecting any claim to exert power over others.

THE DESIRE

Humor has a lot to do with humility, in that it shows up the incongruities of human life. Nothing is more absurd than humanity trying to play at being God. Perhaps that is why there are gargoyles on the cathedral roof, as well as at the carved ends of the pews, to remind worshippers that human pride, and even taking ourselves too seriously, is really comical. As Malcolm Muggeridge once observed, it is significant that modern high-rise office blocks don't have gargoyles. Compared with the court jesters and other evidence of comedy in medieval life, modernity takes itself very seriously!

"Learning by heart" is therefore being "poor in spirit"—not dispirited by our failings, but humbly realistic about ourselves. It is acknowledging that all our energies should be directed to God, as Catherine of Siena expressed it:

> That Thou shalt be, and that I shall not!

It is summed up in the attitude of Pascal, that we should not fabricate our own intellectual gods, but walk with the living God, giving our love

> Not to the god of the philosophers, but to the God of
> Abraham, Isaac and Jacob![18]

The humble delight in God, praise him for his goodness, and live lives of worship that stand in awe of his divine character. They acknowledge their indebtedness and dependence upon God, saying with the psalmist:

> Know that the LORD is God.
>> It is he who made us, and we are his;
>> we are his people, the sheep of his pasture.
> Enter his gates with thanksgiving
>> and his courts with praise;
>> give thanks to him and praise his name.
> For the LORD is good and his love endures forever;
>> his faithfulness continues through all generations.[19]

Yet this priority and supremacy given to God in our lives actually upholds human dignity, as we are made in God's image and likeness. Humble godliness is moral realism and expresses the true human condition.

EDUCATING THE HEART

I have now reached the proverbial three score years and ten. I can look back upon my life and see the tricks we play upon ourselves, suppressing bad news, repressing pain, and doing everything we can to keep ourselves from being vulnerable. I have observed the different ways in which people try to satisfy their deeper desires. When the wrong means are used, the results can be disastrous, with abuses and excesses of every kind that gradually destroy the inner person.

Indeed, it is my belief that we cannot trust ourselves to infinite desires without that faithful, transforming relationship of divine love and friendship with God. The desire that really gives life is to know God. This desire is never satisfied, for it is one that grows with its fulfillment; and our relationship with God changes and leads to a constant deepening of our desires.

This book has been written in an attempt to explore that life-giving, vital desire God gives each of us. As it does so, it encompasses each of the three aspects of learning by heart: seeing God within a historical perspective; living in touch with symbols; and walking in humility. In the first part of the book, in chapters two to six, we shall trace the consequences of misplaced desires—idolatry, addiction, romantic love, and rationalism—and will see how the lure of despair leads to the death of desire.

The second part of the book begins with the awareness of Jesus as the true fulfiller of the heart's desires. His coming opens us to the possibility of desires that really do lead to a full life. In following chapters, great symbols of the Christian life are explored, which express our deepest longings as human beings.

There is the desire to be a witness to the truth, felt strongly by the martyrs of the early church. There is the motif of the desert as the place of freedom from our addictive past, used by the Desert Fathers of the fourth century onwards. The desire for divine love shown by the symbol of the garden of love was an important motif of the High Middle Ages. The symbol of the pilgrim is also fundamental to the desire for life beyond the material world, never more so than toward the end of the Middle Ages. Perhaps the symbol of the child is the most distinctively Christian symbol, expressing a basic relationship of trust between God and his people. It is also a modern symbol. The wounds of childhood can have profound effects upon our well-being in later life.

The first task, then, is to discern the false desires of the heart and free us from them, while at the same time enflaming our true desires, so that we long instead for the authentic relationship with God which alone can fulfill our lives.

> Desire indeed is the desire to know, for we are known,
> and into this we grow.
> —Sebastian Moore[20]

*Do we not all naturally incline to believe
in that which satisfies our desires?*

—Miguel de Unamuno

2

OUR DESIRE
FOR GOD

H ow did God make the world?" "Where does God live?"
"Why can't I see him?" All these questions that a child
asks quite naturally are frustrating for an adult because they are
unanswerable. But a child has the ability, which we must relearn,
to live with unanswered questions. Whether we believe in him or
not, God still lies within the boundaries of our lives. We may know
no more of him than that: that he lies at the edge of things unex-
plored. For that reason God quite naturally arises as a question.

In many religions "God" takes the form of "the Beginning"
or "the Beyond": clearly God has to do with vital matters of life
and death. But God has to do also with values, what is worth-
while, what is meaningful, what is good, what is lovable. So
when we are sitting by the bedside of a desperately sick child
through the night or walking by the seashore or looking into the
intricate beauty of a small flower, our hearts are moved to ask
unanswerable questions about God.

For philosophers there are two central questions: "Why is there something and not nothing?" and "Why do things have to be as they are and not different?" One answer was provided by the eighteenth-century German philosopher Leibniz: "The ultimate reason to things is called God."

Primitive Gods

The oldest religions seem to have been polytheistic. One criticism of early tribal polytheism is that it trivializes people and God alike, because instead of looking toward the Absolute, the human eye is deflected toward earthly, finite things, which are raised to the stature of gods. These are the idols that the psalmist derided, saying:

> Their idols are silver and gold, made by the hands of men. They have mouths, but cannot speak, eyes, but they cannot see; they have ears, but cannot hear, noses, but they cannot smell; they have hands, but cannot feel, feet, but they cannot walk; nor can they utter a sound with their throats. Those who make them will be like them, and so will all who trust in them.[1]

Such idolatry degrades both worshippers and their objects of worship. The result is that the natural human desire to look beyond earthly things withers away in futility and superstition. When rivalry between tribes generates rivalry between the tribal gods as well, warfare becomes legitimate and even desirable.

Another way of answering questions about God is pantheism—the worship of the universe as a whole. This has appeared attractive to people longing for a meaning beyond the material world. But pantheism depersonalizes human beings, as they merge into the great "it." They are mere drops in the world's great ocean, tiny specks in the vastness of the universe. And though they may seem to be submerged and absorbed in the impersonal Absolute, this is a cover for pride: Hidden humanity is now on a level with the gods.

Pantheism distorts the bond between Creator and creature. Human beings are robbed of their distinctive character as persons created in God's image for a relationship with him, and thus of their human dignity. Pantheism may reflect a transcendent desire, but its "absolute" is a sham in which the uniqueness and holiness of God is nowhere to be seen, and the apparently high position given to human beings is in fact their moral degradation. In this scheme of things there is no scope either for humility or for the search for ultimate values. People cannot be seen as moral agents capable of responding in love to their Creator and Lord.

There is also a political side to pantheism. This was to be seen in the quest for order and rule in the great ancient civilizations of Egypt, Babylon, China, and the Inca-Aztecs. Imperial rule was interpreted as bringing a divine-cosmic order to bear on human society. By this argument the empire was the only form of rule where people could live in harmony and truth with their gods. There was no place for political disorder, which would destroy the divine scheme of things. Tension, precariousness, and anxiety were characteristic of such faiths, since no political order is eternally stable. What is more, they could not cross national boundaries to become universal. As a Babylonian text puts it: "When kingship was lowered from heaven, kingship was in Eridu." Creation was seen as merely restoring order and rule to human affairs, not as making the whole world from nothing.

When political disorder did come, people became increasingly confused. The poem *Dispute of a Man Who Contemplates Suicide with His Soul* was written in Egypt in about 2000 BC. It tells of a man who is driven to despair by the disorders of his day and considers putting an end to a life that has become meaningless. But first he must struggle with temptation, for is his life not the gift of the gods, and not his to throw away? Then he ponders the fact that no one has returned from the dead, so who knows what it is like anyway? When neither conventional belief nor skepticism can comfort him, he is forced to meet his anguish head-on, and acknowledges that his suffering stems from a serious, realistic approach to life.

This is not unlike the predicament that many people face today: Should they accept without question an unthinking, uncaring society? Or become detached and cynical? Either way leads to alienation:

> To whom can I speak today? One's fellows are evil: The friends of today do not love.
>
> To whom can I speak today? Faces have disappeared: Every man has a downcast face toward his fellows.
>
> To whom can I speak today? There is no one contented of heart: The man with whom one went, no longer exists.[2]

In a society dominated by evil, the human self is lost.

GOD IN THE HISTORY OF ISRAEL

The biblical view of reality is very different. When the people of Israel experience God (Yahweh), they are living as slaves in Egypt. To leave Egypt is more than a political exodus; it is also an exodus from a pantheistic view of the world. The Israelite experience is set within the historical context of Moses' experience of God in the burning bush, in the wilderness of Sinai. Subsequent encounters with God affect individual lives as well as changing conditions for the whole nation. Because of the exodus, history can be interpreted as a relationship between humanity and God, based not on power, but on fellowship.

The story has been handed down through Jewish history in the form of an ancient memory:

> My father was a wandering Aramean, and he went down
> into Egypt with a few people and lived there and became
> a great nation, powerful and numerous. But the
> Egyptians mistreated us and made us suffer, putting us to
> hard labor. Then we cried out to the LORD, the God of
> our fathers, and the LORD heard our voice and saw our
> misery, toil and oppression. So the LORD brought us out
> of Egypt with a mighty hand and an outstretched arm,
> with great terror and with miraculous signs and won-
> ders. He brought us to this place and gave us this land, a
> land flowing with milk and honey; and now I bring the
> firstfruits of the soil that you, O LORD, have given me.[3]

This memory is continually renewed in worship, sacrifice, and liturgy. We should not confuse the story with the natural cycle of death and rebirth. It stems from personal experience. Thus the beginning of the history of Israel comes to us as a result of personal reflection on past events, not as a survival of pantheism.

Thereafter the history of God's personal dealings with people expands to include all humanity, rather than for those who follow a particular political ideology or for some privileged city or state. However, the significance of this emerges only gradually. In Psalm 136 this unfolding takes place in three stages. The psalm begins by describing God's nature of covenant love:

> Give thanks to the LORD, for he is good.
> > His love endures forever.
> Give thanks to the God of gods.
> > His love endures forever.
> Give thanks to the Lord of lords:
> > His love endures forever.
> To him who alone does great wonders,
> > His love endures forever.[4]

The drama of the Creator-Redeemer then follows in three acts: the creation of the world from nothing; the rescue of the slaves in Egypt—nobodies who became the people of God; and the gift of the Promised Land, through the conquest of Canaan. God continues his work of creation in history, and human existence is lived under the guidance of God.

Prophets like Hosea added the symbolism of "covenant" or *berith* to that of continuing creation. It expressed the faithfulness of a personal God: "His love endures forever." In the covenant God bound himself to his chosen people. But while covenants in the ancient world were political agreements, God's covenant with Israel involved people in a personal relationship with him, through their promise of loyalty and obedience. From then on the history of Israel was interpreted in terms of this intimate covenant relationship. "Good" and "bad" rulers in Israel were assessed by the covenant, and the fall of Jerusalem and the people's exile in Babylon in the sixth century BC were attributed to their failure to live out their covenant promises.

At about the time of the exile, prophets such as Ezekiel began to talk about a "new covenant." This renewed relationship between God and his people would depend on the eternal love and faithfulness of God himself. When the new covenant failed to materialize, later prophets such as Haggai, Zechariah, and Malachi reasoned that this delay was caused by the sins of the people. This caused a new development in Israelite faith, the gift of a dynamic hope based not so much upon the future as on the personal nature of God. It is sometimes known as "eschatology"—though it is a personal notion, not an abstract one.

Eschatology represented a shift in Hebrew thought from a purely historical interpretation of events to a new future perspective, with the promise of a universal Messiah who would bring in the kingdom of God. This was still a historical hope; it lay within the bounds of history; but it looked to an ultimate conclusion beyond history. The new covenant expressed above all an ethical hope, that humanity would be transformed. Thus the focus was no longer on the human viewpoint, but on the personal character of God who calls his people to fulfill his purposes.

This call to look at life from an eschatological point of view was not intended to stimulate curiosity and speculation about the future, but to arouse the individual's conscience, so that people would live in the present in relation to God—a way that is radically different from the standards of the secular world. It was the hope of the faithful and obedient few who survived the exile; the true servants of God.

These teachings were entrusted to the prophets' disciples (*limmudim*), who were said to be divinely "taught." Isaiah echoes this theme of being "taught" such divine obedience and trust in God when he says:

> The Sovereign LORD has given me an instructed tongue
> [i.e. taught], to know the word that sustains the weary.
> He wakens me morning by morning, wakens my ear to
> listen like one being taught. The Sovereign LORD has
> opened my ears.[5]

In turn, the promised Messiah, the symbolic Servant, was the one who would teach everyone to become the *limmud* of God (see Isa. 54:13). This teaching had already been described as the "sealing of instructions" to be treasured in the heart (Isa. 8:16). Indeed, the prophet Jeremiah anticipated that "a new heart" would be needed in order to fulfill the covenant relationship with God, while Jeremiah spoke of "a new heart and a new spirit." Yet, as Isaiah predicted, the people still failed to recognize the Servant-Messiah who was to suffer on their behalf:

> Who has believed our message and to whom has the arm
> of the LORD been revealed? He grew up before him like a
> tender shoot, and like a root out of dry ground. He had
> no beauty or majesty to attract us to him, nothing in his
> appearance that we should desire him. He was despised
> and rejected by men, a man of sorrows, and familiar
> with suffering. Like one from whom men hide their faces
> he was despised, and we esteemed him not.[6]

For the next five centuries it seemed that the prophet's message itself had been lost or "despised." But the hope of a Servant-Messiah still lingered on, as we know from the story of the Ethiopian eunuch described in the book of Acts, who asked Philip: "Tell me, of whom is the prophet speaking, of himself, or of someone else?" And Philip could tell him the good news about Jesus.

GOD IN THE CLASSICAL WORLD

Israel's exile in Babylon was followed in the ancient Near East by the rise and fall of the Assyrian and Persian empires. Then in the fourth century BC, within the lifetime of one man, Alexander the Great of Macedonia, a new concept of empire arose that devoured all human civilization from the Greek city-states in the west, through Palestine and Egypt, into eastern Asia and India. This was the idea of *oicumene,* literally "the inhabited world" or "cultural world," and referred to the many peoples of diverse ethnic and religious origins who were drawn into the expanding empire. This "empire," however, preferred individualism to pantheism. History now became pragmatic—rather than seeing God's influence in the past, people looked to draw lessons from historical events for the future—and philosophers had differing ideas on transcendence and God.

The new empire left its mark on Greek philosophy. The Greek states had never before been able to organize themselves into one large power, so now their thinkers were given a different perspective on the changes of life within this new political system. As they reflected on life and death, they realized that the act of thinking is a whole world in itself. So the soul or *psyche* became all-important as the interface between the individual and the world, as did the mind or *nous* which became the conscious awareness of perceiving reality. Our word "philosophy" comes from the Greek word for the love of wisdom.[7]

New "gods" were introduced into human consciousness—

different systems of philosophy competing to explain the world. Much later, the philosopher Bacon called them "idols of the theater." "For," he said, "we regard all the systems of philosophy hitherto received, as imagined, as so many plays brought out and performed, creating fictitious and theatrical worlds."[8] It is a perceptive comment; the Greeks saw that people still needed to have the truth communicated to them by images. Socrates here refers to the myth of Prometheus, who stole fire from the gods to benefit humanity:

> There is a gift of the gods to men, so at least it appears to me. From their abode they let it be brought down by someone like Prometheus, together with a fire exceeding bright. The men of old, who were better than we are, dwelt nearer the gods, and passed on this gift in the saying: That all things that are ever said to exist have their being from One and Many and conjoin themselves Limited and Unlimited.

The "Unlimited," or *apeiron,* for Socrates meant unending creation that released things into being and then received them back when they perished. In this scheme of things human beings are placed between the two realities of the Limited (the rest of the world) and the Unlimited. So the philosopher who is in search of truth is somewhere between knowledge and ignorance. Later Aristotle affirmed that human consciousness is the area of reality where the divine intellect moves human intellects to engage in the search for our deepest motivations. Whereas the Hebrews had focused on the personal nature of the heart, the abstract nature of the human *mind* was now preeminent. Aristotle also recognized that people are motivated by restlessness, confusion, and ignorance to search for knowledge. Yet in spite of his philosophical achievements, toward the end of his life he wrote this:

> The more I am by myself, the less I am, and also, the more I have come to love myths.

That is to say, the conclusions drawn by an isolated thinker need to be supported by the myths and archetypes of tradition. When Alexander's death brought Macedonian expansion to a halt, the Roman empire expanded eastward to fill the power vacuum. But no pantheistic worldview emerged, and once more we read of the importance of myth. According to Polybius, the most important trait of the Roman commonwealth was the *deisidaimonia,* or religious superstition of the common people. On a more sophisticated level, though, he also recognized that religious superstitions and idols had already been superseded by the gods of the intellect—concepts and principles. Polybius expresses it very loftily:

> If one could form a polity of wise men, this course
> would not be necessary; but since every multitude is
> unstable, full of lawless desire, unreasoned passion, and
> violent anger, the many must be reined in by invisible
> terrors and such like pageantry.[9]

Thus the popular beliefs in gods, the terrors of the underworld, and the mystery religions were seen pragmatically; *pietas,* or popular religion, would hold the empire together.

THE PULL OF NATURE

Perhaps the most popular and persistent god we accept today without really thinking about it is "Mother Nature." As C. S. Lewis observed, perhaps of all the gods of the pantheon of the Western mind, "Nature" has been the hardest to get rid of,[10] although as early as the seventeenth century the scientist Robert Boyle tried hard to discredit the idea. In Greek the word for nature was *physis* (our word physics comes from it), meaning a "coming to be." The Latin word *natura* also had a biological connotation of being born. It was in the Renaissance that the notion of "nature" as the sum total of all things came to the fore. Nature was personified as proud, mighty, and glorious, lending a deeply emotional quality to reality.

"Nature" in this sense includes ethical values, as when we say, "But it is natural" to do so and so, as opposed to what is unnatural, abnormal, or even unhealthy. The rationalism of the Enlightenment and the early romanticism of the eighteenth-century philosopher Rousseau both referred to "natural man" as reasonable, honest, and altogether admirable. "Nature" and the "natural" express something ultimate that cannot be argued against. With a "natural cause" there is no further inquiry to be made. Nature has come to mean all that is immediately evident and indisputable.

For many people, Nature with a capital "N" has taken on a divine character. This was present to some degree in classical thought, which saw the uncivilized barbarians as living a "natural" life and thus being in tune with the gods of Greek mythology. It is not surprising, then, that in the eighteenth century Nature took on a religious association. This was already true of the thought of Giordano Bruno, and he was followed by Spinoza, Goethe, Holderlin, and Schelling in the Enlightenment and after. The "natural" came to be identified with "holy" and, indeed, with God in the Romantic movement.

The alternative to this point of view was positivism, which is concerned only with the observable existence of things and rejects any form of transcendence. But here too, human beings as part of objective reality belong to nature, the sum total of all things.

There is a problem with this view when we think of the human race as observers of nature, for when we observe nature we are detached from it. Environmentalists, for instance, who are alarmed at "what we do to nature" and give us dire warnings to "get back to nature," are clearly standing outside "nature" to talk to us like that. Indeed, we need to stand aside from nature in order to control it, whether to put out petroleum fires in Kuwait or to fight pollution in our cities.

However, in general the universal supremacy of nature goes unchallenged, whether it is seen as holy or as the whole of observable reality. What does this implicit worship do to our desires? It actually stifles them and makes them focus on our life in the here and now. Just as nature is seen as the beginning and end of things, so our human personality is where we begin and end. We focus only on ourselves, assuming that we stand alone and have absolute freedom. We become the "subject" and everything else is interpreted accordingly as "objects." We see ourselves as the primary authority on what is meaningful and valued. If something "makes sense" to me, or if I "feel good" about it, this becomes my pronouncement about reality. As a result we exist only for ourselves. This subjective way of viewing the world began with Kant's notion of the autonomous self; yet even Kant admitted the significance of "the moral law within" and "the starry heavens above," which he saw as mysteries given to humanity.

Once we begin to see ourselves as our own makers, our horizons are sharply reduced. We lose our sense of mystery; awe and wonder disappear, and ultimately there is no one to turn to in gratitude for the blessings of life and the beauties of the physical world. We also lose touch with the spiritual help which we associate with a loving creator God. Nature alone exists, around us and in us, and what we see is all there is.

But making nature into a god is not a purely intellectual exercise: Our hearts are involved as well when we reject the Creator and worship his creation instead. We no longer have to take responsibility for our stewardship of nature; we have no ultimate standards of morality. The French philosopher Pascal summed it up like this:

> As a man has lost his true nature, anything can become his nature. Likewise, since the good is lost, anything can be adopted as what he deems good.[11]

The apostle Paul had a similar warning for the Colossians:

> See to it that no one takes you captive through hollow
> and deceptive philosophy, which depends on human tra-
> dition and the basic principles of this world rather than
> on Christ.[12]

These "basic principles," *stoicheia,* were the axioms of logic and mathematics. The rules of behavior in human society, or patterns in nature, are also *stoicheia.* One natural example is the mathematical ratio 0.618036 that we still find associated with the rectangular shape of playing cards, and is the mathematical basis for the shapes of such varied phenomena as snail shells, sunflowers, the curl of the surf, pineapple scales, elephant tusks, lion claws, and even the cochlea of the human ear.

Other natural patterns may influence human behavior, such as the positively charged ions that are intensified in "bad" winds like the Mistral, Foehn, or Santa Ana, that are popularly believed to bring higher incidences of crime, mental illness, and certain other sicknesses. Negatively charged ions, on the other hand, are supposed to speed up growth and healing. Therapeutic effects are also associated with certain natural environments—water-falls, deserts, the seaside, and mountains are often favorite locales for contemplatives of various religions. Clearly there are basic shapes and patterns that reflect an intrinsic ordering of reality. But do we see in them only nature or nature's God?[13]

Early in the Christian era Clement of Alexandria was critical of the atheist Greek philosophers for seeing the divine in the material world:

> Some philosophers left us the elements (stoicheia) as the
> first principles of all things ... with a show of wisdom
> they worshiped matter ... overlooking the Great
> Original, the Maker of all things and the Creator of the
> first principles themselves, God without beginning.[14]

Perhaps it is worth a few minutes' reflection at this point to ask yourself a couple of questions. Is this my view of reality?

What difference would it make to me and the nature of my desires if I saw all nature as the creation of a loving God?

A striking object lesson of this was given to the fourteenth-century nun Julian of Norwich:

> And in this he [God] showed me something small, no bigger than a hazel-nut, lying in the palm of my hand, and I perceived that it was round as any ball. I looked at it and thought: What can this be? And I was given this general answer: It is everything that is made. I was amazed that it could last, for I thought that it was so little that it could suddenly fall into nothing. And I was answered in my understanding: It lasts and always will, because God loves it: and thus everything has being through the love of God.[15]

From this experience Julian saw that the hazelnut, symbolizing the whole universe, was created by God, sustained by God, and loved by God.

I once gave just such a hazelnut to a dear friend close to the end of his life, whose body was racked by the pains of cancer. After his death the hazelnut was found cracked under his pillow. It had cracked as he held it daily through the pain, yet the simple symbol had comforted him that the God of the hazelnut was his God too.

Paganism Today

As we have seen, the Renaissance was a period when nature became a focus of worship. It was also the time when people realized that the purely intellectual, academic approach to God did not do much for the soul. This led to a fresh outbreak of paganism, and a fascination with the occult and with mystery religions.[16]

There is an obvious parallel in today's world. People have been disillusioned first by the rationalism of the Enlightenment, then by the promise that technology would solve all our problems, only to become fascinated by so-called "sacred psychology." "This psychology," claims one Jungian analyst—it is usually Jungian, because of its fascination with symbols—"reflects the richness of our human nature and hints at the divinity we experience when what we do comes out of our depths and we sense the sacred dimension to our lives."[17]

This psychology allows us to give expression to our desires, usually sexual, by virtue of our "god or goddess quotient." This high-sounding language relates our passions to an example from classical mythology, such as Zeus, Apollo, or Aphrodite. We seek a higher authority, an archetype or myth, to put ourselves in the right, though we do not know a personal God. Another writer goes further when he claims that the pagan gods are necessary psychic forms for very real presences and powers.[18] This is part of New Age thinking, which accepts demonic possession and "spirit guidance," and sees pagan worship as making human beings into gods. Today the number of registered witches is rising rapidly, while in our secular world the cult of satanism is by no means suppressed.

It may be argued that human myths are simply the public outworking of our private dreams and fantasies. However, they need to be kept in bounds. As G. K. Chesterton expressed it:

> He who has no sympathy with myths has no sympathy with man. But he who has most sympathy with myths will most fully realize that they are not, and never were a religion ... they provide a calendar, they do not provide him with a God.[19]

As C. S. Lewis realized on becoming a Christian, "myth became fact when God became man." And when myth becomes history, in the sense discussed earlier in this chapter, then human desires are deeply fulfilled. But when hearts are empty, and souls are restless, then myth can return in a dangerous way.

This is illustrated in a novel by Charles Williams, *Many Dimensions*.[20] It is the story of a wild English scientist who buys a mysterious jewel, "The Stone in the Crown of Suleiman," in a Persian bazaar, and smuggles it into England. A member of the Iranian Embassy hears of this and is desperate to have it returned because he is aware of its terribly destructive powers. Its magic is that it can fulfill the personal desires of those who use it. It can transport its owner to other places; it can move back in time; it can fulfill all manner of self-gratification, and can even heal. The Stone in fact mirrors and extends the motives and desires of all who are in contact with it.

"He wants to see what it will do." Thus the reckless curiosity of the scientist, Sir Cues, begins the story. A young relative of his finds out that chipping the Stone makes it divide into duplicate "Types," thus multiplying its powers. It does not take him long to see how he can make a fortune in selling them. But there is also an economic interest in not selling too many and flooding the market with Stones. The local mayor hears of the Stone's healing powers and realizes that this solution to health care in the community gives him immense political power. The general secretary of the trade unions also hears about the Stone, and fears its magic will undermine the transport union if too many people travel by its magical powers, so unlike the mayor he wants not publicity, but secrecy. Meanwhile the Foreign Office is nervous about the political consequences of riots erupting in the Middle East because the Stone has been taken to England.

In the end it is the Lord Chief Justice and his secretary Chloe who save the day. He is "all for law," and she is "wholly obedient"; together they make a conscious decision "to believe in God and to control the Stone for God." Deliberately Chloe takes possession of the Stone, wills its reunion with the duplicated Types, and by her death ensures seclusion once more for the Stone.

This can be taken as a Christian parable of how self-sacrifice is necessary if we are to be saved from the power of infinite desires that lead us to behave without regard to the common good. It is only the end of desire, fulfilled by finding God, that brings peace and order once more.

Today there is a spiritual vacuum within Western secularism, with the loss of absolutes and the disappearance of boundaries. We have the frightening prospect of human desires being extended by magical powers, paganism combined with technology. The relativism of our age marks it as "beyond virtue," as one serious thinker has described it. There is a loss of faith in progress, and a disillusionment with rationalism. It is a time which encourages the return of the gods, the renewal of paganism, and invasion by the dark shadows of the demonic.

HOW REAL ARE OUR GODS?

We have seen how the ancient Near East created gods that corresponded to political needs and desires. As forms of government evolved from tribalism to empire, so the gods became more complex. The polytheism and pantheism of the religions of Egypt and Babylon were reflected in their religious symbols.

But the historical faith of Israel clearly rejected these invented gods. "The Egyptians are men and not God; their horses are flesh and not spirit" (Isa. 31:3). The king of Tyre might boast: "I am a god; I sit on the throne of a god," but when his enemies came to defeat him, nothing could help him, for "you are a man and not a god" (Ezek. 28:2). Moreover, as we have seen, creating idols cannot turn people into gods. Although these idols may be massive, those who make them are condemned by their unreality:

> All who make idols are nothing, and the things they
> treasure are worthless.[21]

Yet although the idols themselves are unreal, their presence is real enough to their worshippers. As Carl Jung dryly observed, the gods never die, they merely become myths.

Idolatry has a very real effect; the prophet Ezekiel called the gods "dung pellets," because of the besoiling effect they have upon their worshippers. Idols do bring their worshippers into contact with demonic powers.

A young friend told me about his experience of practicing transcendental meditation. Given a mantra, he prayed to the name of his god regularly for some months. Then he began to have out-of-body experiences and erotic desires, until he gradually became aware that he was being possessed by evil powers. Fortunately he stopped in time to realize what was happening to him, terrified by the yawning depths before his spirit.

It is significant that the history of Israel described earlier is not judged by "progress" as we now judge secular history. Rather it is judged by "idolatry." Either the people and their king "did that which was right in the sight of the Lord" or else they were idolatrous in their worship. It was essentially a matter of the heart in God's presence. As the prophet Isaiah expressed it: "These people come near to me with their mouth and honor me with their lips, but their hearts are far from me" (29:13).

Israel was frequently distracted by both syncretism and suppression, and easily tempted by paganism. *Syncretism* meant the adoption of alien beliefs which led to the dilution and eventual loss of the true faith. Without the distinctive characteristics of a personal God, Yahweh, Israel's worship became a meaningless, impersonal, ritual idolization that would do for any god.

Suppression occurred when idols and gods were ignored, rather than faced and challenged. We do the same thing in our secular society when we act in ignorance of evil forces which are, in the words of T. S. Eliot, "not known, because not looked for." Then the headlines of our local newspaper tell of another serial killer, another incident of child abuse, perhaps another incident involving satanism. There are dark forces, and those who worship them take on the nature of their idols. People can become as hard and metallic as Mammon, or as soft and sensuous as Eros, or as diabolical and evil as Satan.

It is appropriate, then, that the sovereignty of God should call for the *subordination* of idols. "You shall have no other gods before me" was Yahweh's command to the Israelites. Other gods may become real powers when worshipped, and then we take a false view of reality; but God belongs to a separate order. He is the Creator of all things. "Who is like unto Thee, O God, among the gods?" God alone is the Sovereign of the universe:

> For the LORD is the great God;
>
> The great King, above all gods.[22]

Lesser gods are restricted in time and space, but God created both space and time. The depths of the earth and the mountain peaks belong to him, "The sea is his, for he made it, and his hands formed the dry land" (Ps. 95:5).

In the early Christian church the principle of subordinating idols to God came into play. At Corinth, the Christian community was divided over whether to eat meat offered to idols. If there is only the one true God, some argued, then the gods to whom the meat was offered do not exist and there should be no scruples about eating it. But others in the community had had very real experience of these gods, and they feared contamination through such a meat supply. The apostle Paul, while not interested in the question of the gods' existence, was aware that whatever is worshipped is indeed a god who is real to the worshipper. So he testified that even if there were so-called gods, whether in heaven, or on earth, yet for Christians:

> There is but one God, the Father, from whom all things
>
> came and for whom we live; and there is but one Lord,
>
> Jesus Christ, through whom all things came and through
>
> whom we live.[23]

The charge against idolatry is always born of hostility to whatever falsifies God and his lordship over creation. Thus sacred sites and sacred festivals were not suppressed, covered over as if they had never existed, but rather subordinated to the worship of the true God. On the same site where temples to Mithras once stood, the Christians built churches. Dates in the pagan calendar were taken over for Christian events and Christian saints.

The believer must always realize that any material principle or power or any psychic force can be interpreted as a "god." They focus intense human emotions when diverted away from desiring God. These emotions do not weaken or disappear, but are directed to other "gods." They cannot be suppressed or neutralized in any way other than by subordination to the personal God. When we have forgotten our genuine aspiration for a personal relationship with God and end up involved in false allegiances, we feel disenchantment and loss.

For G. K. Chesterton this apparent loss was really good news. Life is not the frustrating meaninglessness it can appear—we simply "belong" somewhere else.

> We have come to the wrong star ... that is what makes life at once so splendid and so strange. The true happiness is that we don't fit. We come from somewhere else. We have lost our way.[24]

What Kind of Gods Do We Make?

Francis Bacon, an architect of the "new science" of the Renaissance, eventually became disillusioned with the consequences of intellectual system building. In the *Novum Organum*[25] he describes four types of gods: the idols of the tribe; the idols of the cave; the idols of the marketplace; and the idols of the theater. These all illustrate ways in which Western civilization has made its own gods and still worships them today.

First, says Bacon, "the idols of the tribe are inherent in human nature," in other words the natural human perception of things is faulty. So, he continues, "all the perceptions both of the senses and the mind bear reference to man and not to the universe." People have a habit of turning everything toward themselves; we all tend to make even God into our own image. As a friend recently confessed to me:

> I suppose I want a God I can control. He can be all powerful, but he should use that power to do as I say. He can be all knowing, but he should use his knowledge to help me out. He can be loving and faithful, and this should be evident by his caress and support of me.

Perhaps that is why so many people choose idols they can make themselves. A group of scholars once decided in England that they wanted a God *who did not speak and who would not judge.* That is an idol. It permits a spiritual dimension to our lives without us losing control. With idols we can choose our own sacrifices, write our own story, and decide our own destiny.

Of course nobody likes to be out of control. We all have our own way of exerting control, and the more chaotic things appear, the more control we want. Faith is the opposite. It demands that we hand over control to God, and we are fearful of this disorientation, of being turned inside out and upside down. That is why idols are seductive; they give the illusion of choice, of control. We can make them to fit our own psyche. They are the mistaken ideals of our own imperfect nature, which is why religious idols tell us nothing about God. Like the intellectual idols of philosophical systems, they express instead something about human beings. This was what Feuerbach had the honesty to confess, that often our theology is merely anthropology.

Second, Bacon speaks of the "idols of the cave," those profoundly intimate feelings of the individual that dwell in one's own heart or "den." Such idols are predictable, because we are so open to being influenced by other people and because we admire respected authorities and "experts." They are often so fundamental as to be instinctive, but can be traced to our upbringing and culture, and are characteristic of who we are and what we want to be. My friend confessed as well that:

> I used to say my deepest desire was for truth. Indeed I felt tormented by my separation from it. "It doesn't matter so much which belief system I adopt," I would say, "as long as it is true." In my mind, if there was one that was true, all others were false, and I hated to be deceived. So I persisted on my quest, relentlessly questioning and pursuing.
>
> I'm not so sure now that my desire for truth was genuine. The word of God is open to most, and where it is closed, the trees and the mountains proclaim him. Pure truth is available to all who seek. The obscurity, the opaque cloud surrounding it, must be something we have contrived ourselves. I wanted truth on my terms, and my terms were that I understand it before I accept it. So any truth larger than my mind was not permitted. My desire to control battled with my desire for an experience bigger than and outside myself. That was the source of torment—not the noble quest for truth. In all my talk about earnestly desiring to avoid deception, I was most deceived. Truth is life-giving and fulfilling, not an agonizing search for illusive light. My desire was real, just stifled and misdirected by my own pride and fear. I had put a lid on it, created a box with a ceiling so that I could observe it more efficiently, and with my own tools. Now I see that it was God who I had "boxed."

Why do we want to put God in a box? For my friend the "god of the cave" was obvious. Without emotional intimacy in the family that reared her, she was terrified of unleashed desire. Emotionally malnourished, she could not bear to lose everything by giving up her mind as well. To relinquish intellectual control would be suicide to her. She concluded, "With such misplaced desires, I was in no condition to know my deep need for a personal relationship with God." That was to come later. Yet she could glimpse "how sadly alienated we are from God's abundant desire for us."

Third, Bacon talks of the "idols of the market," which are "formed by the reciprocal intercourse and society of man with man." Our friend's confession has also touched on that, since the negative feelings we have inherited from our parents shape God's image into our neurotic histories. (I have discussed this at length in a previous book, *In Pursuit of Happiness*.26) But there are also the gods of mutual self-interest, of profit and gain, of self-aggrandizement which are pandered to by "unionism," "professionalism," and "commercialism," and the propaganda, jargon, and—of course—the desire for money that go with them.

Kierkegaard could see this whole problem proliferating in the age of science and industry. He observes that "in our age because of the great increase in knowledge, we have forgotten what it means to exist, and what inwardness signifies." Even in Christian churches, to be an "amateur Christian" is an insult, as in the outside world it is repulsive to be just "ordinary." We are all enveloped in the thick haze of pseudoscientific jargon, of professional status and functional roles. Knowing nothing about our own hearts, we hide our facelessness, our lack of inwardness, behind the masks of our own idols.

Finally, Bacon speaks of the "idols of the theater." "For we regard," he says, "all the systems of philosophy hitherto received, as imagined, as so many plays brought out and performed, creating fictitious and theatrical worlds."

Perhaps one of the most serious theatrical performances was put on by Hegel, who spent a great deal of effort on uniting reason and faith. To find a Christianity that was rationally acceptable and objectively valid seemed, to all appearances, to have pinned down religion within the hospitable walls of a system. But at what price?

Rationalizing Christianity led to its virtual suppression. Confronted by the demand of reason that everything should be explicable, God is stripped of mystery and "unknowing," so that in the end he is reduced to a non-necessity, a superfluous appendix in our past. This procession of "the idols of the theater," of intellectual imagination, reduces theology to theory. Its practitioners are no longer theologians, but sociologists, anthropologists, or historians of a sort. Thus a Canadian sociologist, Reginald W. Bibby, has observed, "the poverty and potential of religion" is simply about "fragmented gods."

This poverty has emerged out of the vast numbers of human options—the option of the "electronic church," the "new religion" option, the "private god" option, the "no religion" option, as well as all the *à la carte* options open to the regular church attender. Religion has become a matter of selective consumption—or entertainment—or just plain business. In our self-absorbed generation, self-centered, impersonal, having access to reality only through "techniques," we are well qualified to produce idols on an unprecedented scale.

In sharp contrast, William Cowper's hymn stands as an earnest plea for a posture of self-sacrifice, humility, and a profound awareness of God's deeply personal nature:

> The dearest idol I have known,
> Whate'er that idol be;
> Help me to tear it from Thy throne,
> And worship only Thee.

Mephistopheles: *In this world I will bind myself to cater,*
For all your whims, to serve and wait on you;
When we meet in the next world, some time later,
Wages in the same kind will then fall due.

Faust: *The next world? Well, that's no great matter;*
Here is a world for you to shatter ...
If ever to the moment I shall say:
Beautiful moment, do not pass away!
Then you may forge your chains to bind me,
Then I will put my life behind me ...

—Goethe, *Faust*[1]

3

WHO ARE THE ADDICTS?

F aust's insistence on having everything this life can offer
and his disregard for the life to come express a universal desire. We can trace it back to our very beginnings and
Adam's desire for forbidden fruit, as he sought the divine power
of knowledge without the presence of God.

The unsatisfied longing for God is what drives human beings
above all else. Perhaps no thinker has seen this so passionately
as Augustine. "Longing," he observes, "is the heart's treasury."
For the Christian this means pushing our longing to the limits.
Or, as Augustine put it: "The whole life of the good Christian is
a holy longing. What you desire ardently, as yet you do not see
... by withholding of the vision, God extends the longing;
through longing he extends the soul, by extending it he makes
room in it ... So ... let us long because we are to be filled ... that
is our life, to be exercised by longing."[2] The heart is homesick,
and only the journey home will alleviate its longing to be with

God forever. It is thanks to our mortality that we are beings of desire; heaven is still our ultimate destiny.

In his *Confessions,* Augustine also sees desire as the response of those created to their Creator. So he prays: "Since he [mankind] is part of your creation, he wishes to praise you. The thought of you stirs him so deeply that he cannot be content unless he praises you, because you made us for yourself and our hearts find no peace until they rest in you."[3] Yet Augustine was also well acquainted with the distractions of the world. "Who will grant me to rest content in you? To whom shall I turn for the gift of your coming into my heart and filling it to the brim, so that I may forget all the wrong I have done and embrace you alone, my only source of good?" Then he asks God, "Why do you mean so much to me? Help me to find the words to explain. Why do I mean so much to you, that you should command me to love you?"[4] Despite his learning, Augustine was completely overwhelmed by the idea of God really loving him.

> My soul is like a house, small for you to enter, but I pray you to enlarge it. It is in ruins, but I ask you to remake it. It contains much that you will not be pleased to see: this I know and do not hide.[5]

One thing Augustine believed with certainty was that if God is not the center of our desires, then they run amok in all directions, as passions and sensual pleasures, to debase and imprison us in futility and despair. If we do not adore God, with all our desire focused on him, we can only live enslaved like addicts to our senses. This was Augustine's own experience as a young man: "The briers of unclean desires grew rank over my head, and there was no hand to root them out." Indeed, he rejoiced in his waywardness and in "that tumult of the senses, with which the world forgets God its Creator, and becomes enamored with the creature."[6] All too easily we become intoxicated by the "invisible wine of self-will" and turn aside to indulge in selfish desires.

There are many stories in the Bible of people who deny God

like this. Esau, hungry after the hunt, sold his birthright to Jacob for a meal, and to this day there is animosity in the Near East between the descendants of Jacob and Esau. Samson's passion for Delilah made him a prototype of rulers enticed away from the duties of public life by private pleasure. And Judas Iscariot sold his master for thirty pieces of silver. These and many other stories tell of desire that comes not from God but from human imagination. The biblical phrases "walking in the imagination of their own heart," or "becoming vain in their imaginations," comment on this cause of human willfulness and idolatry. And idolatry leads to addiction to our idols.

WHAT IS ADDICTION?

Originally, the Latin word *addictus* meant handing over goods to someone else, either by sale or by legal decree. It was something given by debtors to their creditors. From this it came to mean devoting or surrendering one's life, as one might to one's gods or to loved ones; and then, by extension, giving oneself to some habit or substance. The modern French word *accroché*, like the English, means being "hooked" by an addiction.

Addiction means being so completely possessed that one is enslaved, deprived of inner freedom, and ultimately of personal integrity. It is the ghastly process of "losing one's soul." Unless one wrestles to overcome the addictive habit, no change is possible, only destruction. Addiction, then, means being caught, taken possession of and then destroyed, but it requires the first step, namely the willingness to be taken. This can be seen in the story of Dracula, where victims offer to expose their necks for Dracula to suck their blood. Once bitten, they become Dracula's slaves.[7]

The beginning of addiction is not usually as dramatic as meeting a vampire. It is the first drink, the first cigarette, the first sexual encounter, the first wrong emotional response. It is denying that anything is wrong, losing sight of reality, unaware of life's true goals and needs, until one's soul is also lost. If we are not able to confront our own dark side—the capacity for evil within ourselves—we remain unaware of how destructive our addiction has become.

Recent medical thinking has distinguished two basic categories of addiction: substance and process. Substance addictions, sometimes called "ingestive addictions," are addictions to substances such as alcohol or cocaine and other hallucinatory drugs, which are usually artificially refined to concentrate the efficacy of the drug. Not all such substances are illegal; the tobacco industry tries to reduce the harmful effects of smoking with filter tips or other devices. But it is not enough to safeguard our physical health; our emotional health requires attention as well. Physical dependence on whatever induces mood change, including caffeine or chocolate, springs from deeper emotional issues.

Process addictions are ways in which one becomes hooked on some series of actions and interactions, such as making money, gambling, sex, work, sports, physical exercise, relationships with other people, even religious activities and creative writing.

The only real difference between these two forms of addiction is the nature of the agent. Otherwise the results are similar: loss of reality, compulsive behavior, and personal deterioration. We all tend to be "hooked" on something; in some way or other we are all addicts. This is why it is so important to reflect on the reality of desire and how it works, so that our spiritual lives may be deepened and liberated. It is not just a "drug problem" for the FBI or the military in dealing with the drug barons. Addiction is our problem, yours and mine.

TOTAL ADDICTION

These days we hear a lot about holistic medicine. The increasing association of sickness with "psychosomatic" illness has led us to consult not only traditional doctors, but also chiropractors, naturopaths, and counselors. In other words, body and soul are understood as being interdependent, and this is well illustrated in addiction.

The human brain is said to consist of billions, even trillions of cells called neurons. These are living colonies, like a beehive, each with its own unique life and environment. Brain activity involves thousands, or even millions of these neurons interacting in local groups or in functional systems to give us our habitual thoughts and attitudes.

Body chemicals such as alcohol, caffeine, and other drugs are powerful influences upon the neurons. The natural ecology of the body's own chemicals is upset by the invasion of the foreign chemicals, so the brain's first reaction is to stop these cells from being unduly stimulated. But increased toleration of the foreign chemicals can produce a new balance of neurons; this is what we recognize as "attachment" or the beginnings of addiction. Other systems are then called in, recruited to create wider and wider adaptations within the whole body. Thus the human body's great gift for adaptation (an ability greater in humans than in animals) contributes to the ultimate tragedy of addiction.

In addition, we have to take account of the psychological consequences of the process just described.[8] For addictions operate not only physically, but also psychologically and spiritually within the person. One day we may learn much more of how all addictions leave their imprint upon brain and body chemistry, addiction not only to drugs, but to the emotions precipitated by money, sex, power, and work.

The brain never forgets what it has learned. That is why past addictions have potential for our future behavior that we never lose. As Gerald May, a psychiatrist, has stated in his book *Addiction & Grace* (Harper S anFrancisco, 1991): "From a neurological viewpoint, it means the cells of our best intentioned systems can never eradicate the countless other systems that have been addicted. And from a spiritual perspective, it means that no matter how much grace God has blessed us with, we forever remain dependent upon its continuing flow."

In the cycle of addiction, the experiences of pleasure, relief, the search for new experiences and increasingly frequent indulgence in the addictive substance or process all reinforce each other. They all combine with the psychological and moral tendencies we have in our own personal makeup, our temperaments and the behavior we have learned from personal relationships with parents, siblings, and friends. Our character traits reinforce addictive attitudes and behavior, so that the addiction seems gradually to dominate our whole life in some form or other. Even our daily routine, we may discover, tends to follow its own addictive cycle. Certainly the dominant traits of our personality reveal how our emotional and relational addictions tend to govern us.

Neurologically, then, addictive habits and attitudes readily form part of our constitution. Indeed, we could call this the "Neurotic Bias," for it is caused by our unconscious desire to avoid pain and to seek what is pleasurable, both in our emotions and in our bodies. We may criticize Freud for exaggerating what he called the "Pleasure Principle," but it undoubtedly exists as a vital element in the character of all forms of addiction. Just as matter is pulled down by gravity, so human beings gravitate toward what is pleasurable. Often enough we hear the passing remark, "I have a right to enjoy myself, don't I?" And then there is our willful tendency, heard in heated argument: "It's none of your business! I can do what I like!" Reinforcing this primary bias we also have an "Egotistic Bias," of "looking after Number One," that is toward one's own self-interest.

Third, we also have a "Group Bias." I remember once asking Malcolm Muggeridge, toward the end of his life, what other significant book he would have written if he had had the time and creative energy. His response was to "write against consensus" in our society. It is so easy to "follow the crowd," to "go with the tide." How many teenagers fall into addictive traps because of their overriding need to gain social approval? Whether by drinking or petting or other "herd mentality" activities, it is all too easy to fall into addictive social traps, with "Everyone is doing it" as our justification.

Finally there is the "Common Sense Bias," our tendency toward pragmatic, immediate, and shortsighted solutions and objectives. It is what we see in the characters already mentioned— Esau, Samson, and Judas—each searching for a pragmatic solution as a quick fix. It is summed up nowadays in what we call ourselves: "the technological society."

If addiction is our common human condition, it makes sense also to call it "sin." Evil within us takes many forms: rebellion and willfulness, falling short of the appropriate standards, and our own selfish and self-centered inclinations. None of these tendencies can be permanently eradicated, because they penetrate every level of our being. Likewise, addiction as sin is a disease of the whole person—bodily, emotionally, and spiritually.

At the same time, recent studies of codependence, addictive families and, indeed, addictive societies, all provide evidence of addiction operating on all levels: personal, familial, and social, and being passed on from generation to generation. When we begin to explore how even church fellowships and religious ministries may be addictive we shall be looking at the far-reaching dimensions and depths of addictive life in human behavior; and Saint Paul's statement that "we have all sinned and come short of the glory of God" will take on new meaning.

There are three levels of addiction to be dealt with.

Personal Addiction means that I have to take far more responsibility for myself as a moral agent than I may have realized. More humility is needed as a mirror to my heart, to see myself as others see me, and above all as God sees me.

Family Addiction means recognizing "conspiracies" or patterns of concealed abnormal behavior that may have been perceived as normal within family life. These patterns should not be perpetuated by family myths. It may be the rebel in the family who begins to see what was wrong: physical or mental abuse, or other deep-rooted, oppressive, and even pathological behavior.

Societal Addiction means recognizing widespread abuse within the previously unexamined or unjudged standards of society. We have touched upon it in commenting on the "commodity mentality" of our consumer society. There is a certain social hypocrisy that focuses on the "drug problem" while ignoring many other kinds of addictions that our society not only tolerates but actually encourages, such as workaholism, professionalism, consumerism, pornography, sexism, militarism, and many more.

Once we accept that an "addictive way of life" goes much wider and deeper than this, we will, of course, need to extend our understanding of repentance. What the early church called *metanoia,* literally turning around and facing in the other direction, has to become much more radical—a transformation of people, families, and society. In other words, a once-for-all, personal "born again" experience is not enough! It may be a wonderful and authentic new beginning, but there has also to be a constant, daily process of transformation, every day for the rest of one's life. We shall consider this in more detail in the second half of the book.

ADDICTS IN LITERATURE

I have always had a certain sympathy for Don Quixote since we grew up in the same region of La Mancha. I loved the tales about him recited to me by my father. For a child, life is full of potentials of desire, and Don Quixote is, tragically, nothing but desire. For him it begins at home, as he spends all his time reading novelettes of medieval chivalry; not the real stuff of history, but the fantasies told about the past. So he sets out into the world to live out his own fantasies. He creates the name of his lover, Dulcinea, or "sweet one," which is symbolic of that "pleasure principle" we have been describing. His romance is all make-believe, as are both his own military prowess and his political dreams. His author, Cervantes, was writing at the end of an age and was poking gentle fun at outmoded romantic chivalry, itself one of those addictive patterns of behavior condoned by society.

In its turn, *Don Quixote* is the first great novel to introduce us to another realm of fantasy, to be called "the modern world," with its own patterns of addiction.

There is a fine line between creativity and addiction. After all, artists are also "knights of Desire," creating their fantasies in stories, drama, and art. And many artists have been addicts themselves. De Quincey was an opium eater, and the addictions of Jack London and Jackson Pollock killed them as young men. Dostoyevsky was addicted to gambling and love. Tennessee Williams, Faulkner, Dylan Thomas, F. Scott Fitzgerald, and Hemingway were all heavy drinkers. Others have described how the process of creative writing became an obsession. The novelist Thomas Wolfe wrote about being possessed by his writing:

> I cannot really say the book was written. It was not constructed word by word or line by line or chapter by chapter. It came from me like lava pouring from the crater of a volcano ... It was something that took hold of me and possessed me, and before I was done with it— that is, before I finally emerged with the first completed part—it seemed to me that it had done for me. The tenement of one man's heart and brain and flesh and bone and sinew, the little vessel of his one life, could not possibly endure, could not possibly be strong enough or big enough to hold this raging tempest of his own creative need.[9]

Van Gogh's life was a similarly volcanic existence that eventually turned him mad. It is in striking contrast with that of Augustine, who, as we have quoted, also saw the restrictions of his earthy dwelling place. Augustine was not interested only in his own self-based creativity; he wanted to make room for the presence of God. It does make a difference when an artist like Bach or Rubens works to God's glory. But when creativity takes God's place, it can become a demon. Boris Pasternak admonishes us:

> Keep awake, keep awake, artist,
> Do not give in to sleep ...
> You are eternity's hostage
> And prisoner of time.[10]

If writers, especially great artists, have their own addictive tendencies, then their works will mirror these symbols or archetypes of addictive behavior. Faust is such an instance. The Faustian archetype is that of "the Debtor." Mephistopheles offers "to cater for all your whims, to serve and wait on you." Through a first "high" we are egged on to have ever greater expectations. In the end all meaning and all hope hinges on a single substance or relationship.

Since we are "relational beings," meant for one another, this appeals to our deepest nature. The promises are limitless—power, fame, money, success, sex, you name it. But what stories of such seductions show us is that the original character, who thinks he is the player, is in fact duped. He is much less real than the sinister figure or the shadowy servant who stays obligingly in the background. Mephistopheles and Sancho Panza are much more real than Faust and Don Quixote; addiction depraves and deprives the real person and ultimately causes their downfall. All that is left is a profound disillusionment with pipe dreams. All our assets have been changed into the wrong currency.

Dostoyevsky's novel *The Gambler* is a particularly vivid portrayal of an archetype, since the author was a gambler himself.[11] For eight years Dostoyevsky was glued to the roulette wheel, and he died leaving great debts. It was to help pay his gaming debts that Dostoyevsky wrote *The Gambler*.

In the novel, Alexei, the gambling character, reveals some of the dynamics of desire that gambling produces. Even before the first die is cast Alexei knows of his fascination with gambling. He describes his initial emotions:

> I confess that my heart was pounding in my breast and that I didn't feel at all cool and detached; probably I had felt for a long time already that I would leave Rouletteberg a different man and that something was about to happen that would radically and irrevocably change my life. I felt that it was bound to happen. Although it may seem ridiculous to say that I expected so much from roulette, I find the generally accepted opinion that it is stupid to expect anything from gambling even more ridiculous.[12]

Alexei began to stake his all upon it, for it is the addiction of the gambler to go beyond all reasonable limits in reckless abandonment to the fate of the wheel or the dice. In the United States this is seen nightly on television in the "Wheel of Fortune" that so many worship. We see it too in the fever that grips the bingo hall or the millions of tickets bought in national sweepstakes.

Money wasted is one thing, but the ultimate disaster of the gambler is finally to challenge fate. So Dostoyevsky confesses through his character:

> I believe I had something like four thousand gulden in my hands within five minutes. That's when I should have quit. But a funny feeling came over me, some sort of desire to challenge Fate, an uncontrollable urge to stick my tongue out at it, to give it a flip on the nose.[13]

"The Romantic" is one of the more attractive archetypes of literature, and yet also one of the more dangerous ones precisely because of its attractiveness.

The legend of *Tristan and Isolde* has been interpreted many times, culminating in Wagner's operatic interpretation. The prelude to Wagner's opera expresses one single emotion, the longing of the addict to be drugged with romantic love. So Wagner himself said of the *Prelude*, "Let that insatiable longing swell forth from the first, timidest avowal to sweetest protraction, through anxious sighs, through hopes and fears, laments and desires, bliss and torment, to the mightiest forward pressing, the most powerful effort to find the breach that will open out to the infinitely craving heart the path into the sea of love's endless delight."

Tristan and Isolde are the representatives of two countries that have been each other's enemies; in fact Tristan was the killer of Isolde's betrothed husband. But looking into each other's eyes, they fall in love, and then later as lovers try to bring about political peace between the two states. After they have drunk a love potion, sealing their love for each other, the lovers sing out their defiance of the day, longing only for the night. Isolde fears marriage, and they both turn their backs on ordinary existence. Like addicts, they want a potion that replaces the conflicts and tensions of reality, and indeed all the duties and frictions of being free and truly alive. Instead of life they choose absolute love, a dream world that means death. Tristan sings the romantic ode of *Liebestod:*

> So let us die
> And never part,
> Die united,
> Heart to heart,
> Never waking,
> Never fearing,
> Nameless,
> Endless rapture sharing,
> Each to each devoted,
> In love abiding![14]

Another key archetype is "the Trickster," the part of the character which maintains the illusion of well-being in the life of the addict. Whenever addicts sense there is something wrong, or dangerous, or when they wake from their dreams, this archetype takes over to lull the senses and put them to sleep again. In Jack London's novel *John Barleycorn* the alcoholic writer reveals the tricks he learned to perform upon himself: "For so John Barleycorn tricks and lures, setting the maggots of intelligence gnawing, whispering his fatal intuitions of truth, flinging purple passages into the monotony of one's days."[15]

John Barleycorn recounts his growing years, when he first drank the forbidden beer, loathed it, but persisted when he was laughed at, though as a teenager he preferred soda. Going to sea at fourteen, he lived with old salts who drank and drank, implying that only beer was the mark of manhood. "Oh, it was brave. I was beginning to grasp the meaning of life.... tipsy young gods, incredibly wise, gloriously genial, and without limit to our powers."[16] Moreover, it was easy to change the gloom of a companion simply by buying a few drinks. "I had got behind men's souls. I had got behind my own soul and found unguessed potencies and greatnesses."[17]

Because of Jack London's strong constitution and the intelligence that enabled him to become successful, the novel concludes with him denying he ever was or is or will be a drinker. He says: "I regret John Barleycorn flourished everywhere in the system of society in which I was born, else I should not have made his acquaintance."[18]

Literature is full of many more archetypes of addiction. There is the "Underground Man," whom Dostoyevsky depicts full of hidden resentment in his *Notes from the Underground*. He is indeed the "betrayer of life," sapping all his creativity through unacknowledged bitterness. There is "the Outsider" or "the Outlaw," as in Hermann Hesse's *Steppenwolf* trying to stand proudly above the ranks of ordinary men, a misfit of society who wishes to be seen as a god. There is Camus' "Rebel," who through rebellion plunges deeper into a life of addiction, because his attempts at self-justification blind him to the traps that endanger him.

Camus, though irreligious himself, concluded that "the only original rule of life today" is "to learn and to die, and in order to be a man, to refuse to be a god." This means sacrificing one's ego.

THE CHILDREN OF ADDICTION

We are becoming increasingly aware of the discord and unhappiness of addictive families. Alcoholism, sex, gambling, workaholism, romanticism, and many other addictions all create extended emotional havoc in the home. Our choices and habits affect not only ourselves, but have an impact on everyone else around us.

One work of literature which has made a profound impression on modern consciousness is Dostoyevsky's *The Brothers Karamazov.* This is partly because it is an indictment of the failure of socialism and the worldliness of organized religion, and partly because of our contemporary preoccupations with freedom and happiness, both of which are thwarted by addictive lives.

Each main character in Dostoyevsky's book, Fyodor Karamazov, his three sons, Dmitri, Ivan, and Alyosha, and their stepbrother Smerdyakov, symbolize different archetypal figures within the psyche of the addict and his family. As we have seen, the author was himself an addict (depicted clearly in his lesser novels, *The Gambler* and *Notes from the Underground)* and no one can describe the psyche of addicts better than another addict. So *The Brothers Karamazov* represents us all, in our different addictions.

Fyodor Karamazov is a merciless and violent drunkard. He was cruel and lecherous to his dead wives, and has wounded each of his own sons by unbridled, dissolute desires. Each member of the family must either succumb to the demon of addiction, or else be transformed. There can be no neutrality. The missing mothers and their abused femininity must be redeemed.

Fyodor is crude, cruel, and cynical, an unconscious hostage to his addictions—alcohol, sex, and money. He is given many opportunities to repent. Father Zossima, the soul friend and spiritual father of the youngest son, tries to help Fyodor. "Do not be so ashamed of yourself, for that is the root of it all ... Above all, don't lie to yourself. A man who lies to himself and listens to his own lie comes to a point where he does not discern any truth either in himself or anywhere around him, and thus falls into disrespect toward himself and others. Not respecting anyone, he ceases to love and having no love, he gives himself up to passions and coarse pleasures, in order to occupy and amuse himself, and in his vices reaches complete bestiality, and it all comes from lying continually to others and to himself."[19] But Fyodor is completely immersed in his depravity. His sons hate him and wish him dead, and in the end he is murdered by his bastard son Smerdyakov.

Dmitri, the oldest of the brothers, lives in open contempt of his father. It is not surprising that his public hatred of his father causes him to be unjustly convicted of patricide. After a disorderly childhood, he grows up to be wild, sensual, a drinker and a gambler, with a life of orgies and duels.

He suffers from guilt, shame, and self-hatred. But underneath, Dmitri has a romantic spirit and a desiring soul. The conflict between good and evil rages deep and long within him. As he confesses to Alyosha:

> I can't bear it that some man, even with a lofty heart
> and the highest mind, should start from the ideal of the
> Madonna and end with the ideal of Sodom. It's even
> more fearful when someone who already has the ideal of
> Sodom in his soul does not deny the ideal of the
> Madonna either, and his heart burns with it, verily, verily burns, as in his young, blameless years. No, man is
> broad, even too broad, I would narrow him down.[20]

For Dmitri the heart is a battlefield between God and the Devil. His romanticism, however, gives him big eyes for what he desires, but a small conscience.

Ivan, the middle brother, has suffered from his father's rejection. He uses reason and logic to defend himself from the pain of childhood, and therefore loves from a distance, in the abstract. Yet he knows he cannot understand the way the world is arranged by logic:

> With my pitiful, earthly, Euclidean understanding, all I know is that there is suffering and that there are none guilty; that cause follows effect, simply and directly; that everything flows and finds its level—but that's only Euclidean nonsense. I know that, and I can't consent to live by it.[21]

Full of resentment, trapped in a nonrelational world, Ivan yearns for love and forgiveness, but he rejects both because of his need for control, power, and mastery. Ivan is not quite sure whether the Devil is a real entity or merely an emotional extension of his own personality. He is in danger of utter despair and insanity.

The stepbrother Smerdyakov is deformed in every way. He is a trickster, and self-destruction personified. As a nihilist, he despises everyone. He puts himself outside the law, giving himself over to demonic self-will, and commits suicide after he has murdered Fyodor, his hated father.

Only Alyosha accepts the sufferings of his family without condemnation. He is the gentlest, the most modest, an even-tempered and gracious character. He has the gift of loving people because shortly before his mother died, when he was four years old, he remembered her lifting him up before an icon of the Virgin Mary, to consecrate him to her special care. He remembers his mother's love vividly all his life, but he comes to love Father Zossima, Alyosha's archetype of a redeemed life, most in all the world.

As a young man Zossima, too, had been ruled by his passions, proud, drunken, debauched. But he humbly acknowledges his guilty past and has been transformed to live a life of sacrifice and service. From him, Alyosha learns that hell is "the suffering of being unable to love."[22] Many of the twelve steps of the recovering addict are exemplified in Zossima's spiritual transformation which in turn inspires the life of Alyosha, the mediator between his brothers and their one anchorage within a turbulent family. Yet Alyosha, too, needs to be redeemed from his own idealism before he can truly reach out to his brothers.

In the end Dmitri is also transformed, after imprisonment and exile. But he has to permit his jealous heart to become trustful, aided by his love for Katerina Grushenka, who had faith in Dmitri when he did not have it for himself. Ivan, who tells the famous story of the Grand Inquisitor, remains at odds with God. In the end his addiction to judgmentalism and to resentment is never redeemed. He is the one who is most like his father— proud, money-hungry, sensual—and eventually he succumbs to mental breakdown.

The best understanding of the nature of addiction in the novel comes from Zossima, the converted addict. He recognizes that it is by "interpreting freedom as the multiplication and rapid satisfaction of desires" that "men distort their own nature, for many senseless and foolish desires and habits and ridiculous fancies are fostered in them. They live only for mutual envy, for luxury and ostentation." So he asks,

> How can a man shake off his habits, what can become of
> him if he is in such bondage to the habit of satisfying
> the innumerable desires he has created for himself? He is
> isolated, and what concern has he with the rest of
> humanity? They have succeeded in accumulating a
> greater mass of objects, but the joy in the world has
> grown less.[23]

Zossima recognizes the growth of addictive tendencies. He observes that a life of addiction results in the abuse of children. We now see ever more clearly that when "the fathers have eaten sour grapes, the children's teeth are set on edge." Addiction breeds addiction.

"Yours will be a long pilgrimage," predicts Zossima to Alyosha. As a monastic novice, Alyosha is told he has to get out into the world. "And you will have to take a wife too." Significantly, it is the women in the novel, Katerina Grushenka and Lise, who, by their understanding, feeling, and love, provide inner freedom from addiction. "Love children specially," Zossima continues, "they live to soften and purify our hearts and as it were to guide us. Woe to him who offends a child!" A kingdom of children represents an alternative society for reformers. Then Zossima adds: "There is much to do. But I have to trust in you, and so I send you forth." How sweet is that expression of trust, how creative it is for the feeble-intentioned, after a life littered with broken promises! Then he concludes: "Christ is with you. Do not abandon him, and he will not abandon you. You will see great sorrow, and in that sorrow you will be happy. This is my last message to you: in sorrow seek happiness."[24]

Zossima dies shortly after these words and Dostoyevsky, too, died before he finished his novel. The theme running through the novel are the words inscribed on his tombstone, the words of Christ: "The grain of wheat must die, in order to bear much fruit." We must die to our addictive lives, so that Christ's resurrection life may become ours.

In the *Diary of a Writer,* Dostoyevsky, both as psychologist and theologian, envisages that in the future "to be an authentic Russian means nothing else but to strive definitively to reconcile in oneself the European contradictions, to show how the longings of Europe may find a way out in the all human and all denying Russian soul. It means to accept them all in this soul, in brotherly love, and thus perhaps to speak the last word of the great, universal harmony of brotherly concord of all people in keeping with the evangelical law of Christ." Were these words exaggerated, ecstatic, fanatic? Or were they prophetic of the soul of Russia, now opened to the same temptations of neurotic materialism and addictive consumerism as the West?

Perhaps it is the poor of the earth in the Third World who are least ravaged by addiction, as they strive to meet more basic needs. Yet children everywhere are the victims of our vices as well as representing the hope of new virtues. As Jesus said, "Let the little children come to me ... for the kingdom of heaven belongs to such as these."[25] Thus in the last scene of *The Brothers Karamazov,* Alyosha, among a group of children, says to them:

> You must know that there is nothing higher, or stronger, or sounder, or more useful afterwards in life, than some good memory, especially a memory from childhood, from the parental home. You hear a lot said about your education, yet some such beautiful, sacred memory, preserved from childhood, is perhaps the best education. If a man stores up many such memories to take into life, then he is saved for his whole life. And even if only one good memory remains with us in our hearts, that alone may serve some day for our salvation.[26]

DEALING WITH OUR ADDICTIONS

Nowadays we can use personality tests to point out our strengths. But the careful use of the Enneagram can point out more clearly where our addictive weaknesses lie. Are we perfectionists? givers? doers? idealists? scholar-observers? fun-lovers? controllers? or appeasers? Each of these are really emotionally addictive personality traits.

Ask yourself the following questions:

- What compulsions do I have? What gives me most pleasure when I wake up in the morning and anticipate what I want to experience? How does this relate to what may be addictive in my daily life?

- What binds and holds me back concerning my past? Do I have a persistent sense of failure or pain? Do I have a negative self-image or a sense of shame, guilt, fear, frustration, or anger? What negative feelings seem to haunt me constantly?

- Do I have, in fact, an inferiority complex? Do I feel inadequate to cope with daily life, to make decisions, to feel assured? Do I protect myself from criticism by judging others instead? Do I feel unworthy of friendships and take no initiative in relationships?

- Do I invest too much in other people's lives? How does the opinion of others affect me personally? Do I control others too much, always wanting to take control or appease or to give to others?

- Do I repress my feelings too much? Did I grow up in a family that likewise never showed their emotions very much? Do I still find it hard to let myself go? Has self-repression played a significant part of my life?

- Do I tend to go to extremes? Do I take strong risks? Do I want to dramatize things and feel afraid of being an ordinary person? Do I oscillate between being too authoritarian at work and too submissive in the home or with close friends? Are my emotions all either highs or lows?

- Am I always looking for something missing in my life? Am I seeking after my lost childhood? Do I feel as if I have a hole in my heart—that there is something missing? Is enough never enough? Am I always restless, discontented, uncertain about life?

- Do I feel as if I am always running around in circles? Do I feel trapped? Am I frustrated, as if I am tilting at windmills, like Don Quixote? How quickly do I pass from one fad to another?

- Do I deny too much? Am I always defensive, and guarded

within myself? Do I find it inconceivable that I might have any addictive behavior whatever?

- Do I suffer constantly from depression or sadness? Do I find it hard to smile or to have a deep sense of peace within? Is the experience of joy a rare emotion in my life?

Perhaps this kind of inventory will help to identify more openly where you (like the rest of us) suffer from addictive patterns of behavior.

A number of my student friends have also tested themselves on a daily or weekly basis like this. Draw a round circle like the face of a clock. At the noon hour of this circle, write down the immediate pleasure that makes you tick. It may be the new day's experiment in the laboratory, if you are a scientist. Or it may be the new man or woman you anticipate getting to meet and date. Or it could be the next person you want to help. Clearly there are many differing things that give us most pleasure—the next "fun" thing to do, the next duty to do well, the next person who needs to be kept "in place," or the next person to please.

By a quarter past the hour, imagine that you have reached your objective emotionally, and record your immediate feelings of satisfaction, disappointment, frustration that it was over or not done well enough or that it was not exciting or beautiful or "fun" enough.

By the half hour you are getting into the dumps, for the addiction has failed to satisfy. Perhaps the resultant sore head from over-eating or drinking or the guilt of doing what you did or the resentment that it was "blown," or the anger that you are still not recognized or rewarded or still misunderstood sends you off into a secondary spin of addiction. This might be as innocent as eating too many chocolates or taking a couple of aspirin or going off by yourself. Or it might have more serious consequences—perhaps going on a shopping spree or over-drinking or masturbation or letting rip in a fight or violent quarrel. Record these secondary consequences.

By a quarter to the hour you are really in a mess: Your emotions are drained, your shame and guilt are intensified. Maybe you feel remorse; maybe depression and anxiety increase so much that you have to get away, even run away or just go to sleep. This is really a time for suppression, to bury the whole cycle and start again as if from scratch. We get restarted when once again we reflect on what gives us pleasure, because otherwise we are lonely or useless or lack significance or need security. So the circle of addiction begins once again.

Like a repeated cycle of exercise you may begin to recognize by this analysis what is repetitive in your own daily and weekly behavior. But to identify your own addictive desires properly, consult your best friends about what *they* see of you. Then you will see the cycle for what it really is, addictive behavior that keeps us in some form of bondage. None of us is truly free.

STRONGER BONDS

Our brief look at literary archetypes of addictive living has shown us that certain vices bind us particularly strongly. There are three that we need to consider further: resentment, covetousness, and self-deception.

Resentment, or "frozen anger," is probably the prime killer of emotional health. For if we are created to be relational beings, then this destructive force in our relationships is indeed dangerous. No wonder then that in the Big Book of Alcoholics Anonymous, resentment is judged as "the number one offender" that destroys more addicts than anything else. Many forms of spiritual disease stem from resentment. The handbook of AA states: It is plain that a life which includes deep resentments leads only to futility and unhappiness.

Resentment kills creativity in the soul and destroys any incentive to recover from addiction. It can take many forms: cold silence, envy, emotional rancor and bitterness, being spiteful and vindictive; it is repressed through condemnation, judgmentalism, cynicism, jealousy, and even self-deprecation and a show of false humility. As the opposite of love, resentment expresses the vapors of an underground world, close to hell.

When Jesus taught his disciples to pray, "Forgive us our debts, as we also have forgiven our debtors," he went on to add the only commentary to any of the petitions of the Lord's Prayer: "For if you forgive men when they sin against you, your heavenly Father will also forgive you. But if you do not forgive men their sins, your Father will not forgive your sins" (Matt. 6:14–15) It is therefore vital that we overcome the spiritual malady of resentment, if we are to surmount all kinds of emotional, mental, and spiritual obstacles, and above all sort out our own relationship with God.

Covetousness, avarice, and *greed* are particular forms of material selfishness, all referring to the "itch for more." Usually the desire to have more relates to material possessiveness. Jesus warned us: "Watch out! Be on your guard against all kinds of greed; a man's life does not consist in the abundance of his possessions" (Luke 12:15). Yet covetousness is also a psychological obsession, a strong desire that is hurtful to others, maybe emerging as intense rivalry or theft, even as stealing the heart of another person's spouse. In the Bible, covetousness is always viewed as a very serious threat to the welfare of humanity. It was one of the first sins to surface when Israel settled in the Promised Land, and again when Christians became established in the early church.

The "itch for more" begins in apparent innocence. In C. S. Lewis' novel *Perelandra*, the main character, Ransom, wakes up to the intoxicating sight and smells of the exciting environment of the new planet he has entered:

> Looking at a fine cluster of bubbles which hung above his head, he thought how cozy it would be to get up and plunge one's self through the whole lot of them, and to feel all at once, that magical refreshment multiplied ten-fold. But he was restrained ... He had always disliked the people who encored a favorite piece of music in the opera—"that just spoils it" had been his comment. But this now appeared to him as a principle of far wider application and deeper moment. The itch to have things over again, as if life were a film that could be unrolled twice or even made to work backwards ... was it possibly the root of all evil? No, of course, the love of money is called that. But money itself—perhaps one valued it chiefly as a defense against chance, a security of being able to have things over again, a means of arresting the unrolling of the film.

That's it. Ransom recognized that we all crave for euphoria, for the intense delight of staying always in Wonderland or Disneyland. So "one more drink for the road," one more salary increase before contentment, one more sexual adventure, and soon we are rushing headlong into an addictive lifestyle.

Human beings have a tremendous capacity for imagination. Our ingenuity and creativity give us wonderful flexibility, but they also rob us of contentment. As Samuel Johnson observed: "Were it not for the imagination, Sir, a man would be as happy in the arms of a chambermaid as of a Duchess." The unyielding inbuilt pattern of the behavior of animals is both salvation and tyranny for them; so, perhaps, it is imagination which both saves and tyrannizes us. It gives us liberty, but perhaps more than we can handle. Falling in love, climbing great heights, dreaming exalted dreams, playing as a way of life can get us into serious trouble at times. Addiction begins when, like Oliver Twist, we ask for more, if the need for "more of the same" becomes a tyrant.

Addictive behavior is also reinforced by shame. We have already heard Dostoyevsky's warning: "Do not be so ashamed of yourself, for that is the root of it all." Shame is not the same as guilt. Guilt is about behavior that has harmed others, while shame is about not being good enough in one's own self-esteem. So, yes, a repentant addict may wake up to the guilt of having hurt other people; but we have to say that whereas I am guilty for something, I am ashamed *of myself.* Shame may be induced by things that do not appear to have moral value, such as our need to conform, to be socially acceptable, fear of rejection, embarrassment, humiliation, failure. Shame will drive me into myself and make me afraid to trust others or to confide in them.

During the last decade there has been compelling evidence of the power of shame to cripple our inner lives from childhood onwards. It is now recognized that the eating disorders bulimia and anorexia are largely caused by shame. Deep down, people feel that something is profoundly wrong with their own self-image. Poor people may suffer from class shame, and find alcohol a powerful shame-reliever, at least for a while. There is self-absorbed shame, when parents' love is a sham as they encourage children in self-indulgence without fully loving or accepting them.

When people feel worthless or unwanted, their pain and depression may be readily alleviated by the pleasure that becomes an addiction. Addiction may then begin with the shame caused by a particular situation in which one is constantly discouraged by other people's criticism and judgmental attitude.

Self-deception begins slowly. In its early stages the addiction is something desirable, so the mind is deceived into thinking it is harmless. Our rationalization that it is pleasant, sensible, or beneficial soon leads to self-deception. Tendencies that form habits and routines, like a daily glass of wine, seem to be safely reassuring, but the will is harnessed to greater and greater appetites. In time, all our precautionary defenses have been demolished, and addiction has begun in earnest. Deep down we may have a dim awareness of danger, but it is repressed.

At this stage of addiction, we give up all attempt at openness and self-reflection. Any sort of expression of our inner self becomes a threat to us. Prayer and meditation are not at all attractive to the addict. Eventually, as our tolerance to the addictive substance or process increases, reality becomes totally suppressed. With so much of our interior lives blocked out, boredom takes over in the face of emptiness and loneliness. As poor, impoverished creatures in a state of weary self-destruction, we seek only more addiction in order to forget our condition, and so the cycle of promise and unfulfillment is perpetuated. Our behavior becomes more secretive, more furtive, and self-esteem is gradually eroded; guilt, shame, and eventually the wish for death are all intensified. In this desperate condition we look for a way out. But we all have to "hit bottom" and experience this complete loss of our inner selves before we can be set free. The wages of Mephistopheles must ultimately be paid.

It is usually ignored in our addictive and secular society that the twelve steps of Alcoholics Anonymous are deeply, though not specifically, Christian. They invite us to surrender our idolatrous fixations, to accept that the goodness of creation is in the higher hands of our Creator, and that we have our place in his scheme of things. They call us to make an ongoing act of faith by placing ourselves in his hands. We are called to open and trusting relationships with our friends and neighbors, to accept our creatureliness and sinfulness, and to reach out to others who are also sinners and in suffering. Indeed, unconditional acceptance of each other is really the celebration of God's forgiveness and gracious acceptance of ourselves.

But once an addict, always an addict. We have to learn what seductive pathways of life to avoid at all costs. The alternatives—depending on God and on one another in the community, giving thanks for divine grace, and resisting the temptation to walk in the imaginations of our own hearts—are all ways in which day by day we can learn about living the transforming life of "the converted," of being free.

As we reflect more deeply on the nature of our addictive lives, we pray in the words of Augustine:

> Tell me why you mean so much to me. *Whisper in my heart. I am here to save you.* Speak so that I may hear your words. My heart has ears ready to listen to you, Lord. Open them wide and *whisper in my heart. I am here to save you....* There is no one but you to whom I can say: *if I have sinned unwittingly, do you absolve me. Keep me ever your own servant, far from pride. I trust, and trusting I find words to utter.*[27]

Sin of self-love possesseth all mine eye,
And all my soul, and all my every part;
And for this sin there is no remedy,
It is so grounded inward in my heart.
—Shakespeare, *Sonnet 62*

4

THE QUEST FOR LOVE

As we have already seen, wrong or unbridled desires lead to destructive addiction. So where does love, the greatest of all human longings, fit into the picture? What makes Christian love so different from other forms of love? And what happens when love breaks down?

Two women published a beautifully illustrated book on the theme of love in art. They confessed that their motive for doing so was "to confront the awesome theme of love after the failure of each in our marriages. In fact, so few of our friends' marriages had resulted in a deepening emotional commitment that divorce began to seem like a cultural cliché."[1]

As we know, many of us from personal agony, divorce has afflicted over a million marriages each year now for over a decade in the United States alone. Other nations of the West have comparable statistics, and in Scandinavia they are even worse. If "love is the act of extending oneself to nurture another," as these ladies have come to believe, then love is the discipline of self-giving, a skill that has also to be crafted. In fact, love is also the only thing that you get more of by giving it away. Yet love is so intertwined with our emotions and will that to give ourselves in love all too frequently means passing on the garbage of our inner lives and personal story as well.

In the years since the Second World War, people have become very pessimistic about love. Indeed, if pop songs have anything to tell us, love is all about broken hearts and disillusionment. "The song of love is a sad song.... Don't ask me how I know" ("Hi-Lili, Hi-Lo," Helen Deutsch and Bronislaw Kaper, 1952). The experience is a common one. Increasingly love has come to mean disappointment for those who grow up in broken homes and then have broken marriages themselves. As a result of their experiences, or of other people's, they believe that "love is dead." They choose to describe love in clinical terms: "a trick to make us vulnerable"; "a projection of infantile needs"; "a travesty of the sex instinct in those who forget that they are just a superior species of animal." This is hardly inspiring for the young, who are eager to try out their own chances of love.

For many, love is reduced to sex, and sex is pursued without love. As Erich Fromm concludes in his book *The Art of Loving,* "Love ... is a relatively rare phenomenon, and ... its place is taken by a number of forms of pseudo-love which are in reality so many forms of the disintegration of love."[2]

Perhaps we have taken love too much for granted. Perhaps we have a tendency to enter too lightly into relationships and marriage. Certainly a generation ago the mania to "date" and "have your girl" or "your man," Hollywood style, was naive and often trivial. Perhaps we are returning to the sobriety of a century ago, when marriage was a serious affair that we expected to last for life and when broken families were unheard of. Rainer Maria Rilke, in his well-known *Letters to a Young Poet,* writes on May 14, 1904, as follows:

THE DESIRE

> For one human being to love another: that is perhaps
> the most difficult of all our tasks, the ultimate, that last
> test and proof, the work for which all other work is but
> preparation.
>
> For this reason young people, who are beginners in
> everything, cannot yet know love: they have to learn it.
> With their whole being, with all their forces, gathered
> close about their lonely, timid, upward-beating heart,
> they must learn to love. But learning time is a long
> secluded time, and so loving for a long while ahead and
> far into life is—solitude, intensified and deepened alone-
> ness for him who loves. Love is at first not anything that
> means merging, giving over, and uniting with another
> (for what would a union of something unclarified and
> unfinished, still sub-ordinate, achieve?), it is a high
> inducement to the individual to ripen, to become some-
> thing in himself, to become a world for himself for
> another's sake. It is a great exacting claim upon him,
> something that chooses him out and calls him to vast
> things.[3]

Rilke gives us here a thoroughly realistic view of the continual effort and striving that love implies. So it is hardly surprising that people who accept the popular clichés about love being "easy" or "natural" soon get disillusioned and fall back on divorce. Their kind of love is like the house built upon the sand which, when the floods came, was quickly undermined and swept away in the storms of life. That is why Fromm concludes his reflections on love in modern life by stating that "people capable of love, under the present system, are necessarily the exceptions; love is by necessity a marginal phenomenon in present-day Western society."[4] In other words, not only is the modern world an idolatrous society and an addictive society, but we are now also a loveless society. Once more we are forced to start at bedrock and examine the nature of our foundations.

We have two great incentives not to give up both receiving and giving love. First, because human life is intrinsically relational; so to become cynical about love is to become cynical about being human. To lose love is to lose also our humanity. Second, today as in the ancient world, love is the point of contact between the human and the divine. In the ancient religions of the Near East, it is true that divine love was interpreted sexually, in the cult of sacred prostitution, and not as a relationship.[5] But in biblical faith, it is impossible to speak of religious life without love. Indeed, we may insist that love is the presupposition of all else in the Christian life. The heart then is the symbol of love; and if we want to be real human beings, both in our personal and spiritual lives, the desires of our hearts will center on love. So like Shakespeare we still take love with the utmost seriousness:

> Let me not to the marriage of true minds
> Admit impediments. Love is not love
> Which alters when it alteration finds
> Or bends with the remover to remove....
> It is an ever-fixed mark,
> That looks on tempests and is never shaken. (Sonnet 116)

HOW LOVE HAS BEEN DISTORTED

The eclipse of love in our world today is often blamed on the structures of modernism. Nowadays people are interested primarily not in relationships but in power, not in love but in money. So we can blame the failure of love on the competitive, dog-eat-dog mentality of the marketplace. We can blame bureaucracy with its blandness, the "technological society" with its engineering mentality, capitalism with its monetary instinct, indeed the "abstract society" with its alienation. When the whole human race is turned into an amorphous mass of consumers for whom big is beautiful and speed is of the essence, we soon get nostalgic. We long for a return to small-scale living, to go back to the old days of country village life, far away from the big cities.

It is conceivable that postmodernity will bring a revolution in our relationships. The time may come when, as the prophet anticipated, everyone will once again know God through the covenant bonds of divine love. Will this ever be so? Will reverence for the uniqueness of the person ever be restored? In short, will love be restored as the center of our lives?

In today's households, where couples are afraid of marriage because they see it as tyranny, where it is commonplace for the children of more than one marriage to live uneasily together, what space is there to unfold the desires of the heart? Love has been distorted, and we blame modern society for the pain and loneliness that this has caused.

The question that we always come back to is whether the hope of love is false and based on idolatry, or whether there is a firm historical foundation for the personal experience of the presence and love of God in our hearts. It is an important question, because we have a double inheritance. As we have already observed, alongside the continuity of Christian tradition we also have powerful influences from the classical tradition in Western society.

LOVE IN THE CLASSICAL TRADITION

For the ancient Greeks love was an inexplicable force that could only ultimately be explained by myth. Notice that it is a force, not a relationship. The Greek mind-set was intrinsically impersonal: Their gods were detached and unfeeling, and even they were ruled by the inscrutable Fates. The classical explanation of human desire is that whole human beings were originally androgynous, both male and female, but were later separated by the gods into their male and female halves. Ever since then they have therefore had a desperate longing for wholeness, through sexual and relational union. Love is the expression of this desire for wholeness.

It may be significant that the Semitic goddess of love, Ishtar, was androgynous. Her Greek counterpart, Aphrodite, was an erotic symbol, from whom we get the word aphrodisiac. Thus the classical influence encourages us to see love as sexual rather than relational. By the fourth century BC, an emphasis on the debased side of Aphrodite's nature had led to her being associated with Pandemous, the patron of the prostitutes. So classical thought turned to the idea of Venus, the Roman form of Aphrodite and a more heavenly being. We are reminded of Venus in the hippies' slogan of the late sixties: Make love, not war.[6]

Another archetype of love was Eros, the son of Aphrodite. With his bow and arrow he has become the popular symbol of romantic "falling in love." As he shoots his arrows at random, love is seen as a matter of mere chance rather than a relationship built on mutual trust. Plato's response to the myth of Eros was to retort that love is not a god, because there is need in love, and no god is needy.[7] Love is certainly a human need, which when it is not met, leaves people unfulfilled, and desire is a longing for completeness.

Under the impact of the rational philosophers, notably the Sophists, Greek myths were gradually transformed into allegories, stories which have a symbolic meaning. In Greek tragedy there is a fuller portrayal both of relationships and internal personal conflict, as in the stories of Oedipus, Prometheus, and Narcissus. As we have already seen, the old gods are superseded by a new god, *nous*, the mind that is conscious of its own thought.

Roman pragmatism took this even further by replacing the notion of love with that of duty. Virgil depicts Aeneas as resisting his love for Dido in order to carry out his duties. After one night of nuptial delights, he goes back to his ship to continue his voyage, bidding farewell to her:

THE DESIRE

> Duty-bound, Aeneas, though he struggled with desire
>
> To calm and comfort her in all her pain,
>
> To speak to her and turn her mind from grief,
>
> And though he sighed his heart out, shaken still
>
> With love of her, yet took the course heaven gave him
>
> And went back to the fleet.[8]

Yet the speed at which Dido's love turns first into hate, then into suicide, suggests that theirs is indeed a pseudo-love.

The Latin poet Ovid tells the story of another pseudo-love—Narcissus, the beautiful youth with whom everyone falls in love, but who rebuffs them all. One day Narcissus discovers, as he looks at himself reflected in a pool, that he is in love with himself. He dies eventually, through not being able to tear himself away from his reflection in the water. The story of Pygmalion, a sculptor who falls in love with the statue he has made, is a variation on the same theme. Under the guise of romantic love he is hopelessly committed to self-love. These are insights we all experience painfully in marriage—that our beloved is not ourself.

However, perhaps the most profound classical study of love can be found in Plato's *Symposium*. Plato believed that sexual desire had no place in love: It was a physical appetite, an urge belonging to man's baser nature shared with the animals. He argued that true erotic love has its origins not in desire, but in the perception of another person's beauty. For Plato, beauty was the visible expression of the immortal soul. Desire which centered on the physical attraction of the beloved was a hindrance to true love, and must therefore be transcended.[9]

Plato then, and Kinsey now, are like the two sides of the same mirror of human self-absorption. Plato frowned on all forms of sexual desire, while Kinsey, on the other side, smiles upon them. For Plato, the purest erotic love ceased to be love for a particular human being and became etherealized in what medieval writers were to know as romantic love. However, the unreality of romantic love has turned modern men and women toward sexual love instead.

ROMANTIC LOVE

Plato was responsible for creating a dualist approach to love, one that still persists, when he separated the world of the senses from the world of thought. However, whether it is my body and my sexual desires or my mind that determines who and what I love, Eros remains fixed as acquisitive love, whose aim is simply self-satisfaction. Even in the Middle Ages, when Eros was elevated to an intellectual desire for what is "good," Platonic love remained essentially egocentric. For if the gods do not need love, they neither give nor receive it, and the entire loving enterprise is only human, not divine. Platonic love then, in its original meaning, is wholly incompatible with Christian love, which is identified as self-giving—an inconceivable reality outside the Christian faith.[10]

In the development of Plato's thought known as Neoplatonism that developed after the third century AD with Plotinus and Porphyry, the world became more religious, more mystical, and therefore more preoccupied with the inner life. The Eros motif came to dominate the soul, with its central longing to return to God, or the Good and the Beautiful. This was interpreted as the soul's ascent, the quest for the better and indeed for the Absolute. But with Plotinus there arose a completely new notion: If the soul can ascend, then it can also descend—into sin and guilt.

This had nothing to do with a Christian understanding of God's descent to rescue and save humanity. It was rather an attempt to explain the ambiguity of human love that can be both good and evil. For when the material world is understood in Neoplatonic terms as unreal, deceptive, and uncertain, at best only a mirror image of a higher reality, then human love remains shadowy and unreal as well.[11]

Various similar movements such as Gnosticism and Manichaeanism contributed to an enlarged vocabulary of erotic love that we know as "Romantic Love,"[12] as did the medieval courtly love tradition. In medieval tradition, courtly love is outside the bounds of the reasonable, the possible, and the legitimate. It requires jealousy to arouse it, a great imagination to sustain it, and adultery to complete it, even though this end was not usually achieved. The seventeenth-century poet Andrew Marvell described romantic love succinctly:

> My Love is of a birth so rare
> As 'tis, for object, strange and high:
> It was begotten by despair
> Upon impossibility.
> Magnanimous despair alone
> Could show me so divine a thing,
> Where feeble hope could ne'er have flown
> But vainly flapped its tinsel wing.

DEFINITION OF LOVE

It is love outside the bounds of wedlock, so Marvell can add:

> For faith with jealous eyes doth see
> Two perfect loves; nor let them close:
> Their union would her ruin be,
> And her tyrannic power dispose.[13]

The love of Dante for Beatrice is one of the archetypes of this romantic love. Dante first met Beatrice when she was a child of nine. By the time he was eighteen, he had fallen deeply in love with her. They were sufficiently well acquainted with one another to meet on the street and talk, but she married someone else and probably never knew of his deep love for her. Dante also married and had children, but during the thirty-one years that he lived after her death, Beatrice remained for him the ideal beloved. He lists the characteristics of romantic love as follows:

- The shock of an intense personal experience of falling in love.
- Inability to avoid the stimulation of sexuality and the disturbance of the emotions.
- The conversion of the person's worldview, as they reinterpret reality, with love as central to their life.
- The experience becomes an end in itself: If positive it may release new creative energies, or if negative it can lead to despair.
- The whole being of the beloved begins to symbolize a greater whole: The beloved is worshipped by the subservient lover and may even be seen as *theotokos* or God-Bearer. This may lie behind the magnified role that was given to the Virgin Mary in the climate of medieval romantic love.

In the second book, *Purgatory,* of his vast poetic work *The Divine Comedy,* Dante learns from his guide, the Roman poet Virgil, what love is. Humanity is created to love, so the mind creates within itself an image of the beloved. When this image is matched by a real person, the mind is captured by love. Thus the internal and the external worlds of the real person are intimately connected by the symbol of the beloved.

Ultimately, romantic love can be seen as narcissistic or self-centered, beginning and ending with the needs of the lover rather than those of the beloved. Medieval Christian literature resisted any such identification, but in the thirteenth-century allegory *The Romance of the Rose* the garden of courtly love is watered by the fountain of Narcissus. A century earlier the Provençal troubadour Bernard de Ventadorn wrote:

> Alas, how much I thought I knew about love and how little I really did know! For I cannot keep myself from loving her from whom I shall have no requital ... Never have I had power over myself nor been mine own, from that moment when she let me look into her eyes unto a mirror that blessed me so much, till now, since I beheld myself in you, my deep sights have killed me, for I have lost myself as the beautiful Narcissus lost himself in the fountain.[14]

The invention of glass mirrors enhanced the pursuit of self-love both in the boudoir and in literature. Self-love is traceable through Spenser's *Faerie Queene*, Shakespeare's plays and sonnets, Milton's *Paradise Lost*, and Beaumarchais' *Marriage of Figaro*. For example, Milton makes Eve confess to Adam her self-love in loving him:

> ... he
> Whose image thou art, him thou shall enjoy
> Inseparablie [sic] thine, to him shalt beare
> Multitudes like thy self, and thence be call'd
> Mother of human Race
> —*Paradise Lost,* Book IV, Lines 471–75

With the Enlightenment, love ceased to be identified with religion, and the idea of human bondage as a result of Adam's sin was rejected. Schopenhauer declared dogmatically that "all amorousness is rooted in sexual impulse alone, is in fact absolutely only a more closely determined, specialized, and indeed, in the strictest sense, individualized sexual impulse, however ethereally it may deport itself."[15] Sexual love was now enthroned and romantic love, already watered down as narcissistic love, eclipsed.

By emphasizing love as an individual experience, Schopenhauer also prepares us for the new interest in psychology, which presupposed that the lover himself had reached a high degree of individuality. An idealized love corresponding with our mental image of the beloved would no longer do. The search was on for a unique person who would meet our psychological needs.

LOVE AND PSYCHOANALYSIS

In the twentieth century, Freud introduced a new interpretation of love, not as a natural human desire, but wounded and neurotic. Freud's new view of human beings sought to rediscover the desires of infancy, and to find new objects of love to heal the childhood wounds inflicted on us by our parents. Freud's *Libido* is a life force which replaces Plato's Greek *Eros* by its Latin equivalent. The Platonic conflict between the intellectual and the emotional parts of the personality was heightened and redefined by Freud as the conflict between the conscious ego and the unconscious id in the mind.

Like Schopenhauer and Nietzsche, Freud saw sexuality as human aggression, which could be diverted and sublimated into nonsexual activities. An example of such sublimation might be the painter Van Gogh, who painted passionately to compensate for the lack of a sexual life. He was clearly not interested in the explanation of normal human love, only in its neuroses or diseased forms. As one critic, T. Gould, has remarked: "To compare love with mere sexual need is almost the worst mistake a person can make. Sexual love is a tension which is easily satisfied and vanishes with the satisfaction; love is exclusive, unpredictable, ever demanding and grows rather than dies when it is fulfilled."

Freud dealt not with love, but with sex. He never attempted to define love, except to make the connection between adult and infant desires, interpreting love for others as a necessity which absorbs a useless surplus of narcissism.[16] Followers of Freudian psychoanalysis have varied opinions about the definition and the nature of human love. There is no explicit religious framework, although a symbolic and mythic emphasis is to be found in the work of Jung and his followers. The origin of the human need for love is seen to lie in people's prolonged helplessness as infants, regardless of their rapid intellectual growth. Longing, in the child, emerges from the alternating presence and absence of the caring parent. In adulthood this longing can never be entirely satisfied. The lover thus seeks to be always physically and psychically available.

Love is also made possible, according to psychoanalysts, by our ability to use symbols. Symbols allow people to transfer love from one object to another, from the animate to the inanimate, and in the end, to direct this love toward abstract ideas. It is possible, then, to love any object or idea to the point of idolatry.

As we have seen, human beings are quite capable of choosing themselves as their own object of love. Some self-love is necessary for healthy self-esteem and personal growth. But when that self-love has an unbalanced component of sexuality, either too much or too little, then physical fantasy or emotional deprivation may inhibit the ability to love another person. Psychoanalysts explore the emotional consequences of such a difficulty by probing into the growing child's awareness of his or her own sexuality, and the wounds of guilt and anxiety inflicted by culture and upbringing in coming to terms with it.

In love for another person, self-love is transferred to the loved one. In lust, on the other hand, there is little or no transference of one's self for the other, hence the usual contrast of lust with love. But Freud saw them not as opposites but as part of a spectrum. He and many after him were drawn to study the causes of the incapacity to love as more complex and more interesting than love itself. We see clearly today the suffering of many who were deprived in childhood of a deep bond with one person who had loved them in the early years of life. Divorce has intensified this situation.

Altogether there is a great variety of distorted love in society today: loveless sex, masochistic and sadistic love, narcissistic love, romantic idealism, and even childless love where an intrusion into the all-consuming focus on the partner cannot be tolerated. Many long-held values, illusions, and delusions incorporated into the idea of love by previous generations have been shattered by our post-Freudian world.[17]

THE CHRISTIAN EXPERIENCE OF LOVE

What in classical thought was called the highest "Good," the *summum bonum,* Christians call "Love," divine love. Christian love is not the same as the erotic love or the friendship valued by the classical world, because it starts with the love God has for us rather than with human speculation. It is the experience of love, not just a discussion about it. As Kierkegaard says in one of his prayers: "How could love be rightly discussed if you were forgotten, O God of Love, source of all love in heaven and on earth, you who spared nothing but gave all in love, you who are love, so that one who loves is what he is only by being in you!"[18]

There is a contrast between earth—where love tends to be isolated in a few acts and relationships—and heaven, where all is love, between the human and the divine. The Christian desire for love is prompted primarily by the heavenly character of God himself. It is the primacy of divine love and its expression in forgiveness and reconciliation that overarches all Christian understanding of human love. Since God loves us first, the Christian desire for love does not come from deprivation, but from the experience of love, seeking more of it. We have already "tasted and seen that the Lord is good."

Divine love is the revealed nature of the Holy Trinity: God who is the source of love, Christ our Savior and Redeemer who is the communication of love, and the Holy Spirit who is our reminder of that sacrifice of love. In the Old Testament the word mainly used for love expresses the spontaneity and fullness of the love of God. It is not a love which must reject some in order to be able to choose others, but an overflowing abundance. Another word for love is that used of the covenant agreement between God and his people, usually translated by "loving-kindness," which shows God's loyalty and mercy to us. Such love is a firm and reliable foundation for the new way of living to which Israel was called. It stresses the unfailing willingness of God to help and comfort his people. To show such loyalty to others is to reflect the attributes of God himself. A third word is used to express compassion and therefore empathy with the feelings of others, in intimacy. Its root literally means being "born from the same womb," such are the fellow feelings understood and shared in love.

These words represent three key emphases in the Old Testament on the nature of love: "Its spontaneity reflects the infinite love of God; its loyalty and mercy express the covenant God makes with his people; and its compassion is an expression of the perfect intimacy of God's love for us."[19]

There is no place in Scripture for the ecstasy and madness of addictive love. Instead there is the command to love God with all one's heart, soul, and might. It is the fitting response to God's own nature, and therefore to the outpouring of his love to us. It is expressed in loyalty, so that as a man "cleaves to his wife," so he is to "cleave unto the Lord." The commandment "You shall love your neighbor as yourself" also reflects God's love for us. Love, then, does not express an unknown, inarticulate desire, but a known and experienced pattern of divine love, which, the apostle Paul tells us, "has been shed abroad in our hearts by the Holy Spirit."

In the New Testament, the manifestation of God's love in Jesus Christ has two vital consequences. First, God's love is seen more clearly than before to be an atoning love; it brings sinners back to God, overcoming the estrangement caused by our pride and rebellion. We are shown that to be self-sufficient and pretend we do not need God is to deny our humanity. But secondly, Christian love is shown not to be a feeling or an emotion aroused by a person who is found to be lovable, and therefore desirable.

Christian love does not mean winning the person whom the lover desires, getting one's own way and satisfying one's own desires. It can be neither self-sufficient nor self-contained: It has been called "the radical personalism" of the Christian life.[20] The Christian ethic is not the individual acquisition of certain virtues, but the expression of those virtues to "one another."[21] Our relationships with each other and with God can never be overemphasized. Christian love is a fellowship of doing good to each other, redeeming each other, reconciling ourselves with each other, loving each other, sharing with each other, sacrificially assuring and building up each other to grow together in community.

The example of Jesus shows us that this love is not restricted to one family or nation: it is for all the world, even for one's enemies. Paul's hymn to love in 1 Corinthians 13 celebrates a love so distinctive in its quality that the human notion of "love" is not exalted enough, and translators have often preferred to call it "charity." Yet Jesus teaches that it is precisely such "charity" that expresses "the Kingdom of his love," into which we are invited to be his children. Christ's release of this divine love is the creation of a "new race." In it there is a new responsibility to love each other. As Paul put it: "Let no debt remain outstanding, except the continuing debt to love one another" (Rom. 13:8).

This is Christianity in action. To love like this is to receive God's love in our hearts, so great a gift that we are infinitely indebted to God. This is the love we share with others, so that we live in community, in what Charles Williams calls "co-inherence," each-for-the-other. We never cease to be in this debt of love to one another, because it links us with the eternal love of God. As Paul said, love remains[22]—it never wastes away, nor is it ever disillusioned, disappointed or betrayed.

It was when the classical world of late antiquity was crumbling, and Rome itself had fallen, that Augustine took up again this theme of divine love, which he symbolized as "The City of

God," in sharp contrast to "The City of Destruction." Plato's god had been an ideal that could be argued about or even dismissed with impunity. But to speak of the love of God is to speak about the reality of God, who exists whether we want to believe in him or not. To dismiss him is to exclude ourselves from this quality of life and love, which will leave us infinitely impoverished, indeed, "dead," said Paul. As Kierkegaard observed:

> To cheat oneself out of love is the most terrible decep-
> tion; it is an eternal loss for which there is no reparation,
> either in time or in eternity ... one who is deceived has
> locked himself out and continues to lock himself out
> from love.[23]

This is the state that Augustine calls living within "The City of Destruction." No other father of the church has been so profoundly "otherworldly" as Augustine, who constantly used the symbol of the pilgrim or traveler to signify the person who seeks the heart and love of God. In the end, there is no resting place, no purpose in life other than that of abiding in God's love.

Yet as we shall see in a later chapter, Augustine's interest in the symbol of the pilgrim also reflects his cultural heritage of Neoplatonism. This philosophy not only emphasizes the unchanging nature of God; it lays too much stress on human striving, on the human part of the journey. As a result there is not enough awareness that a loving God has descended and is alongside us in our efforts. Human desire is seen as something which is not yet attainable, which we must continually succeed in climbing upwards to reach. And the insistence on the "immutability of God," his unchanging nature, makes it difficult for changing human beings to be fully aware of God's love.

If we look closely at the philosophy of his day, we can see that Augustine was steering a middle way. On the one hand there were the Manichaeans, whose evasion of the responsibility of being human and denial of the goodness of creation led to despair; and on the other there was the rigorous self-righteousness of the

Pelagians, seeking to earn their way to heaven. Augustine saw that the only safe rule was: "Make neither of your own righteousness a safe-conduct to sin." Instead, grace, humility, and love are the rules for the Christian life. Yet we are still travelers who have not fully attained our goal, and so a holy longing for what is to come is also characteristic of the Christian. In Augustine's words: "Longing is the heart's treasury."[24]

The Augustinian heritage in the church has left us with some confusion as to how much love of self is compatible with the love of God. A Lutheran theologian, A. Nygren, has suggested in his book *Agape and Eros* that love of God and love of self are in irreconcilable conflict, just as Augustine's two cities were. But in response, a modern Augustinian Catholic, Father M. C. D'Arcy, in *The Mind and Heart of Love*,[25] has argued there is no contradiction in these two views of love. He confesses:

> We want to know how a man who is by nature bound to love himself can also love God more than himself. If it can be shown that in loving himself truly he is in fact loving God more than himself, then the difficulty is answered.

D'Arcy seeks to show that *eros* is natural human love, but *agape* is love that goes beyond the bounds of the merely human. Reflecting upon our own self-consciousness requires the use of our minds, so in this sense all self-seeking love (*eros*) is identified with our minds—it makes rational sense. But self-giving love (*agape*) that goes far beyond the ways of the mind, even to the point of appearing irrational, is also called for. The New Testament epistles urge us to follow this ethic of personal sacrifice in our behavior to each other.

How can *eros* and *agape* be integrated? Augustine would say it is only possible in God. D'Arcy would agree, but the real problem lies in identifying what it is about God that makes it possible for us to be both self-loving and self-giving at the same time. Neoplatonist philosophy cannot help us: It is a metaphysical straitjacket that does not permit this combined love to flow between God and humanity.

Perhaps it is the apostle Paul who had the most relevant comment. He said:

> God demonstrates his love for us in this: While we were still sinners, Christ died for us.[26]

Could anything be said more plainly? It is not we who begin negotiations with God to convey to him our desire for love. It is God himself who continually presents his love in an assurance beyond argument. He lets the full force of evidence break through our hardened hearts and deaf ears. The logic of God's love shown to us is intended to penetrate our very depths.

As Paul argued, what motive could we possibly have to die willingly for another? It is, perhaps, conceivable that we might be so attracted to a particular friend that in light of his or her goodness we might be prepared to die. But can we imagine dying for those who despise or ignore us? Yet this is the overwhelming love of God: Jesus died for us while we were still sinners.

This love breaks down the defenses of our hearts, to permit a new openness of being, a new existence in God's love. Paul continued:

> I am convinced that [nothing] will be able to separate us from the love of God that is in Christ Jesus our Lord.[27]

Yet we fear love. Love is a threat to our self-will. Love involves sacrifices, compromises, and a consideration for others that we don't want to make. Perhaps for a young married couple the stumbling block may be merely the irritation of an open toothpaste tube lying in the bathroom or the clothes left lying around the bedroom.

For another person it might be the unwilling realization that their false relationships are based on self-love, or the discovery of a self-willed desire to do things on one's own terms. Exposures like this may lead to a sequence of broken relationships, a parade of brief friendships through life, and an increasing resort to self-deception to avoid facing the truth.[28] It is what in the Middle Ages was called "concupiscence," the self-based love of sinners who hide rather than being found out. No wonder we prefer romantic love, love that is blind and purports to be blissfully unaware of such sinful shortcomings.

If, however, we do have the humility to be exposed as "sinners," how do we come to recognize the evidence of God's love in our hearts, in place of our self-love? Numerous writers in seventeenth-century France saw the evidence of God's love in the process of self-abandonment to his will. One of these, Jean Pierre de Caussade, spoke with relevance to our society and its obsession with the cult of self-fulfillment when he observed:

> The clearest evidence that we are not mistaken about the love of God is:
> 1. When we wish everything that happens to us will please God.
> 2. When we can suffer without a murmur to please God.
> 3. When we have a great horror of sin, even of the most trivial kind, and do our best not to commit any consciously.[29]

So divine love leaves us with a great repulsion for and sensitivity to sin.

Humility is needed if we are to experience God's love, for we must then face God's cleansing Spirit of truth. We need the sense of memory so dear to Augustine, that consciousness of the living God who rules in the affairs of human beings and loves each one of us. And in the end, as the poet Thomas Traherne affirms, it is God who takes the initiative: He is not unmoving but active in love.

He courts our love with infinite esteem,
And seeks it so that it doth almost seem
Even all His blessedness. His love doth prize
It as the only sacrifice.

'Tis death, my soul, to be indifferent;
Set forth thyself unto thy whole extent,
And all the glory of His passion prize,
Who for thee lives, who for thee dies.

There is no goodness nor desert in thee
For which thy love so coveted should be;
His goodness is the fountain of thy worth.
Oh! live to love and set it forth.

Thy love is nothing but itself, and yet
So infinite is His, that He doth set
A value infinite upon it. Oh!
This, canst thou careless be, and know?
—Thomas Traherne

But often, in the world's most crowded streets
But often, in the din of strife
There rises an unspeakable desire
After the knowledge of our buried life:
A thirst to spend our fire and restless force
In tracking out our true, original course;
A longing to inquire
Into the mystery of this heart which beats
So wild, so deep in us—to know
Whence our lives come and where they go.
                                    —Matthew Arnold, *The Buried Life*

5

THE SICKNESS OF MODERN DESIRES

There is a suffocation today, a sense of malaise, like that of a sick person trying to keep alive. We live on the surface of "things"; our lives are easily described, but rarely understood, busy, but going nowhere in particular. We live at the edges of other people's lives, too busy to listen; we are often unappreciated by others. We are like astronauts, each in our own spacesuit, orbiting the earth.

Perhaps that is the grim message of our drug culture; people want the candy of life, not just the paper wrapping, and are prepared to go to any lengths to try to get it. We are a bored culture—bored with the modern world's unreality, with its blandness, its plastic make-believe, its jargon, and its salesmen. We have become sports maniacs, for at least we can admire the physical skills the body can perform. But we are also becoming television and video zombies, creating our own celluloid unrealities.

We plaster up our emptiness with a professional but unreal air of confidence. We shut up our emotional skeletons in the cupboards of repression and denial. We handle the awkwardness of mystery and transcendence by institutionalized religion.

Recently the punk culture has tried to outrage us out of our unreality, but its cynicism will tend to lead its members to join the Hemlock Society and give up trying to live.

CHEATED AND CHEATING LIVES

In his novel *The Paper Men,* William Golding thinly veils biography with the reminiscences of a famous writer, Wilfred Barclay, who is tormented by three witches in his life: Alcohol, Sex, and Immortality. He confesses: "I could describe my whole life as a movement from one moment of farce to another farce on one plane or another, nature's comic, her clown with a red nose, ginger hair, and trousers falling down at precisely the wrong moment. Yes, right from the cradle."[1] It is all a matter of "fixation, frustration, and folly."

The story begins with the visit of an ambitious young professional, Professor Rick L. Tucker, whose only claim to fame is to associate with Wilf as much as he can, interpreting his thought to posterity. After a full dinner, Wilf is thankful to see his guest upstairs and turn in himself. But he is wakened in the night by a sound coming from the dustbin outside. Of course, badgers! But instead he sees the dawn-lit face of a "full professor of English Lit. rifling my dustbin." His first reaction is of offense that his guest, not having had enough dinner, is now feeding on the bones. Then he sees the file of papers he had discarded from his writings, and realizes Tucker is after his originals.

Now Wilf's wife, Elizabeth, enters the scene, picks up one of the papers, and reads aloud, "... longing to be with you, Lucinda." Sniffing a scandal she asks coldly, "And *who* is Lucinda?" That "who is Lucinda?" finishes the marriage, and for the rest of the story, Wilf is pursued by the relentless researcher of fictional glory, while he tries to avoid every new bit of his past being uncovered. This reminds us of the poet Yeats's quest for the illusions of sincerity that betray the dark past of our lives by their insincerity:

> Those masterful images because complete
>
> Grew in pure mind, but out of what began?
>
> A mound of refuse or the sweepings of a street,
>
> Old kettles, old bottles, and a broken can,
>
> Old iron, old bones, old rags, that raving slut
>
> Who keeps the till. Now that my ladder's gone,
>
> I must lie down where all the ladders start,
>
> In the foul rag-and-bone shop of the heart.
>
> —W. B. YEATS, *THE CIRCUS ANIMALS' DESERTION*[2]

Certainly, most of contemporary fiction is rummaging in the dustbin. Yeats's allusion to the loss of the Neoplatonic "ladder of Ascent" suggests that an age has come when people have lost the prospect of heaven, so can only be rag-and-bone merchants, raking over the unsavory garbage of their hearts.

Can we explain our society's garbage bin? Is that what the reaction of "postmodernity" is all about?

Clearly, the term "postmodern" implies disillusionment with modernity, especially with its rationalism and worship of science. Perhaps we are never wholly disillusioned with materialism as such; the vices of possessiveness and avarice are always with us, and our materialistic disillusionment is shallow. We always want more, and it is only diminishing resources that have stopped us claiming more as a right. Now we are realizing we are not entitled to anything that we have not earned for ourselves!

The good old days of rock-solid social ideologies are behind us. In Russia today, the myth that through revolution a superman is born has toppled with the statues of the revolutionary heroes. But our faith in a Western society of credit is also disappearing as nations face bankruptcy; national debt is really the debts of a country's citizens.

However, postmodernism reserves its strongest condemnation for the rationalism and impersonality of the technological society we have bred. We are also becoming disillusioned with a world where information increasingly lacks cohesion and meaning, as the computer spits it all out. "So what?" has become an evasive tactic for the deluge of data now available. The question "How?" has been answered phenomenally well, but "Why?" remains unanswered, leaving us to wonder what is the significance of all this knowledge.

Looking back, we can now understand more clearly why the philosopher Pascal had contempt for the scientist Descartes. For Descartes was one of the first to reduce the human soul to the "thinker." "I think, therefore I am" sounds innocent enough, until we trace its implications through the philosophies of the Age of Reason, where every ideology uses a similar definition, from Marx's "I produce, therefore I am," to Freud's "I am sex-repressed, therefore I am," each narrowing further the potential of the human being. Nietzsche's version, "I rebel against the past, therefore I can control the future," proved to be a disastrous statement when Hitler took him seriously.

Pascal saw that where Descartes was leading would mean the death of the soul. What Descartes did not build into his theories was that man has religious desires, as well as the desire to know mathematically. Humanity's intuitive sense of mystery, of divine presence, Pascal called *esprit-de-finesse;* it is needed to complement and complete the mathematical exactitude of Descartes' *esprit-de-geometrie.* This absolutizing of rationality frightened Pascal and prompted him to say: "Write against the people who press all too deeply into science: Descartes!"[3] For, he affirmed, "we know the truth to be not only with the reason, but also with the heart. The heart has its reasons which reason does not know; we see this in a thousand things."[4] Indeed, the desires of the heart are more real than even the desires of the mind. This is the heritage that Pascal saw Descartes destroying. "I cannot forgive Descartes," he said, "in all his philosophy he would have been quite willing to dispense with God."[5]

Later, at the end of the eighteenth century, when French revolutionaries enthroned "the Goddess of Reason" they were following a logic previously laid down by Descartes and his followers. And in our times, Gandhi has remarked: "Rrationalism is a hideous monster when it claims for itself omnipotence. Attribution of omnipotence to reason is as bad a piece of idolatry as is worship of stock and stone believing it to be God."

Reason became the goddess of the mind because of the assumption, which Descartes had already proposed, that mathematics is the most certain form of knowledge. "Noumenal" or intuitive knowledge is considered a much less trustworthy form of knowing than "phenomenal" or objective knowledge. This of course assumes that we can "know" without the exercise of belief, an argument that is now being challenged. Even our belief that there is a rational pattern to the universe which human intelligence can grasp—an essential assumption lying behind all theories based on scientific observation—is unproven and must be taken on faith.

Of course, Romanticism was in part a protest against the view that all knowledge must be merely factual. As the poet Keats protested:

> O for a life of sensations rather than of thoughts!

Yet he saw no defense against this tidal advance of rationalism, writing to Benjamin Bailey in 1817: "I have never yet been able to perceive how anything can be known for truth by consecutive reasoning—and yet it must be."

Rationalism puts up a barrier between ourselves and life, making everything into "things-out-there," detached from the observer. Just as Pascal detested Descartes for his threat to the human soul, so Kierkegaard scorned the arch-rationalist Hegel who wished to reduce God to a concept, "the God-idea." As Kierkegaard commented:

> The danger of abstract thought is seen precisely in respect of the problem of existence, the difficulty of what it solves by going around it, after boasting that it has completely explained it. It explains immortality in general, and it does so by identifying it with eternity— with eternity which is essentially the medium of thought. But with the immortality of each human being, wherein precisely the difficulty lies, abstraction does not concern itself, is not interested in it. And yet the difficulty of existence lies just in the interest of the existing being—the person who exists is infinitely interested in existing. Abstract thought accepts immortality only in order that it may kill me as an individual being with a personal existence and so make me immortal.[6]

Thus Kierkegaard exposes the fallacy of the purely rational point of view by irony. "For the rationalist takes away our fever by taking away our life and promises us, instead of a concrete, an abstract immortality that consumes us, as if it were an abstract and not a concrete hunger!"[7]

The revolution of consciousness that thinkers like Hegel and Nietzsche created was in fact the deformation of metaphysics and theology in order to make human beings into supermen. In place of "understanding," literally standing under the nature of the object studied to learn from it, there was now "overstanding" in speculative thought—the facts were fitted to the theory instead of vice versa. The speculative thinker could claim to have the ultimate revelation, thus playing God with the aid of his reasoning.

This creation of the speculative mind was a profound revolution of human consciousness, for it dismissed all sense of mystery, of the spiritual realm, of divinity other than its own godlike powers. It was a deliberate rejection of the historic sense of memory as God's action in history, and of the presence of God in human life. It was not merely a point of view, or even a school

THE DESIRE

of philosophy, but rather it was a change in human consciousness. It reduced thought to a grammar of "things out there," with humanity as the detached observer of reality, as if we had no involvement in the universe. "Reality" became something like the view an astronaut sees of earth while floating above it in outer space—it was all descriptive and speculative, and no longer participatory knowledge in which the observer was personally involved.

This state of mind affects us all today. Perhaps you first looked at the cover of this book, the title getting your attention. "The Desire"! "Hmm," you say, "it's an interesting topic. Perhaps I should look into it and read some more." But the words on the page remain just that—words, ideas, thoughts, the currency of rationalism. And you say, "Isn't that just a waste of time?"

Of course it is, because you and I would gain more by expressing the grammar of friendship in meeting each other, in seeking transformation together into a richer reality than the cheating world of modernity. So you are not a "reader," nor am I a "writer," but we are persons in communication, aware that we are also in the presence of God, enriched by the memory of a historic relationship with God that also has a future. This is participatory knowledge.

Thus, human consciousness should be used not merely to gain an objective knowledge of the truth, but to become part of its reality. This implies that when we speak "the truth" we are committed not just to mathematical accuracy, as in the statement that two times two equals four. "Telling the truth" to someone must also involve communication between us as persons, allowing each other to share part of our lives.

EMOTIONAL POVERTY IN THE MODERN WORLD

The consequence of the rationalistic perspective upon life, Kierkegaard observed, is the cause of the personal and experiential knowledge; "we have forgotten what it means to exist, and what inwardness signifies." But as one of his commentators, Patrick Gardiner, notes, people have often been unwilling to commit themselves to looking for an inner reality: "If they attended to their own attitudes or emotions it was through a thick haze of pseudo-scientific expressions or cliché-ridden phrases which they had picked up from books or newspapers rather than in the direct light of their own inner experience."

One consequence of this has been to assume that "moral reasoning" is the only appropriate way of behaving. This assumes that to think morally is to act and live morally. Writers such as Lawrence Kohlberg have been given wide acceptance on the assumption that it is enough to learn morality and that rational discussion will establish the moral life.[8]

What such writers overlook is that emotions are an integral part of human behavior, and therefore of any real moral understanding. Any system that assumes the primacy of human reason will tend to neglect the emotional life. Yet empathy, the feeling of interrelatedness with other people, is clearly of the utmost value in moral life. In fact the Greek *empatheia* literally means entering into suffering, being "in passion," with one another. It implies sympathy, putting oneself in someone else's situation, and compassion. It is empathy that provides the basis for loving someone else.[9] By contrast, in a morality which has a solely rational basis, there would be no motivation to take the initiative in a relationship, no compulsion to do what empathy sees is necessary.

People's lives today are markedly affected by the atrophy of their affections. This can be seen in the intellectualists who make everything a matter of curiously detached and noncommittal observation. They populate the loneliness and shyness of their inner worlds with facts, figures, and odd observations that appease their intellectual, information-gathering interests, like old curiosity shops, where neighbors or colleagues—clients—are served willingly or unwillingly with their wares. They may be brilliant scientists, or just know all the football stars and scores, but beyond that there is very little to them. Their hearts have atrophied.

Another familiar type, the pragmatists, use their engineering skills to deal with life. They are good at quick fixes, but have no more than a basic utilitarian approach to everything. They find any reference to matters of the heart quite irrelevant and even threatening, and are concerned only with what is useful. They are well acquainted with ambition, energy, power, and organization, but not love.

Then there are the official bureaucrats, for whom life is run according to the "rules." They operate within a legalistic framework and since it is dangerous to deviate from the rules they are also conservative, afraid of innovations. Not surprisingly their emotional lives are reduced to mere satisfaction at doing things "properly."

Another type of emotional atrophy can be found in people whose aim is to control events. They view the emotional life with suspicion, as it "messes things up" and is a sign of weakness. If such people allow themselves to reflect they may pause to wonder why they have so much suppressed anger that periodically erupts beyond their control. Instead, they strive to silence their hearts and to live with power and authority, hiding behind the front of officialdom and professionalism.

Is it any wonder then that modernity has brought so much heartlessness and violence into our lives? In a time of troubles, everyday life becomes an exercise in survival. It appears to be a kind of luxury simply to be oneself, and it is seen as out of place to desire too much, especially from the heart. The society of the "minimal self," as Christopher Lasch has called it, has come.[10] And yet, Matthew Arnold reminds us:

> But often, in the world's most crowded streets
>
> But often, in the din of strife
>
> There rises an unspeakable desire
>
> After the knowledge of our buried life.

The Sickness of Religious Life

The loss of our emotions in personal life today clearly also has a deep influence on the life of faith. As early as the mid-eighteenth century, Jonathan Edwards observed that "as in worldly things worldly affections are very much the spring of men's motions and actions; so in religious matters the spring of their actions is very much religious affection: he that has doctrinal knowledge and speculation only, without affection, never is engaged in the business of religion."[11] It is as if Edwards was listening to Hegel a century later, and protesting against him.

It has been said that the tremendous achievement of Christianity was that it removed the holiness of the universe in order to exalt its Creator. But having a sacred God in a profane universe has encouraged the very process of rationalism that we now deplore. Moreover, as one critic, Thomas Molnar, has noted:

> The Christian religion is exposed to the temptation of an excessive rationalism because of its well-defined doctrine and documented historicity. By eliminating the pagan myth and replacing it with a story with truth content, Christianity compelled the mythopoetic impulse within us to leave the domain of public imagination or to curb itself within certain limits.[12]

Molnar is asking, has conventional Christianity taken away too much of the mystery of life? This criticism is borne out by the fact that we tend to see faith descriptively as something to be "taught" rather than seeing it as a way of life and behaving accordingly.

It is probably no accident that Feuerbach, growing up in a strict Lutheran home, reacted against his intellectual faith and moved toward a "feeling" interpretation of religion, which gave ultimate significance to human needs. He saw the idea of "God" as something that people projected onto the universe to cope with their own needs and fears.

Carl Jung also grew up in a Lutheran pastor's home. The lack of emotional content in the faith he was taught caused him to turn to myth and intuition. Without any historic content to his religious inquiries, he reverted to paganism. In the early days of his friendship with Sigmund Freud, he wrote:

> I think, dear Dr. Freud, we must give psycho analysis time to infiltrate into people from many centers, to revivify among intellectuals a feeling for symbol and myth. Ever so gently we want to transform the Christ back into the soothsaying god of the vine, which he was, and in this way absorb those ecstatic instinctual forces of Christianity for the one purpose of making the cult and the sacred myth what they were—a drunken feast of joy where man regains the ethics and the holiness of an animal. That is the beauty and the purpose of classical religion.[13]

In other words, Jung was advocating the takeover of Christianity by the classical paganism that it had once conquered. Today, the so-called "sacred psychology" is another more overt attempt to do just that, under such names as "scientific therapy."

While the emotional content of the heart has been undervalued for a long time, there has been widespread confusion because it ranges from bodily feelings to the highest spiritual experiences of love, joy, and peace. It is a disastrous misunderstanding to lump all these feelings and emotions together. There is, however, good reason to discredit mere sentimentality or hysteria that cuts emotions off from their original cause, leaving them in some irrational limbo. When that happens, false feelings are rightly denounced as unworthy.

Significantly, the rationalist does something similar in expressing rational argument without the appropriate emotions to clothe it as personal truth. Thus when religious truth is subject to either a floating sentimentalism or a rationalistic fundamentalism, faith becomes an object of caricature and unattractive to secular society.

The impression many people have is that religion is something you either "catch" or you don't, but if you do, then it is either very insubstantial, or else heavily hypocritical. A sad example of the former can be found in the reminiscences of Christopher Robin Milne, son of A. A. Milne, entitled *The Road Less Traveled.* Milne actually wrote his charming children's tales to communicate shyly to his son what he was unable to convey to him directly—a father's love. But he left the general public with the image of "Christopher Robin saying his prayers."

Perhaps the outrage for the child was that if father could not be intimate with his son, how could Christopher be expected on his own to be intimate with God? This is a common distortion for the beginning of faith. So Christopher tells us that he "spent his entire adult life running away from Pooh and his friends." As a private person, Christopher's father could give of his emotions only sparingly, so one suspects he gave his son all he could in his private writing rather than in any personal intimacy. Christopher's relationship with his mother was even worse: he saw her only once in fifteen years of widowhood. The effect of all this on a stuttering, shy, and lonely child is described by Christopher himself:

> As a child I accepted what I was taught. From Monday to Saturday I learned about the Ancient Romans; on Sunday about the Ancient Hebrews. After six days of struggling with my voice in class, on the seventh day I shook it free of its chains and sent it, pure and clear, soaring up into the rafters of the school chapel. In solos and descants I praised the Lord. How could I doubt the truth of what I did so well?
>
> But alas the fleeting treble became the croaking bass, and when my voice broke, my strongest link with the church broke with it. In the end I was left holding a guide book to the Guide whom I had never really met, and a picture which, though it once had satisfied me, satisfied me no longer.[14]

Why had the picture failed?

In part, it was because the visible world seemed more attractive than an unknown God. A detached father, busy writing in his study, and an embittered mother made intimacy with God seem inconceivable to the child.

It is a scandal of our times that the mind and the emotions are in conflict, each separated from the other, and incapable of living meaningfully together, needing each other or recognizing their mutual dependence. An emotional life must be meaningful, and a rational existence must be clothed with appropriate emotions. When this is not recognized, then the apparent clash between them is interpreted as a conflict between science and faith—and the rationalistic faith that has emerged from a Newtonian worldview has proved to be too brittle to compete with a rationalistic universe.

Many people who see religion as purely emotional are led to reject it out of a desire for intellectual integrity. This is illustrated by William Golding's novel *Free Fall*. Sammy Mountjoy is a prisoner of war reflecting in his cell about his past and his fall from innocence. He was a bastard child fostered by a priest, and remembers two teachers at school who have a profound influence upon his life. Their influence grows rather than diminishes with time. "Mine is the responsibility but they are part reasons for my shape, they have had a finger in my pie."

Rowena Pringle is a spinster who teaches religion in the school Sammy attends. She professes "Bible and purity," but the truth of the matter is that she is simply hateful. Her own repressed desires are projected in false accusation onto the small boy, and she humiliates Sammy in front of the whole class. Previously, Sammy had loved the Bible stories of Moses and the burning bush, of Jacob's ladder. But she crushes the awe and wonder of them all, and bowdlerizes them by her insensitive, false manner, destroying an opportunity for faith.

In the classroom next door, Nick Shales, the science teacher, lives in his rational universe. "There was no place for spirit in his cosmos. Consequently the cosmos played a big practical joke on him. It gave Nick a love of people, a selflessness, a kindness and justice that made him a homeland for all people; and at the same time it allowed him to preach the gospel of a most drearily rationalistic universe that the children hardly noticed at all."[15] The burning bush of Miss Pringle's lesson violates the scheme of Nick's rational universe. Crossing from one class to another, the children hold both universes effortlessly in their heads, but give their hearts to Nick's kindness. Both systems are coherent, but both are unreal.

Years later, Sammy reflected upon these two influences in his life.

> Miss Pringle vitiated her teaching not by what she said, but by who she was. Nick persuaded me to his natural scientific universe by what he was, not by what he said. I hung for an instant between two pictures of the universe; then the ripple passed over the burning bush and I ran toward my friend. In that moment a door closed behind me. I slammed it shut on Moses and Jehovah. I was not to open that door again, until in a Nazi prison camp. I lay huddled against it, half crazed with terror and despair.[16]

Miss Pringle was totally unable to dam up the inner lusts and anger of her secret desires and passions: She shared the loneliness of her private life with only a plastic canary in a plastic cage, and plastic flowers on the table. Would prayer and meditation have helped her? Would the beauty of believing have triumphed over the cheap, adolescent calf-love of Sammy's sexual escapades? Instead, religious life for Sammy came to a halt until the crisis of prison camp.

UNCERTAIN LIVES

These stories illustrate that a schizophrenic culture, split between head and heart, thought and emotions, has been deeply destructive of the religious wholeness of being that is fostered by true faith, making us mature people. Instead, this false choice between being rationalistic and being sentimental has produced an anemic "gas and gaiters" or "lollipop" type of religion. John Updike portrays such religion very effectively in his novels. In an interview, he once confessed:

> My books feed, I suppose, on some kind of perverse relish in the fact that there are insolvable problems. There is no reconciliation between the inner, intimate appetites and the external consolations of life. You want to live forever, you want to have endless wealth, you have an endless avarice for conquests, crave endless freedom really, and yet, despite the aggressive desires, something within us expects no menace.[17]

As in the book of Ecclesiastes, which Updike quotes quite often, the universality of death, life's mystery, and God's silence threaten and confuse us. Updike's characters often seem paralyzed, unable to make serious decisions in choosing between good and evil or in accepting God in their lives. Thus in *Rabbit Redux*, Peggy tells Harry (Rabbit), "Living is a compromise between what *you* want and doing what *other* people want." To which he responds, "What about what poor God wants?" Unfortunately what God wants is always an unanswerable question.[18] God is never far away from the conversations of Updike's characters, but they refer to him always as "out there." Moreover, there is silence. God never speaks. There are no "burning bush" experiences.

As a result, God takes the form of Updike's characters' ultimate desires or wishes. Freddy in *Couples* is an agnostic who interprets God as "Big Man Death" but "people are the only thing people have left since God packed up." And "by people," Freddy continues, "I mean sex." Yet on another occasion, Freddy, commenting on Jesus' miracle at Cana, expresses a deep desire:

> Christ. I'd love to believe it … any of it. Just the littlest
> bit of it. Just one lousy barrel of water turned into wine.
> Just half a barrel. A quart. I'll even settle for a pint.

But belief seems far away for most of the characters, and is replaced instead with busyness. In Updike's first novel, *The Poorhouse Fair,* Hook observes: "There is no goodness without belief. There is nothing but busyness." So in *Rabbit, Run,* "… he runs. Ah: runs. Runs." The writer of Ecclesiastes long ago called this a chasing after the wind … vanity, vanity, all is vanity.[19] Some characters like Connor belittle belief, and with their vision redirected to the earth, declare that visions of God can be chemically induced.

John Updike himself does not give us a very convincing estimate of his own faith. "Looked at coldly," he observes, "having been given a Protestant, Lutheran, rather antinomian Christianity as part of my sociological make-up, I was too timid to discredit it. My era was too ideologically feeble to wrest it from me, and Christianity gave me something to write about, and a semblance of a backbone, and a place to go on Sunday mornings when the post offices were closed."[20] After all, "church going in a small town is one of the few places where the people are and the only cultural institution dealing in two-thousand-year-old rites and six thousand years of history." Without concert hall and opera house, church is the social institution. Moreover, "being human cannot be borne alone," argues Updike. "It needs other presences. We need the signs of sustaining Otherness." If it is a choice between atheism or God, then let God be. So Updike made a logical formulation—not perhaps worthy of Anselm or Aquinas—yet suitable for his time and temperament:

1. If God does not exist—the world is a horror show.
2. The world is not a horror show.
3. Therefore God exists.

But behind this logical facade "proving" the existence of God, Updike had to admit:

> The Christian religion I had been born into ... almost no one believed it, believed it really—not its ministers, nor its pillars like my father and his father before him. Though signs of belief (church, public prayers, mottos on coins) existed everywhere, when you moved toward Christianity it disappeared as a fog solidly opaque in the distance thins to transparency when you walk into it.[21]

Fortunately, Updike decided to read a few authors like G. K. Chesterton, T. S. Eliot, Miguel de Unamuno, Søren Kierkegaard, and Karl Barth who helped him believe in something more substantial than fog.

However, even in a more educated Christian environment, where "the truth" is known, Watson's forlorn desire will still haunt us:

> Shall I ever feel at home,
> Never wholly be at ease?
> —SIR WILLIAM WATSON, *WORLD-STRANGENESS*

Even if we are taught "doctrinally" to be orthodox in our religion, if we do not learn also to cultivate empathy and love, we can grow up emotionally deprived. This can have a deadening effect upon people's lives. As one friend whom I shall call Helen confessed, she never felt she had a right to her own feelings, or indeed to express them, while she was growing up. As she told me:

> I grew up in a very strict, rationalistic atmosphere, well cared for physically but where there was little expressed affection, little touch, and thus little perceived love. As a family we have never been able to express or share our feelings with each other. My father was a strict disciplinarian, and very controlling in every aspect of family life.

> My mother was somewhat repressed emotionally. As a result I suffered a considerable degree of emotional deprivation, and my emotional life has been stunted. The religious influence in the home was similarly authoritarian and rigid, so I developed a view of God as stern, harsh, and angry, a view I still find difficult to shed. The early influences shaped a character that was legalistic, judgmental, rigid ... where duty, loyalty to the status quo and bondage to regulations, have all marked my life.

This suggests that when life is reduced to a formula, even if it is a religious formula, it is drab indeed. Heaven is seen only in terms of decency, duty, and a lot of work for the Master, wandering forever beneath the blank stare of the Creator.

THE AGE OF AQUARIUS

Into this anemic, marginalized religious life, a whole new interest in "spirituality" has suddenly burst forth. The promise given by Tom Paine seems about to be fulfilled after all: "We have it in our power to begin the world again."

The human potential movement was first seen in California in the early 1960s. As futurists like Willis Harman called for a radical shift in self-understanding, psychologists like Abraham Maslow, Erich Fromm, and Carl Rogers reached toward new spiritual perspectives for humanity. Holistic medicine made Eastern mysticism look respectable within Western science. Experiments with psycho-neuro-technology and paranormal psychology have created a deepened self-consciousness. The drug culture has intensified the demands for psychedelic experiences. And so the "New Age" is launched! It is assuredly "scientific." It is "global" in its inclusion of faiths from both East and West. It is a "religious impulse for secular man," for it is undogmatic, non-institutional, and intensely individualistic. It is "heightened experience," with a sensational and dramatic emphasis on personal experience. It is desire on a cosmic scale that is danger-ously ecstatic.

One New Ager who spent fifteen years in the movement describes his disillusion with religion as a teenager. Although he grew up looking like a successful all-American boy, inside he was rootless, the result of his father being in the Navy and moving every three or four years.

> "In early teen years my inquisitive mind started to become interested in religion. I started to feel an empti-ness inside and a hunger for truth. At home, we rarely discussed religious issues, mostly leaving such topics to be covered at Sunday school and church." One day, pursuing "a God and Country" scouting award, he asked a Navy chaplain friend with great expectations of real dialogue: "I'd really like to know God, but I have so many doubts." The bewildered, irritated response was "Perhaps some other time, but not now, Randall. You are too young." The boy's frustrations intensified in church attendance, until one day "something snapped in me," he said. "I no longer wanted to attend what I perceived as sterile and lifeless church services and study groups. I suddenly knew what I was looking for wasn't there. In the years ahead, I would hear many New Agers telling a similar story."

There followed regular trips to bookstores in shopping malls to buy books on yoga, meditation, Eastern religions, and philosophy, and then periodic visits to gurus to learn to practice detached self-observation, out-of-body experiences, and much else.

Eventually one night, in a mystical state, Randall felt an overwhelming luminosity that was followed by a face of devour-ing darkness and unspeakable abomination. He woke up the next morning in absolute stark terror, terribly shaken, his mind racing uncontrollably, and yet dimly aware of a profound grati-tude. It was not too late to be delivered from this terrible evil.

In fact, the "New" Age offers age-old occult practices: the use of psychic powers, witchcraft, and magic. It encompasses all aspects of human experience and promises human transformation, exalting the intellectual capacities of men and women as divine. Its framework is a monumental self-centeredness and self-glorification, and as more and more sophisticated devices are developed to manipulate the brain, the high-tech aspect of the New World Order, with its subliminal abilities, parallels the inhumanity of Aldous Huxley's *Brave New World*.

There can be no objection to mystical experiences, to visions and voices; very many such personal experiences have been well documented. But the New Age draws on the mysticism of self-indulgence and self-absorption. There is a real danger of becoming open to evil forces that may be clothed in light, but which, as Randall discovered, are really demonic.

The protest of the New Ager that Westerners have put too much emphasis on reason, have abstracted reality and robbed us of personal experience, is certainly valid. Since the scientific revolution, everyone feels the respectability of science and is intellectually drawn to it. The New Age Movement has recognized that the spiritual component of life has been rejected, and the significance of this is illustrated in the massive positive response to New Age thought. But there are inconsistencies in their proposals. "Spirituality" for them is accompanied by pseudoscientific data, so that their claims do not suffer any loss of respectability. Crystals and gems, "for healing, self-transformation, and accelerated enlightenment," are techniques which are substituted for the disciplines of spirituality. Now "brain-drive machines" as well as hallucinogenic drugs are using so-called "scientific" skills to induce the "spiritual."

What we are witnessing in the New Age Movement is human desire being diverted to a use that is even more frightening than that harnessed and rationalized by political economists in the eighteenth century to turn the private vice of acquisitiveness into a public virtue. The New Age uses sciences such as pharmacology and neuro-techno-psychology to expand human consciousness—for the purposes of self-indulgence. The ambiguity of this trend is that the more that human potential is extended, the more room there is for self-centeredness and sinfulness. It intensifies feelings of alienation instead of promoting human beings' relational needs. It expresses the boredom of an affluent society that cannot take suffering and poverty into account, so it is a movement with no concern for the underprivileged, for the Third World, or for the "losers" within our own society.

THE SICKNESS OF POSTMODERNISM

But is this change in worldview not an overreaction to modernism? Perhaps so. The new vocabulary of "spirituality" has displaced "rationality." "Surprise" has been substituted for "progress." "Sexual freedom" has become a substitute for "personal freedom." "Sinfulness" is now attributed to the modern world, and not a personal responsibility. Like the catastrophic thaw after a great ice age, the rationalism of the Age of Reason is suddenly being threatened by the irrational, changing the face of the whole landscape of modernity.

The "Age of Aquarius" is "Aquarian" because after the turbulence of the twentieth century it seeks peace. It is a "conspiracy" in the original sense of a "breathing together," people discovering that they think alike at a gut level and are desirous of the same things. Yet it is fraught with internal contradictions.

If everything is divine, why seek for some things that are better? Should not pantheism inhibit desire for anything, as it has tended to do in Indian religion? If everything is One, when did it become the many—what is the cause of diversity? If the Divine Reality is impersonal, but union with the One is desired, how will our personal longings ever be satisfied? Surely

Buddhism is more consistent in seeking the complete obliteration of human desires.

In the same way, postmodernism with its emphasis on rational reflection is also full of internal contradictions. It is a desire for new vision, a way to pass from "what-has-been," which we dislike, to "what-should-be." But simply changing the vocabulary, speaking of the "spiritual" where we once spoke of the "rational," does not bring about transformation. To talk about a holistic, harmonious future in purely abstract terms is to evade concrete, personal responsibility for action in specific contexts. For instance, merging with nature is not going to redeem humanity's arrogant disruption of the natural world by its technological power. Our control needs to be expressed not in nature worship, but in stewardship of nature.

What the postmodern spirit cannot abide is specificity, uniqueness, the naked distinction between what is right or wrong, true or false. Postmodernists react strongly against specific values, the maintenance of boundaries, laws, and virtues, and deny the ability of human language, mind, or spirit to establish standards in an objective manner.

The sickness of our culture today lies in our shallow, flippant, and commercial way of dealing with the central and vital questions of our humanity. Our "stainless steel civilization," as it has been called, is sad and empty. The individual is doomed to live a life of quiet desperation, threatened by oblivion and only capable of living from day to day, if not, like our cousins in the Third World, from hand to mouth. Too many people today have to "sell things" to have a job. They don't believe in what they sell, but outward appearances have to be kept up. Busyness is the modern definition of blessedness.

There is a dimension missing from modern consciousness, because we are either over-rationalistic or over-sentimental. We go through life either seeing the stars as geometrical designs or twinkling down at us. Either we live in the mud or else our heads are in the clouds. Either Christmas is our "busy season" or else it is the time when we sing ancient carols without paying too much attention to the words. If we did, they would break our hearts. Perhaps it's time to listen to the Preacher, weary of the world:

> I have seen the burden God has laid on men. He has made everything beautiful in its time. He has also set eternity in the hearts of men; yet they cannot fathom what God has done from beginning to end (Eccl. 3:10–11).

That is the worst moment, when you feel that you have lost
The desire for all that was most desirable
Before you are contented with what you can desire.
—T. S. Eliot, *The Cocktail Party*[1]

6

DESPAIR: THE FATE OF THE DESIRING SOUL

f tragedy shows people better than they are and comedy shows them worse than they are, then despair perhaps shows them as they really are. The effects of tragedy and comedy are biased in one direction, to the external world, but despair is primarily the "disrelationship" in which we find ourselves with ourselves. This is the direction in which we have been heading so far in this book.

We have discovered that when we spend a lifetime worshipping idols in an unreal world, life gets seriously dislocated. We established that we can be addicted not only to drink but to relationships with other people and within ourselves, in the worst form of egoism, self-love. Life is pretty drab as it is, but if, as we considered in the last chapter, our religious life is absolute mediocrity, when "the best lack all conviction," then what is left? Despair.

We enter Dante's "dark wood where the straight way is lost," discovering our illusions, our enslavements, our self-centeredness, and the boredom of our busyness—"our quotidian existence." This is why we experience despair within ourselves. It is inherent in our own nature. Like sin, with which it is linked, despair is the destruction of our own spirit. For it is not so much that we despair about externals; we despair about ourselves. "The fault, dear Brutus," Shakespeare wrote in *Julius Caesar*, "is not in our stars, but in ourselves, that we are the underlings." We see ourselves as "fear in a handful of dust," as T. S. Eliot noted in *The Wasteland*.

Yet, Kierkegaard noted, despair has become quite a rare phenomenon, not because there is less of it around, but because of our casual assumption that if we don't feel despair, then we are not in despair.[2] It is, after all, in our nature to suppress truth that is a threat to our egos.

In the past, when the presence of God was more evident than in our secular world today, the reality of despair was better understood. The primordial picture we have of God's first encounter with humanity is of him taking a handful of dust and breathing into it—the creation of a human being. It is a profound picture of how dependent we are on our Maker; once we turn away from God, all our relationships lose their reality.

Perhaps despair alone can help us see how we are intrinsically in disarray without God's presence. Life becomes more "dust" than "reality" when we pretend we don't need God. Then we are what Eliot calls "hollow" and "stuffed," whimpering alone in the night.

SHADOWS OF DESPAIR

If this state of despair is not readily recognized for what it is, then T. S. Eliot's character Celia in *The Cocktail Party* is particularly unusual. A conversation with her psychiatrist follows:

> CELIA:
>> I just came in desperation. And I shan't be offended
>> If you simply tell me to go away again.

REILLY:

    Most of my patients begin, Miss Coplestone,

    By telling me exactly what is the matter with them,

    And what I am to do about it. They are quite sure

    They have had a nervous breakdown—that is what
        they call it—

    And usually they think that someone is to blame.

CELIA:

    I at least have no one to blame but myself.

REILLY:

    And after that, the prologue to my treatment

    Is to try to show them that they are mistaken

    About the nature of their illness, and lead them to
        see

    That it's not so interesting as they had imagined.

CELIA:

    Well, I can't pretend that my trouble is interesting;

    But I shan't begin that way. I feel perfectly well.

    I could live an active life—if there's anything to
        work for;

    I don't imagine that I am being persecuted;

    I don't hear voices, I have no delusions—

    Except that the world I live in seems all a delusion![3]

Celia then goes on to say that she would really *like* to think that there was something wrong with her, for if not, then there is something wrong with the world itself—or at least the world is very different from what it seems to be—which is much more frightening! As Celia talks further she is made aware that she has always been alone, that one is always alone. It is a revelation of her relationship with *everybody*. She explains that besides her loneliness, she has a second symptom. "And the second symptom?"

CELIA:

> That's stranger still. It sounds ridiculous—but the
>> only word for it
> That I can find, is a sense of sin.

REILLY:

> You suffer from a sense of sin, Miss Coplestone? ...
> Tell me what you mean by a sense of sin.

CELIA:

> It's much easier to tell you what I don't mean.

REILLY:

> And what, in your opinion, is the ordinary sense?

CELIA:

> Well ... I suppose it's being immoral—
> And I don't feel as if I were immoral:
> In fact, aren't the people one thinks of as immoral
> Just the people who we say have no moral sense?
> I've never noticed that immorality
> Was accompanied by a sense of sin.

Like any good analyst, Reilly asks her about her family and their views:

CELIA:

> Well, my upbringing was pretty conventional—
> I had always been taught to disbelieve in sin.
> Oh, I don't mean that it was never mentioned!
> But anything wrong, from their point of view,
> Was either bad form, or was psychological ...

REILLY:

> What is more real than anything you believed in?

THE DESIRE

CELIA:

> It's not the feeling of anything I've ever done,
>
> Which I could get away from, or of anything in me
>
> I could get rid of—but of emptiness, of failure
>
> Toward someone, or something, outside of myself;
>
> And I feel I must ... atone—is that the word?
>
> Can you treat a patient for such a state of mind?[4]

Such is the state of society that Reilly can do nothing for her except send her off to a sanatorium.

What we really need to recognize is that we were meant for personal relationships. If we did not live in what we might term "self-dimensional unreality," we would see more clearly how we make everything around us into "things," and that includes people and, worst of all, God. Yet to make God a "thing" is a natural tendency of theology, which thrives on abstraction. If theologians really had the living God in mind, they would react more violently to William Blake's question: "Tyger, tyger, burning bright ... What immortal hand or eye could frame thy fearful symmetry?" It is, of course, a naive trust in reason's powers when we try to substitute a rational explanation of reality for reality itself. As Dostoyevsky protested at the height of the Enlightenment's influence:

> All these beautiful systems, these theories of explaining his [humanity's] best interests are nothing but sophistry. For the factor that is omitted from all such calculations is the perverse insistence of human beings to choose not what is best, but what they want, regardless if it is good or bad, or even madness to do so.

In this way we even make ourselves into "objects," incapable of knowing how to relate intimately with ourselves, let alone other people. This is why I have called despair "disrelationship," a state of nonbeing. Mary Elizabeth Coleridge has described it like this:

I sat before my glass one day
And conjured up a vision bare,
Unlike the aspects glad and gay
That erst were found reflected there
The vision of a woman wild
With more than womanly despair …

Her lips were open—not a sound
Came through the parted lines of red
What e'er it was, the hideous wound
In silence and in secret bled
No sigh relieved her speechless woe
She had no voice to speak her dread.

And in her lurid eyes there shone
The dying flame of life's desire
And kindled at the leaping fire
Of jealousy and fierce revenge
And strength that could not change nor tire.[5]

Then she whispered the words, "I am she!"

Despair arises within us when, like Celia, the God-shaped vacuum in our lives makes us feel we need to "atone" to someone, or when, like the poet, we come face to face with ourselves. Despair, too, is the result when relationships have been fragmented and there is no promise of repair. Indeed, at this very point I have been interrupted by the phone, to hear a divorced father weeping for the absence of his children, that they are growing up not knowing him.

"Despair is my reluctant acknowledgement," wrote a friend to me recently, "that I am, after all, powerless in a meaningless world. While many around me hold tight to their little empires and power plays, speaking with authority and building material protection, I retreat into my emptiness, clutching as desperately to my honest despair, as they to their dishonest hope." This expresses the kind of "spiritual weightlessness" in which many people spend their lives within their own inner space. We long to control our destinies, but we cannot.

Jean Valjean, the central character in Victor Hugo's *Les Misérables,* finds himself in a similar plight. His God is powerless in the face of fate. "Though we chisel away as best we can at the mysterious block from which our life is made," he writes, "the black vein of destiny continually reappears." And yet the perversity is that we want our conscience on our own terms: not a "knowing with God" as *conscientia* originally implied—but a self sovereignty, in spite of God. Thus Hugo comments: "Jacob wrestled with the angel for one night only. Alas! How many times have we seen Jean Valjean grappling in the darkness with his conscience, desperately wrestling with it."

> Unparalleled struggle! ... How many times had that conscience, furious for the right, grasped and overwhelmed him! ... How many times had his refractory thought writhed convulsively under the evidence of duty. Resistance to God. Agonized sweating. How many secret wounds, whose bleeding only he could feel. How many times had he risen bruised, lacerated, illuminated, despair in his heart, serenity in his soul, and conquered, felt himself conqueror. And, having racked, torn and broken him, his conscience, standing above him, formidable, luminous, tranquil, said to him, "Now go in peace."[6]

"But," says Hugo, after "coming through such a gloomy struggle, what a dreary peace, alas!"

Most of us do not have dramatic expressions of despair, but "lead lives of quiet desperation," like my friend Thelma. She writes:

> Despair in facing aloneness as a single woman was not much of an issue when I had my own business and professional career. I looked forward to retirement, to being freed of my heavy responsibilities, but I was not prepared for the emptiness that replaced it. Gradually the

need to have a valid reason for existing confronted me. I discovered that I had unconsciously believed that my life was primarily meaningful because my work was meaningful—therefore without that work my life was now meaningless. It was terrifying to be faced with the empty days and years of living alone which now stretched before me.

There was the temptation to get involved in some regular activity which would relieve the loneliness and despair. I knew, though, that more busyness would not solve the real issue before me, which was to find meaning and even joy apart from my own efforts, in whatever situation I might find myself now, and in the future. If I didn't face the reality of my fears now, they would haunt me throughout the rest of my life....

Over the next months, the rising terror of despair within continued. Yes, there were brief moments of sheer joy, usually as I walked along the beach, when I exulted in being alive for no apparent reason. But most of the time I despaired of ever seeing any change in my sense of abandonment within me. Then I began to realize I was part of God's creation too, and that seemed good reason enough to feel content. My relationship with Him, for those moments, was all I truly needed to give my life meaning. Then a more specific breakthrough came when I realized that a great part of my problem with loneliness had arisen because I did not consider myself good company. Many times, to get away from myself I had run to be with others, which merely gave me temporary relief and often left me feeling more solitary than before. The lifelong battle with self esteem, which I had thought I had won long ago was still going on at the unconscious level. Once I accepted that and recognized more deeply the gracious acceptance of me by God, then much of the

despair began to dissipate. Further, in accepting myself,
I am becoming better able to accept others.

The story of Marie-Louise is of another despair, caused by an emotional addiction. This young woman has been bulimic for the past fourteen years. She is successful in her profession and well regarded. Yet she despairs in the binding clutches of her addiction. Her weak father never affirmed her femininity in the growing years, nor did she experience any real bonding with her strong, manipulative mother. It was as if *in utero* the unborn infant began life locked into free-floating anxiety that she has never been rid of.

She is still suspended above an abyss with many levels of despair. While she denies that her father was emotionally sick, that her mother was manipulative, that her circumstances were abnormal—forces within her cause her to put her finger down her throat to vomit the food she cannot swallow. It is her intense intuitive nature which makes her so vulnerable, and leads her to reject herself, her body, instead of rejecting the emotional lie that she makes her own by refusing to acknowledge the truth about her family.

Perhaps anorexic or bulimic women like Marie-Louise were once among those burned as witches, because they were seen to be pathetically susceptible to bewitchment, to the invasion of false, despairing spirits that left them unaffirmed and despairing of themselves.

Then I think of John, so familiar with despair in his life that the very notion he should desire anything seems wholly unrealistic. "I don't think that I can actually remember having any relationship with anyone, which would have led me to anything like yearning or deliberately seeking for it," he admitted. He had an unhappy home—a father who did not tolerate the expression of any emotions and a mother who responded stoically like a martyr, accepting in silence her husband's frequent infidelities. Since it was important to her to project to the outside world an image of the perfect family, secrecy was a way of life for John. His Jesuit teachers seemed to confirm that his religion also alienated him from life; God was a stern taskmaster. With so much despair in his life, how could there be any scope whatever for the exercise of desires, even secret ones?

THE DESPAIR OF BOREDOM

For many of us, however, it is simply boredom that dominates our lives. Like Updike's character Rabbit, we just *run, run, busy, busy.* Experienced as restlessness, unease, tedium, dryness, and apathy, boredom is a complex of feelings. When it is a passing experience, we can easily seek pleasurable diversions. When it is more obstinate and deep, it may be paralyzing, and the soul will lose all motivation to desire or change anything. Boredom was well described by Dostoyevsky's *Underground Man.* It undoubtedly became even more prevalent in the twentieth century, precipitating a dangerous, unfeeling numbness and lovelessness that can sink into the deeper darkness of violence and preoccupation with evil. Boredom today can be seen in the criminal acts taking place daily on our streets.

The paralysis of boredom is that the past is blocked by guilt and the future is blocked by anxiety.[7] Guilt is the penalty for what has gone wrong; it is irreversible because it is past. Anxiety is forward-looking, fleeing from potential danger. Yet *anxietas* can also imply a cramped environment, where there is no space to escape. That's why we identify boredom with the "now generation" who want to live for the moment; the past is dead and the future holds no promise. With such a narrowed consciousness life is trivial and superficial, characterized by emptiness. It feeds only upon its own self-perpetuating boredom, like fungi in unventilated darkness.

Boredom can intensify into depression. Virginia Woolf, who suffered from severe neurotic illness, wondered "how a year or so perhaps is to be endured … the inane pointlessness of all this existence ... the old treadmill going on and on for no reason."[8] The time came when she could endure it no longer, and exercised her last act of will in suicide. Arthur Koestler, who wrote of depression in *Darkness at Noon,* calls it "a veritable demoralization" of one's whole being; he, too, saw death as the only solution.

In contrast, there is the example of the German psychiatrist Conrad Baars, who during the Second World War helped Allied airmen to escape through the Pyrenees. When he himself was caught, he was tortured and sent to Buchenwald. There he learned that what is most deadly when people suffer from depression in prison is repressed anger. While it was dangerous to express anger openly, Baars learned to allow it to stimulate his adrenal glands and so provide him with the energy to survive hard labor, a starvation diet, and other adversities. He was one of the few to survive Buchenwald and, as he confessed, "prayer and anger allowed me to see the how of liberation." He found that a great number of his depressed patients recovered when they could ask themselves, "Who is making me feel angry? What is annoying me?"[9] In other words, it is when personal relationships fail, especially a relationship with God, that darkness is created and nourished by despair.

DESPAIR AS GODLESSNESS

To speak of "God"—whether we are religious or not—is to deal with the essence of things, the roots or foundations of reality. So far we have described despair rather than explained it, and now we need to explore it in terms of its nature and root cause. Søren Kierkegaard, who suffered deeply from despair himself, helps us as few modern thinkers can. He confessed about his childhood: "So far back as I can remember, my only joy was that nobody could discover how unhappy I felt"[10] When later he learned of his father's sexual indiscretions, it was "the great earthquake" of his life. Five of the seven children in the family died young, which convinced his father that God was punishing him. Then Søren too "sowed wild oats," and was only reconciled, both to his father and his own religious faith, shortly before his father died—around Søren's twenty-fifth birthday. Later, there was an agonizing break in his romance with Regine Olsen, because Søren could not share his family secrets with her, although he loved her. He never married, but continued to experience loneliness and despair.

Through all his personal experiences Kierkegaard learned how people need relationships, so for him despair reflected a breakdown in one's relationship with God and with other people. People are spiritual beings, and we cannot live without relationships. Yet God has not arranged that we must be relational; we are free to reject our Maker if we so desire. This may cause what Kierkegaard calls "fundamental anxiety," the ambiguity people are placed in when they must choose rightly or wrongly. Despair emerges when our false sense of self leads to sinful choices. For how reliable are our choices after the fall, after Adam sinned? Wistfulness, self-worship, or lack of belief in God are all expressions of the "false self," when in fact God wants people in his image and likeness to relate to himself.

Kierkegaard sees that it is our pride in our autonomy which is sinful. It represents a denial of the being-in-relationship which is truly human, and leads to anxiety. The condition of despair, whether we are conscious of it or not, is to live falsely, denying our relational nature. Having been designed in the image of a triune God, with the desire for relationship incorporated into our very being, we live with restlessness, stress, fear, and loss when we reject either God or other people, who also bear the divine image.

Under these terms, we are all sinners, regardless of vice or virtue. We all experience despair. Yet, argues Kierkegaard, while despair is evidence of our failure in relationships, it also points strikingly to our humanity; we don't live a life based solely on animal instinct. Our despair reflects solitude, which is a result of our failure to relate to other human beings, but highlights the moral dignity of being "human." So profoundly rooted in us is the life of despair that Kierkegaard calls it "the sickness unto death."[11] This does not have to mean suicide; rather it is a despair that can be alleviated only in the death of the "natural man" (as the apostle Paul calls us) becoming alive again as a "spiritual man" and not living for ourselves but "in Christ Jesus." This concept will be discussed in the next chapter.

Kierkegaard described several types of despair. First there is the *despair of possibility,* which is caused when there is too little constraint in one's life. With wide-open opportunities, we feel frightened and choose to operate in a narrow, petty existence, paralyzed by our own freedom.

This type of despair can find expression in the daydreaming of the artist, the dramatist, the romantic, or indeed the idealist. The scholar, too, can live so freely in a world of thought, of creative ideas, that he or she drifts away from the relational world, losing touch with reality. Too much freedom then, without boundaries, will engender this "despair of possibility." Psychologists have noted that small children, when left to play in a large, open yard, will stay cautiously in the center, but when placed in a fenced yard will run courageously to its limits. For many people, despair arises out of the dizzying sensation that we are free to choose. We are, as Sartre put it, not only free, but "doomed to freedom." We are cursed not so much by what we must do, but by what we are free to do, and this leads us into despair.

For Sartre, freedom meant the absence of an absolute—nothing to live *by* and nothing to live *for.* In Sartre's play *The Flies,* the hero Orestes says to Zeus:

> Suddenly out of the blue, freedom crashed down on me
> and swept me off my feet. My youth went with the
> wind, and I knew myself alone ... and there was nothing
> left in heaven, no right or wrong, or anyone to give me
> orders ... I am doomed to have no law but mine ... Every
> man must find his own way.

Freedom in this sense has a terrifying implication: It means that there is no ground beneath us, only a void, an abyss. Too much possibility was awful for Sartre because it meant the loss of any meaning to life. Dostoyevsky, through the "The Grand Inquisitor," accuses Christ of bringing about the ruin and despair of humanity by guaranteeing them freedom of choice. While we long for freedom when we don't have it, the weight of unlimited possibility is too much for us to bear.

Then there is the opposite kind of despair, where there are too many constraints, too little freedom. It is the *despair of finitude*. It results from constricting narrow-mindedness and oppression, seen in the despair of women in a male-dominated world. The sexual insensitivity of male chauvinism has left many women embittered, frustrated, hurt, or just repressed in the denial of their true femininity and of their own personal identity. But there are two versions of this despair: when someone gives in to social conformity, and their pain is hardly noticed by the world; and when someone simply adopts a fatalistic attitude so that their despair is even more inwardly hidden.

Since the world thrives on outward consensus, these two forms of despair are hardly recognized by society until crisis point is reached—such as the pain of divorce, or "feminist rebellion," or the sudden awareness of child sexual abuse, or the whole issue of family codependency, people conspiring to protect the addiction of one family member. But the damage has been done, and people continue to live lives of despair like actors on the stage of tragedy or as mute sufferers in a family conspiracy of unreality.

All these forms of despair clearly affect and may even determine our personalities. We respond, consciously or unconsciously, to misfortune and pain. Kierkegaard tended to see this, in his own culture, in terms of sexual differentiation: the masculine more conscious and defiant, the feminine more unconscious and submissive, with unconscious, "feminine" despair being the more dangerous of the two forms. It is also the more common, in a world that remains unaware of its sinful state. In fact, one of its worst manifestations is the blandness, the blindness, and the deadness of much of organized religion, of what Kierkegaard calls "Christendom." The church is pathetically unconscious of its moral deadness.

When despair is conscious, however, one form that emerges is the *despair of weakness.*[12] This means deliberately rejecting the reality of one's true self and choosing to live falsely, as for example when people find their entire identity in their job or career, or social status. When one's career fails, when one's aspirations fall through, or when one's relationship breaks up, this identification with what has been lost is nothing short of disaster. The despair of weakness reveals the low self-image with which many people live. Having lost any sense of our true uniqueness, we become faceless conformists, impersonal functionaries, little more than social statistics.

Other people may not fall into this trap, but succumb instead to the *despair over the eternal.* Whereas the former is the despair of weakness, this is the despair *over* weakness. People with a low view of themselves feel despised by others and loathe their own company. Like Thelma, they dread loneliness because they cannot bear coming face to face with themselves. This may partly be due to the tendency we all have to wound ourselves as we have been wounded. If I was rejected as a child, then I will tend also to reject the child within me, and when I find myself in the pit of despair, something in me makes me just dig a deeper pit. Completely absorbed in our own perceived weaknesses, we become even more despairing of them.

Finally, there is the most intense form, the *despair of defiance.* This is "the despair of willing despairingly to be oneself." It begins with people not wanting to be themselves because they hate their own weakness. Then they despair because they have chosen created, earthly things to satisfy their eternal desires. Soon they despair over their bias toward self-seeking in place of spiritual and eternal values. And finally they use the power of their eternal longing to strengthen their defiance, and sabotage their whole existence. As Jeremy Taylor has put it, "Despair is the proper passion of damnation." Disraeli has said more bluntly: "Despair is the conclusion of fools." For it is supreme folly to turn all our human aspirations into despairing defiance. Yet this is the spirit of existentialism. It is the spirit of being one's own god, seen in the thought of Nietzsche and Sartre. It is the self-actualization movement of the 1960s that is further exaggerated in "New Age Consciousness." As Kierkegaard says:

> It recognizes no power itself, therefore ... like
> Prometheus stealing fire from the gods this is stealing
> from God the thought—which is earnestness—that God
> pays attention to no one.[13]

LAMENT: THE ANTIDOTE TO DESPAIR

The crucial distinction between the view of the universe as divine and the possibility of a personal God is the difference between an abstract and a relational interpretation of events. We may smile at the notion that in the ancient world all human events had a heavenly counterpart. Yet science today is not so different when it claims that it is physics, chemistry, and biology that are the ultimate and only building blocks of our impersonally interpreted world. Whereas in the past the gods were the ultimate standard of reality, now we have the scientific equivalent.

In the ancient civilization of Sumer, when political catastrophes occurred, people looked for cosmological interpretations. Reflecting upon the attack of Elam, it appeared to the Sumerian poet that it was really the god Enlil who had been carrying out his revenge:

> Enlil called the storm—the people groan.
>
> The storm annihilates the land—the people groan.
>
> The great storm of heaven he called—the people groan.
>
> The great storm howls above—the people groan.
>
> The storm ordered by Enlil in hate, the storm which
>> weeps away the land
>
> Covered Ur like a garment, enveloped it like a linen
>> sheet.[14]

That is to say, a cosmic shroud was thrown by the god Enlil over the city of Ur, so that its streets were filled with corpses. Then the people cried in despair that the god Enlil, like all the other gods of the ancient world, was arbitrary and callous, indifferent to human affairs.

The people groaned publicly, and indeed there was much communal lamentation. The literature and cultic life of these ancient peoples is full of outcries against death, destruction, plagues, famines, and wars, as well as sickness and the guilt of sin. As an integral part of ancient Semitic life, lamentation had a threefold character: It was directed toward the gods (a religious dimension), toward the community (the social dimension), and toward the individual (the psychological dimension). As Claus Westermann has astutely observed:

> Using modern categories, we could say that the three elements of lamentation presuppose an understanding in which theology, sociology and psychology have not been separated from each other.[15]

But for us today lament no longer seems wholesome, because our grief, pain, and suffering are much more internalized, kept locked away within us. Thanks to our modern culture we have separated out the religious, social, and personal dimensions of our humanity, yet all three are part of our total being. We have separated the knowledge of God from that of society and that of the self. We might say, then, that modern despair has an intense inner destructiveness that was unknown to the peoples of the ancient world. While they seemed able to share their burden with the rest of the community, we, with our focus on self-actualization and self-fulfillment, have accelerated the inner self-destructiveness of despair in ways unknown even to Kierkegaard's generation.

As part of the ancient Semitic world, Israel participated in the communal expression of lament. Professional mourners beating the breast, rolling in the dust, putting on sackcloth, wailing loudly, and fasting were common manifestations of suffering everywhere in antiquity. Yet in Israel there was a profound difference. Lamentation was not set within a cosmological framework of indifferent, capricious gods. Instead, in an extraordinary rupture of this view of reality, God had revealed himself as good, personal, loving, and faithful. The God of Abraham, Isaac, and Jacob cared for his people. Psalm 8 then is a very different poem from that of Sumer:

> When I consider your heavens, the work of your fingers,
> the moon and the stars, which you have set in place,
> what is man that you are mindful of him, the son of
> man that you care for him?[16]

Compared to the immensity of our universe, we who are here today and gone tomorrow are minute! Yet God cares for us!

For the people of Israel, the cry for help to a personal God was an integral part of their experience. From the beginning, God heard the spilt blood of Abel calling out from the earth. He heard the wailing sobs of Hagar and her child in the desert. He saw the affliction of the Hebrews under Pharaoh. Indeed, throughout the history of Israel, lamentation was an appropriate expression of suffering, since "God hears his people" and "he is attentive to their cry." The strong emphasis of both lament and praise in the Psalter, Israel's prayer book, symbolizes God's everlasting faithfulness.

The psalms of lament have a threefold address to God:

They complain of the enemy; they are aware that the whole community will benefit in being heard and delivered by God; and the individual, too, will be comforted. All three dimensions of lament lead into a realization of the goodness and might of God's salvation, and of God's covenant character of faithfulness and loyalty to his people, in love and grace. Laments in Scripture almost always end in praise. It is still true today that:

- God-directed lament saves us from self-despair.
- Communal lament saves us from self-pity.
- Personal lament saves us from unconscious despair.

However, the Bible also draws attention to the lament of God. God is grieved that the animal world shows more consistency than the fickle waywardness of humanity—which was created to glory in the unsurpassed glory of God.

> The ox knows his master,
>
> the donkey his owner's manger,
>
> but Israel does not know,
>
> my people do not understand.[17]

"Ah, sinful nation," laments Yahweh, the covenant God—you have turned, in denial of relational life and a personal God, to worship what is impersonal, what is creaturely. Again the prophet Jeremiah expresses the lament of Yahweh:

> Why then have these people turned away? Why does Jerusalem always turn away? They cling to deceit; they refuse to return.... Even the stork in the sky knows her appointed seasons, and the dove, the swift and the thrush observe the time of their migration. But my people do not know the requirements of the LORD.[18]

The divine laments bear witness to a deeper pain than we could ever imagine. "Israel does not know," "my people do not know," discloses the total breakdown of the relationship between a covenant-keeping God and rebellious humanity.

Yet if God loves us so much that he laments our sinful perversity, then the Suffering Servant described in the book of Isaiah reveals further that God is prepared even to suffer for our sins. In the lament of the Suffering Servant, so movingly interpreted in Handel's *Messiah*, the Servant is confirmed by God in his suffering. He intercedes for his enemies—no longer accusing them—and the community believes that his suffering and dying was on their behalf. Lamentation becomes profoundly redemptive and healing.

What clearer connection could there be between Old and New Testaments, between Jew and Christian, than the reality that God is personal, that his covenant continues with the human race? That takes us from despair to hope, from death to life, and from self to fellowship. Indeed, it is the restoration of life in relationship and an escape from alienation and despair that God planned for us in his mighty act of salvation. This is the extent of his desire for us.

A PRAYER

Father in heaven ... Grant that we may each one of us become in good time aware what sickness it is which is unto death, and aware that we are all suffering from this sickness. O Lord Jesus Christ who came to earth to heal them that suffer from this sickness ... from which You are able to heal only those who are conscious that they are sick in this way; help us in this sickness to hold fast to You, so that in this sickness, if we honestly desire to be healed remain with us so that for no single instant we may to our own destruction shun the Physician but remain with Him—delivered from our sickness. For to be with Him is to be delivered from our sickness, and when we are with Him we are saved from all sickness.

—Søren Kierkegaard, *The Sickness Unto Death*[19]

Part Two

BREAKING THE SPELL—
THE PROMISE OF
CHRISTIAN SPIRITUALITY

... were we led all that way for Birth or Death?

—T. S. Eliot, *Journey of the Magi*[1]

7

JESUS CHRIST: THE HEART'S RESURRECTION

We might well pause here and ask ourselves, what is the goal of our desire? Are we longing for life or for death? If, as we have seen, our desires mislead us into idolatry, enslave us in addiction, disillusion us about "love," and then cheat us further with a rationalistic universe in which we are empty and bored, no wonder we despair.

"Were we led all that way for Birth or Death?" Clearly both, for we shall all die, as we were born. This is inevitable, but "dying as we were born" has another meaning besides the "natural causes" of a coroner's statement. For what if the desires of the heart should lead us deep to desire "a lost memory," before our birth and death? What if those memories died as we were born?

Of course, we know all about being born. We are launched into a new, unknown realm of being, very different from the warmth and security of our mother's womb. It was that first cry of birth, we are told, that gave us breath—a paradox indeed, that such distress should bring us life.

Yet distress is a real part of every birth, since to be born is to be separated from the womb, to be brought into the unknown and into insecurity. From then on we grow up as beings led by desire, first for our mother's breast, then for the love in her eyes, then many more desires until our very identity seems to be "I desire, therefore I am." The early "bonding" of a child with its parents and the prolonged weaning of the human infant surely indicate that human desire is love seeking to relate.

Yet we are also born with memory—that is, with the ability to be a "self," to experience the presence of "myself"—a story of a continuous history of experience.[2] I am not trapped in the present moment, nor by a life based on instinct like the animals, for I can go beyond these limitations, the immediate sensations of the body, by exercising my memory.

Augustine called this ability to override the immediate impressions of our senses "that vast court of my memory ... For there are present with me, heaven and earth, sea and whatever I could think about, besides what I have forgotten. There I will meet with myself, and recall myself, and which, where and what I have done, and under what feelings."[3] Augustine, in his *Confessions*, reminds us of the power of the human memory in our experience of personal identity, even though our conscious minds cannot contain all this experience. From this "memory" we bring out the "four emotions of the mind, desire, joy, fear, and sorrow."

But this cannot be the only function of the memory, to explain us to ourselves. In Plato's allegory of humanity—people cowering in a dark cave, refusing to face the sunlight of Truth outside—what can the shadows know of the light outside the cave? Can memory lead us to a truth beyond ourselves?

It was Jung's intuition that our dreams and fantasies are fed by some great primordial and universal reservoir of the "unconscious," which is a common inheritance from our ancestors.

THE DESIRE

Those who believe in the "historical consciousness" of God's presence in his world, however, will not be convinced that our own explanations give a complete account of human memory, whether they are the explanations of Plato or of Jung.

THE BROKEN IMAGES OF MEMORY

Today, we are learning new insights into the memories of childhood, as, for example, "the child within" us becomes more aware of sexual and other forms of emotional abuse suffered in childhood.

Since our memory underlies a great deal of how we think and act, a crucial issue is how we use it. We can use it destructively, and be swamped with remorse for our past misdeeds. Or we can end up feeling defeated because we remember failure. Shame can be the result of a crippling series of memories, of what we recall about ourselves; guilt can spring from the reflection of bad relationships with others. Memory reveals, too, how we have been trapped in life, remaining "stuck" with little hope of change. The storehouse of memory can be a collection of "bad" memories, as well as of endless deceit.

Memory is "the heavy burden of the growing soul,"[4] that perplexes and offends us more and more, day by day. So we need humility both to be open to a deepened memory, and also to be willing to accept the help of others. Without humility, the soul remains small; the memory is restricted, actively repressing the past. For the proud, the pain of living is too much without some narcotic to dull the remembrance of past failure.

We tend to have a "bad memory" about "bad memories." We deceive ourselves very readily about what really happened. As we saw earlier, we play down the damage we have done to others and distort reality by manipulating people. We rationalize our false desires, making excuses for our actions; we create stereotypes, and look on people with prejudiced eyes, unaware of their personal uniqueness. We externalize problems by blaming other people for our failures, but we are unable to control or suppress our internal emotions. We compartmentalize our lives by looking only at some areas, and we idealize ourselves when we view ourselves in a particular light that distorts reality. We go to great lengths to defend our weaknesses and protect our own self-image. All these things create "broken images" of reality, through which a mixture of truth and lies is fed into our lives.

And what do we make of our religious memories—the memory of birth at Christmas, and of death and resurrection at Easter? Is it all suppressed by the frantic shopping, children's pantomimes, intoxicating partying, and all those "tissued fripperies, the sweet and silly Christmas things"? The poet John Betjeman asks the question that our memories shy away from:

> And is it true? And is it true,
> This most tremendous tale of all,
> Seen in a stained-glass window's hue,
> A baby in an ox's stall?
> The Maker of the stars and sea
> Become a Child on earth for me?
> (JOHN BETJEMAN, CHRISTMAS[5])

As William Blake reminds us, "Life's dim window of the soul distorts the Heavens from pole to pole, and leads you to believe a lie, when you see with, not through, the eye." We have seen how very different our interpretation of reality is when we look at life with a "cosmological" mind-set, instead of with a "historic consciousness" of the ever-present God.[6]

The wise men had to travel many miles to find the "young child," whereas the shepherds needed only to cross the fields of Bethlehem to come and adore him, but once there, they all took Jesus as they found him, a real baby. But that simple reality is also dense with symbols: the guiding star, the worshipping voices of angels, gifts that speak of kingship, sacrifice, and death, even the claim of the Virgin Birth, without which the incarnation makes little sense.

THE DESIRE

These strange stories are not instances of "wish projection," as Enlightenment thinkers have argued. After all, who would be so crazy as to conjure up such "wishes," to surround an ordinary baby with such a weight of symbolic meaning? Our problem is that Jesus came in such simplicity, as a human child, that for the majority of people today he still remains hidden: "Like one from whom men hide their faces he was despised, and we esteemed him not."[7] That rejection is certainly "wish projection," as we seek to eliminate someone who upsets our way of looking at life. Yet curiously, although many people have been only too glad to reject Christianity, they have also hesitated to defame or reject Jesus. Albert Camus, D. H. Lawrence, and even Nietzsche still admired the person of Jesus, in spite of their very different philosophies.

It is difficult to do otherwise, for the memory of Jesus also arouses our nostalgia for what is good, true, loving, and beautiful. Reject these values, and life is hell indeed. Why? Because the heart has a memory of them; we recognize them from our own desires. Can there be a more beautiful, more balanced, more profound, yet more sympathetic and loving expression of what it means to be genuinely human than Jesus Christ?

JESUS CHRIST KNOWS OUR HEARTS

If we go to such lengths to conceal reality from ourselves, what about Jesus? Does he see the human heart? And if so, what is his response?

All four Gospels assert that Jesus knew people's hearts.[8] On one occasion, when he healed a lame man, he asked the religious leaders, "Why are you thinking these things in your hearts?" At other times the phrase is used of Jesus "knowing their thoughts" in the light of the questions they asked him. When the disciples argued among themselves as to who should be the greatest, Jesus, who saw the thoughts of their hearts, took a child and placed him in the midst, saying, "He who is least among you all—he is the greatest." Indeed, John reports that "Jesus would not trust himself to them, for he knew all men. He did not need man's testimony about man, for he knew what was in a man."

In talking to the woman who had had five husbands, Jesus revealed that he knew all about her. He perceived when people were demon-possessed. Seated at the Last Supper, he knew what would happen—that Judas would betray him and Peter deny him. Indeed, such was the disciples' awe of Jesus' apparent omniscience that their response was: "Now we can see that you know all things and that you do not even need to have anyone ask you questions. This makes us believe that you came from God." After the resurrection Peter confessed: "Lord, you know everything; you know that I love you."

But there is a perverse streak in us that prefers darkness to light. John's gospel speaks of how light has come into the world, but even so people love darkness rather than light because their deeds are evil. The blindness of the willfully blind is intensified, and the hardness of the heart of those bent on iniquity gets worse. It was this public exposure of people's evil hearts that also exposed Jesus to public hatred, as he challenged the vested interests of public religion. As Paul later declared, this thing was not "done in a corner"!

The light that Jesus shed on the darkness of humanity was not restricted to first-century Palestine. It also revealed his future role as Judge. In the book of Revelation John recorded an apocalyptic vision of Christ, "with eyes like a flame of fire," judging the church. Paul, in his vision of Jesus on the Damascus road, heard Jesus speak deep into his heart, "Saul, Saul, why do you persecute me?" And writing to the Corinthians later, the apostle described the future power of Christ: "He will bring to light what is hidden in darkness and will expose the motives of men's hearts."[9]

It is then with "fear and trembling," a theme eloquently taken up later by Kierkegaard, that we are "to work out our own salvation," within a depth of our being that we shall explore for the rest of this book. Jesus came into this world not to condemn us, but that "the world through him might be saved." "I judge no one," he said; but his presence among us as "the memory of God" is enough to expose and condemn the "evil memories" which possess us and hold us in bondage. For who can stand in the presence of God in Christ without condemnation?

While it is clear that Jesus Christ stands in judgment over us and against us, knowing and bringing to light our "thoughts and intents of the heart," nevertheless he also stands *alongside us* in our temptation. As the writer to the Hebrews put it: "We have one who has been tempted in every way, just as we are."[10] We can approach his grace "with confidence, so that we may receive mercy and find grace to help us in our time of need." Jesus himself shared in our humanity, to free us from the bondage of our sinful nature, and "because he himself suffered when he was tempted, he is able to help those who are being tempted."[11]

Jesus knows our stories well and is fully acquainted with our weaknesses. The fact that he was tempted as we are means that our "bad memories" of shame and guilt can be replaced with the memory of divine forgiveness and acceptance by his love. When we share our memories with him, we are given a new story, which is about the transformation of our lives.

Jesus knows our hearts because he freely accepted the condemnation and the judgment of death from which no one can escape, by dying in our place. "He became a curse for us" is a statement beyond our imagining. We cannot begin to penetrate the awesome mystery of what it means, that "he bore our sins in his body on the tree," but this is what happened. Our only real response can be that of Isaac Watts, who exclaimed:

> When I survey the wondrous cross,
> On which the Prince of glory died,
> My richest gain I count but loss,
> And pour contempt on all my pride.

Christ penetrated the darkest places of our hearts, the demonic depths of human existence, and even robbed death of its terrors. His death has set us free from our old desires: from ambition, greed, and self-centeredness. We are transformed by Christ, given a new heart, a new spirit, new desires that come from living in the light of our memories of God. Nevertheless, we are still beset by temptation.

The Temptations of Jesus Christ

Then Jesus was led by the Spirit into the desert to be tempted by the devil. After fasting forty days and forty nights, he was hungry. The tempter came to him and said, "If you are the Son of God, tell these stones to become bread."

Jesus answered, "'It is written: 'Man does not live on bread alone, but on every word that comes from the mouth of God.'"

Then the devil took him to the holy city and had him stand on the highest point of the temple. "If you are the Son of God," he said, "throw yourself down. For it is written: 'He will command his angels concerning you, and they will lift you up in their hands, so that you will not strike your foot against a stone.'"

Jesus answered him, "It is also written: 'Do not put the Lord your God to the test.'"

Again, the devil took him to a very high mountain and showed him all the kingdoms of the world and their splendor. "All this I will give you," he said, "if you will bow down and worship me."

Jesus said to him, "Away from me, Satan! For it is written: 'Worship the Lord your God, and serve him only.'"

Then the devil left him, and the angels came and attended him (Matt. 4:1–11).

Did the Devil not know the true nature of Jesus Christ, that his life was spotless, as he carried the memory and desires of God always before him? Was the Devil wasting his time, as has been suggested? Or could it be that, at a much deeper level, the Devil was attacking everything of God's own nature and purpose in his Son? Indeed, was this the Devil's confrontation with all that was implied in the incarnation, God becoming human that we should become like him?

Clearly, Jesus was being tempted as a human being; he was hungry after fasting forty days and nights. He was also being tempted as to the nature of his ministry, which, the Devil suggested, could be carried out more effectively if he did not attempt to transform the natural human desire for wonders, but worked with it. Finally, he was being tempted to take on the pragmatic and political roles of president of World Vision, chairman of British Airways, and secretary-general of the United Nations, all at the same time. Then things would really get done, according to human expectations!

It is something like this that Dostoyevsky had in mind in the story of "The Grand Inquisitor," told by Ivan in *The Brothers Karamazov*,[12] which was uncannily prophetic of contemporary events in the former Soviet Union. He saw clearly that the ideologies of the Enlightenment, which aimed to produce a utopian society for Russia, would be disastrous.[13]

Dostoyevsky's story begins in Seville in the sixteenth century, when the Church is fearful of the effects which the Reformation might have in Spain. With the Inquisitor in control, "fires blazed every day to the glory of God," burning heretics.

The day after an *auto-da-fé* or burning, a stranger quietly appears. He is quickly noticed as he blesses and heals the sick, and when he raises to life a little girl in a coffin, on the way to the cathedral for her funeral, the Inquisitor orders his arrest. On the following day he puts Jesus on trial before him. The Inquisitor asks Jesus:

> "Is it you? You?" But receiving no answer, he quickly
> adds: "Do not answer, be silent. After all, what could
> you say? I know too well what you would say. And you

> have no right to add anything to what you have
> already said once. Why, then, have you come to inter-
> fere with us?"[14]

There follows a monologue from the Inquisitor, who takes the Devil's part, rejecting the whole foundation of Jesus' character and ministry as being incompatible with the world's ways and with human nature. It is a confrontation between socialism, curiously in league with the church, and the consciousness of Christ's presence in the world. The gist of the Inquisitor's argument is that human beings are rebels by nature, so to offer them freedom, as Jesus does, is highly dangerous; all the Devil can see is the need for bondage.

It is the dilemma of any totalitarian state that fears a Tiananmen Square incident or a Russian *glasnost*. To offer freedom is to open the door to anarchy. That is why Jesus' response to the Tempter is so dangerous in the eyes of the secular world. Love can operate in society only when Christ, not Caesar, is enthroned in our hearts. The Inquisitor says sternly to Jesus:

> "Was it not you who so often said then: 'I want to make
> you free'? But now you have seen these 'free' men. Yes,
> this work has cost us dearly," he goes on, looking
> sternly at him, "but we have finally finished this work
> in your name. For fifteen hundred years we have been
> at pains over this freedom, but now it is finished, and
> well finished."[15]

"Well finished"? After twenty centuries we still face the same temptations and alternatives that confront the free human being.

In the first temptation, the issue is bread or virtue. Don't we all believe that virtue cannot be taught to empty stomachs? This is practical common sense. So the Inquisitor speaks to Jesus and to all his disciples:

> You want to go into the world, and you are going empty-
> handed, with some promise of freedom, which they in
> their simplicity and innate lawlessness cannot even com-
> prehend, which they dread and fear—for nothing has
> been more insufferable for man and for human society
> than freedom! But do you see these stones in this bare,
> scorching desert? Turn them into bread and mankind
> will run after you like sheep, grateful and obedient,
> though eternally trembling lest you withdraw your hand
> and your loaves cease for them.[16]

The thrust is clear: Human desires are primarily material, not spiritual. But to echo our previous discussion, both the worldly Inquisitor *and* the Devil lack all awareness of the "historic consciousness" of the Word that commanded all creation into being and still creates the world now. It is by the Word in our hearts that we can pray, "Give us this day our daily bread," where "bread" means being fed at every level of our being, both physical and spiritual.

The second temptation also reflects worldly ways of coping with rebellious humanity. Give them bread, yes, but give them miracles as well. They love the sensational and the dramatic. "Cast yourself from the pinnacle of the temple … your angels will lift you up, bearing you aloft." This is the temptation to desire godlike powers so that we can control the minds and hearts of other people. So the Inquisitor accuses Jesus:

> You did not come down from the cross when they
> shouted to you, mocking and reviling you: "Come down
> from the cross and we will believe that it is you." You
> did not come down because, again, you did not want to
> enslave man by a miracle and thirsted for faith that is
> free, not miraculous. You thirsted for love that is free,
> and not for the servile raptures of a slave.[17]

The Inquisitor can only reckon with the natural craving for miracle, mystery, and authority, not the supernatural values of faith, hope, and charity; so now he attacks Jesus one more time. Do not human beings desire above all to be "universal"? Is not this the reason for empire building? Is not this what the "ecumenical consciousness" of the Hellenistic and Chinese empires was all about? Is not this what science and technology, along with a certain spiritual longing, are doing today, that will bring all humanity together in the rebuilding of the Tower of Babel?

> Oh, this work is still in its very beginnings, but it has begun.... And yet you could have taken the sword of Caesar even then. Why did you reject that last gift? ... Great conquerors, Tamerlanes and Genghis Khans, swept over the earth like a whirlwind, yearning to conquer the cosmos, but they, too, expressed, albeit unconsciously, the same great need of mankind for universal and general union. Had you accepted the world and Caesar's purple, you would have founded a universal kingdom and granted universal peace.[18]

JESUS' SILENCE

As Dostoyevsky clearly saw, the Devil was defeated by Jesus' silence, and that silence meant "taking up his cross." In the Gospels Jesus speaks out and rebuts every temptation of the Devil with the authority of the Word of God. But before a man, Pilate, Jesus is silent. And the Inquisitor is still a man, though demonic in his intent. So Jesus is silent as he stands before a human being.

We always know when God is far away from us, when our spirits are dry and his presence is withdrawn from us: it is when we are withdrawn from him, in our attitudes and in our hearts. As the Lord declared: "These people worship with their lips but their hearts are far off."

God's silence can expose what is false within us. His silence shows us up when we protest too much—when we communicate a false view of the world, when our motives are all wrong. Pilate wanted it both ways; he wanted to appease the crowd and keep his own authority, yet he also wanted to keep a good conscience. Jesus cannot communicate in the face of such deviousness.

The silence of Jesus also means a refusal to argue with us on the level of rationalism and our Enlightenment mentality. As Dostoyevsky wrote to his brother, when he was eighteen:

> Reason is a material capacity, while the soul or spirit lives
> on the thoughts which are whispered to the heart.
> Thought is born in the soul. Reason is a tool, a machine,
> which is driven by spiritual fire. When human reason
> penetrates into the domain of knowledge, it works inde-
> pendently of the feeling, and consequently of the heart.
> But when our aim is the understanding of love or of
> nature, we march toward the very citadel of the heart.[19]

Reason and the heart need not come into collision, unless we make an exclusive claim for the truth of human knowledge. Jesus is silent when the eternal Word confronts the talk, theory, and ambition of Organization Man or Woman. This is not to posit an opposition between reason and faith; it has to do with the absence or presence of God in our lives. His silence is his judgment upon our ways and our thoughts.

There is, however, a still deeper level at which we may interpret the temptations of Jesus. They are to be seen as demonic attacks on the very nature of Jesus Christ as Savior and Lord.

In dealing with his temptations Jesus refuses to be a magician with special powers to impress other people. He refuses to use magical power for a quick fix. Just like lust, magic is a refusal to accept life in relationship with others. Both want power, not love, and both therefore stand in opposition to personal relationships. Through its power over other people, magic simply encourages us down the path of addiction, which ultimately leads to hell.

He rejects the idea that material things can feed the heart's desires, the idolatry of materialism which leads to addiction, whether to money or drugs. "Man shall not live by bread alone." Christ is not Condorcet's "progressive Superman," nor Marx's "materialistic Superman," nor Nietzsche's "dionysiac Superman." He is God, revealing his eternal love for humanity in human form, "humbling himself, even to the death of the cross."

Jesus Christ cannot be interpreted from "below," that is from our human perspective; he is to be seen from "above," from the perspective of divine revelation. Knowing him is not given us by magical arts, or even by objective information, but by the Spirit of God within our hearts. That is why this book is focusing especially on memory (the memory of God in our lives), symbols (our attention directed to divine realities), and humility (our openness to God in daily life).

In confronting temptation, Christ also refuses to reject his humanity in favor of his divine nature. Anyone who is thus tempted to make the incarnation an ideal or a speculative idea is rejecting the "historicity of God," God made human. We have touched on what kind of life this was: "a babe wrapped in swaddling clothes," laid on real straw that cattle eat. Jesus' body was touched in loving tenderness by his mother, and a woman washed his feet with her tears of contrition. The incarnation, life, and resurrection of Jesus all belong on the level of human reality—Jesus was not enticed by the Devil into operating in the angelic realm by making a dramatic leap from the temple that a human being could not have survived.

This temptation to make Jesus Christ into "the Christ idea" is kept by many religious liberals at the top of their heads, with no substance to it in the bottom of their hearts. As T. F. Torrance, a true theologian, says at the beginning of his great book *Space, Time and Resurrection*, "I make no apology for taking divine revelation seriously."[20] If we do not take God's action in the world seriously, religion becomes mere illusion. Our desires can be freed from idolatry and addiction by nothing less than the reality that God became a human being, in the person of Jesus Christ. Only then can all the symbols of Christ's birth, his earthly ministry, his death and resurrection, make any sense at all. Like his seamless garment, given in its wholeness to one of the soldiers at the crucifixion, the reality of Jesus of history is intrinsically one with that of the resurrected Christ.

Jesus' last temptation shows us his refusal to be anything less than the Savior and Lord of all creation. The sovereignty of Christ is as Creator, as well as Savior. His saving work began when the Word spoke in the midst of what was *tohu* (chaos) and *bohu* (void). The double meaning of "creation" is first to order reality by giving it bounds, as light separated from darkness, or heaven from earth, or earth from sea, and then to make reality fruitful, to the praise of its Creator. As Lord of creation Jesus Christ has no place within the Devil's restricted horizon of "being." Yet the Devil offered Jesus the temptation of universal rule.

Our temptation is to seek a "lord over us" whom we enthrone to be *our* king—our own limited perspective upon life. It is no different from having a puppet we carve or an idol we create and bow down to worship. But Jesus Christ cannot be less than the Creator and Redeemer of all reality. He alone can set our desires free from their deformity, and give us a "new memory," by which our lives can begin afresh.

THE DEATH AND RESURRECTION OF JESUS CHRIST

"This Birth was hard and bitter agony for us, like Death, our death." The record is clear that Jesus was not privately murdered by some hired hitman, but publicly executed with the consent of the state, the religious leaders, and the people. It took place, ironically, in Jerusalem, which had been a symbol of

God's presence with Israel when the temple was built. The result was absolutely devastating to those who loved Jesus.

When we have watched our own loved ones die, the sight is awful! People who talked and walked with us are dead corpses with gray faces, rigid limbs, and frozen lips. But the dead Jesus! To see the nails driven through his hands and feet, the spear thrust through his side, the brow mottled with the thorns that crowned him in mockery; how that must have overwhelmed his followers.

Cremation would have been far more civilized, with the death certificate delivered impersonally through the mail. There are times when we don't want to see or know. There is also the grief of irrevocable separation that afflicts husbands and wives, children and parents. But the "end" of never seeing Jesus again, that surely must have felt like the "end of the world."

The one crumb of comfort was Jesus' silence. Does that tell us anything? There had been witnesses to narrate the temptation of Jesus Christ; witnesses had seen his glory in the transfiguration. Could the disciples be witnesses of more to come? So it was that the risen Jesus appeared to them, in Jerusalem and in Galilee.

In his book *Resurrection*, Rowan Williams beautifully shows us that "God is the agency that gives us back our memories, because God is the 'presence' to which all reality is present."[21] But when God gives us back our memories, we are profoundly discomfited. In Eliot's words: "We returned to our places, these Kingdoms. But no longer at ease here, in the old dispensation, with an alien people clutching their gods." Then begins the "pain of the re-enactment of all that you have done, and been."

One aspect of the resurrection is therefore Jesus Christ bringing God's memory back into our distorted human memories. It is as if, having failed in examinations, we start the next academic year from the beginning again. There has been no graduation after all. Old lessons have to be relearned in a new way that must now transcend death, old relationships have to be given a new and deeper basis. Everything is changed by the death of Jesus. That is why death is a vital aspect of all life: There has to be death to our addictions, death to our idols, death to our habitual thoughts and sinful ways. We do not become extinct but, like the butterfly emerging from the chrysalis, we become "new persons."

This "newness" does not merely plaster over old cracks in our lives. Every therapist knows the tyranny of buried images of our past that hold us captive to our emotional history. Instead, we have to go back to our "roots," to find where our memories began. They might reveal the early loss of "bonding," childhood abuse, or inadequate relationships. Whatever they are, all these "stories" go to make up the way in which we perceive reality now.

After his resurrection Jesus went back to Galilee, to where he first encountered the disciples, fishing on the lake, and they suddenly realized: "It is the Lord!" The memory returned as from "the beginning," when he had called them from their nets. Now Jesus appeared again, to give them "daily bread," with a lakeside breakfast. Truth is always recognized, for once it has been lodged in the heart, the mind can respond. The disciples had already "followed Jesus in the way"; but on the resurrection morning their call to follow him took on a new form. For them and for us, hearts are reborn, hopes transformed, and memories are of God and no longer merely human. Vocation—our calling in Christ—utterly changes our desires and our lives, and nourishes us in a new way.

Restitution and forgiveness followed as well. Peter was taken aside by Jesus, for the meeting place between God and human beings in matters of salvation is in the privacy of the heart. "Simon," he remembered, had been his old name, his old identity—confident, boastful, impulsive, weak—the one who denied his Lord. How he had wept in bitterness over that former identity, when Jesus simply "looked at him" at the moment of Peter's public denial that he knew him. Now, beyond death, that memory was also changed. Simon was made new as "the apostle Peter," forgiven, restored—himself risen to new life.

Peter learned that our betrayal of God is never God's betrayal of us. Death, our death in Christ, has swallowed up our past betrayals.

Mary was also changed by her meeting with the risen Christ, outside his tomb. She heard him call her name in such a tone of love that the speaker was unmistakable. Her response, "Rabboni!" (Teacher), was her recovery of memory, of all that the "Teacher" had indeed taught her; of being healed and loved by her Master. Yet Mary was still not aware of the radical "newness of the new." Jesus had to warn her, "Touch me not." We must not go back so quickly to old ways of behaving.

In all valid mystical experiences we may have of Jesus, there will always be a fresh command from him. That is one way in which we test their reality. So Mary was told: "Go tell my brethren." What freedom such a commission gave to a woman in that culture, to share the good news of the risen Lord Jesus with the male apostles.

Finally, we consider Jesus returning to the upper room. The disciples had been confused and bewildered by Jesus' words, his strange claims and promises. During his lifetime, Philip, Thomas, and Judas Iscariot had scarcely understood some of his words. Now, in the shining light of the cross and resurrection, they could understand. And it was all so "real." Jesus met them in their state of confusion and gave them the chance to touch reality: "Thomas, doubt no more, but stretch your hand into my wounded side."

Legal proofs of the resurrection have their place as useful books—but they remain books. The real "proofs" of Jesus' resurrection are resurrected lives, transformed by the living Christ in their hearts. That was Jesus' work in his forty days among the disciples. How different they were from those forty days in the desert when the Devil tempted him. Now his "silence" could be fully understood in the light of his resurrection.

T. S. Eliot understood all this when he could make the wise men say, "I should be glad of another death." And yet George Herbert can correct us against either masochism or confusing the death of Christ, the death of deaths, with our own deaths:

> Kill me not ev'ry day,
>
> Thou Lord of life; since thy one death for me
>
> Is more than all my deaths can be ... (*Affliction [II]*)[22]

Instead, we can witness to our changed lives in singing:

> Rise heart; thy Lord is risen.
>
> Sing his praise
>
> Without delays,
>
> Who takes thee by the hand,
>
> That thou likewise
>
> With Him mayst rise:
>
> That, as his death calcined[23] thee to dust,
>
> His life may make thee gold, and much more just.
>
> (*Easter [I]*)[24]

Jesus, a great desire have we
To walk life's troubled path with Thee:
Come to us now, in converse stay;
And O! walk with us day by day.

—Edwin Paxton Hood[1]

8

TRANSFORMED
DESIRES

Wh
hen the death and resurrection of Christ have
affected our lives in such a way, our transformed
desires will inevitably witness to the change within us. Such witnessing, however, may be a costly process.

A friend of mine was once involved in a court action. I still
remember the shame I felt, listening to the stories of other
people's lustful lives. Outside the court we were greeted by a bat-
tery of photographers, and I had to stand in front of my friend
to prevent her face from appearing in the newspapers. She and I
both learned that it is frightening to be a witness confronting a
hostile world. It is one thing to share past memories with a gentle, understanding therapist, and quite another to stand up in
front of a court of law and promise "to tell the truth, the whole
truth, and nothing but the truth, so help me God!"

Few people are willingly going to volunteer to be grilled and
roasted by a clever lawyer, to become vulnerable to a society that

looks only for the sensational, that exposes people to public curiosity, and allows them to be hounded ruthlessly by the press. So what about people whose lives are drastically affected by the testimony they make, people like Whittaker Chambers, in the midtwentieth century, who was tempted to put an end to it all by suicide?

Whittaker Chambers (1901–1961) came from a Quaker background. He was the elder of two sons. His mother pampered them, and his father was distanced from them by the failure of his own life. As a teenager Whittaker ran away from home. Eventually he was converted to the communist cause in the United States at the age of twenty-four. In 1932 he was drafted into Soviet military intelligence in New York. He soon became disillusioned with the communist ideology, and for ten years beginning in 1938 he planned how to escape.

He was subpoenaed by the House Committee on Un-American Activities and willingly disclosed everything he knew, thus implicating Alger Hiss, assistant to the assistant secretary of state. The outcome was a battle of "two men's faiths, Communism and Freedom, that came to grips in the persons of two irreconcilable and resolute men ... neither would nor could yield without betraying not himself only, but his faith; and the different character of these faiths was shown by the different conduct of these two men toward each other throughout the struggle."[2]

Chambers, with no legal background, would lay himself open: "I am for stating the facts." Hiss, a debater and skilled lawyer, would repeat *ad nauseam* his appeal to the Fifth Amendment, or say "I would have to consult counsel before responding to that line of argument." That is to say, Chambers presented nothing but *himself* as a witness, whereas Hiss presented a *legal defense* of the nation's brightest lawyers and hired detectives behind his "campaign of protection."

The issue, as Chambers saw it, was the threat of a system of thought that is humanity's second oldest faith. "Its promise was whispered in the first days of Creation under the Tree of Knowledge of Good and Evil—Ye shall be as gods." It is the great alternative to Christianity. It is what we described earlier as part of the great conspiracy of the nineteenth-century philosophers, to promote a consciousness that excludes any necessity of thinking about God or of living in his presence.

There is always a choice between freely exercising our infinite desires before God, or sabotaging those desires by denying God and living without him. For Chambers, to break away from the latter was to be like "Lazarus, the impossible return. I began to break away from Communism and to climb from deep within its underground, where for six years I had been buried, back into the world of free men. When we dead awaken … I used to say to my wife … awakened from fears, uncertainties, self-doubts, cowardices, flinchings of the will, natural to every man who undertakes to reverse in mid-course the journey of his life."[3]

The struggle was such that one night, during the heat of the battle, Chambers nearly committed suicide. Sensing something wrong, his two children ran out into the night, where he was hiding—ready to do away with himself—and cried out desperately for their "Papa." Walking over to his small son, Chambers felt as if he were making "the most terrible surrender I should have to make on earth. 'Papa,' he cried, and threw his arms around me, 'don't ever go away.' 'No,' I said, 'no, I won't ever go away.' Both of us knew that the words 'go away' stood for something else, and that I had given him my promise not to kill myself."[4]

Jesus, however, the God-man, knew and accepted that he was going to be killed, and repeatedly told his disciples in the upper room at the Last Supper, "I am going away." As "the true and faithful Witness" described in the New Testament book of Revelation, he has by his death transformed the character of the witness for ever. The witness of Christ is unlike any other witness before or since, since he both died and rose again from the dead. If we are to be similar witnesses, we too must "die and live again" in Christ.

THE WITNESS OF JESUS OR OF BARABBAS

When Pilate sat on his judgment throne, he had at about the same time two prisoners presented to him, Barabbas and Jesus. According to the Gospels, Pilate would have had no difficulty in pronouncing the sentence of death by crucifixion on Barabbas, for he was a notorious prisoner, among rebels in prison who had committed murder in the insurrection and was called a robber or brigand.[5] Clearly, violence was his alter ego. Then Jesus was presented and false witnesses were bribed by the religious leaders to testify against him. Their case was weak—"I find no fault in this man," said Pilate. But the Jewish leaders incited the mob and demanded his death, so Jesus was crucified. We have no further record of what happened to Barabbas.

In the novel *Barabbas,* by the Nobel prize-winning novelist Pär Lagerkvist, Barabbas watches the crucifixion from a distance, and for the rest of his life he keeps Christians at a distance. Barabbas is afraid of a faith that speaks of a "God of love." In the course of the story he is enslaved in the mines and finds himself chained to Sahak, who becomes a Christian. One day, Sahak engraves crudely on the metal disk that claims him as state property the name of Jesus. Intrigued, Barabbas requests him to put the name on his disk too. Later, they are both caught with the name and found guilty of treason. To Barabbas, the name of Jesus means nothing so he is released. Sahak cannot recant and deny his faith, and he is crucified.

Barabbas is later promoted to being a slave in the governor's palace, where he overhears Christian slaves whispering about a rendezvous in the catacombs. Intrigued, Barabbas steals out into the night and reaches the entrance undetected. He hears muffled voices, but gets lost and in panic flees out of the presence of the dead and returns toward Rome. In the suburbs he sees a house in flames, then more houses ablaze. The cry goes up, "It's the Christians! The Christians are setting fire to Rome!" Barabbas believed their "hour had come." Their Savior had come! Grabbing a torch he set fire to house after house in the name of the Christians. This was his finest moment! He would not fail as he had before, when Christ had needed him. This was the great hour of a glorious destiny, when "the whole world was ablaze! Behold, his kingdom is here!"[6]

After his arrest, he finds himself in the same dungeon as a group of Christians and their leader, possibly Peter. The old apostle recognizes Barabbas and begins to talk to him. Barabbas admits that he wanted to help them and their Savior set the world on fire. Shaking his head sadly, the apostle tells him it was Caesar himself who started the fire. "'It was your worldly ruler you helped,' he said, 'him to whom your slave's disk says you belong, not the Lord, whose name is crossed out. Without knowing it, you served your rightful master. Our Lord,' he added gently, 'is Love.'" Then he tells the Christians that this stranger in their midst is Barabbas. "Nothing could have astounded or upset them more than this! Barabbas, he who was acquitted in the Master's stead."[7]

Alone with his thoughts, Barabbas asks himself if there has been any meaning in the life he has led. When he is crucified, he outlives all the Christians crucified with him. Then, as death approaches him also, he speaks into the darkness, "as though he were speaking to it:—To thee I deliver up my soul. And then he gave up the ghost."[8]

The novelist Pär Lagerkvist is himself an enigma. He revolted against his upbringing in a devout Lutheran home in order to become a socialist, "a believer without faith, a religious atheist." He depicts a Barabbas who is so close to Christians, and yet so far away from their personal faith that his death cry can only echo the words of Christ on the cross. In the end we do not know whether Lagerkvist delivered himself into the darkness or into the hands of Christ.

The story illustrates poignantly that to be a true witness of the Christian faith one must know Jesus Christ personally, not simply espouse a cause or undertake a crusade in his name. Each witness must express in his or her own life that which is consistent with the death and resurrection of Jesus Christ. So it is wholly appropriate to read books such as *How to Share Your Faith without Being Offensive*[9] or *Explaining Your Faith Without Losing Your Friends*.[10] The desire to witness to the truth must be part of the deeper desire to live in the truth shown in Christ.

On the other hand, it is a natural human failing to be like Barabbas and take up causes and even a ministry on behalf of Christ without really knowing him personally. It is perfectly possible to bear witness to a religious faith in a manner that is neurotic, ideological, and even toxic, one that wholly betrays the reality of the "truth that is Christ Jesus." Our very witness can be a lie about Jesus. Our manner of witness can so contradict his character and life that, instead of giving life, its rigid doctrinaire spirit saps life from others.[11]

MAINTAINING THE WITNESS OF JESUS CHRIST

In Lagerkvist's story, the great difference between the Christians and Barabbas was that the Christians suffered and died because of the testimony they bore to the "Name," the symbol of the character of Jesus Christ, whereas Barabbas knew nothing of the character of that "Name." This is historically accurate; when Pliny gave the Emperor Trajan a report of the legal proceedings in his territory, he declared that he tested people accused of being Christians by whether or not they recanted the "Name" of Christ. This became the criterion for the persecutions that followed throughout the Roman Empire.

The writer of the book of Revelation did not go into detail as to how Christians were loyal even to death in upholding the "Name," but nonetheless spoke for suffering and persecuted Christians throughout Asia Minor toward the end of the first century. They were said to suffer not just because they witnessed *to* Christ, but because of the witness *of* Christ himself within them. Their testimony was his testimony;[12] in witnessing for Christ the first desire has to be to "maintain the testimony of Jesus," to allow him to speak through you.

In the book of Revelation Jesus was first named as "Jesus Christ, the faithful witness, the firstborn from the dead." Similarly, John's gospel records Jesus' testimony before Pilate: "For this reason I was born, and for this I came into the world, to testify to the truth."[13] To bear witness to the truth of Jesus will involve suffering like him. As we have seen in the confrontation between Chambers and Hiss, truth is a terrible threat to those who want to maintain a life of illusion. It can bring suffering and death at the hands of those who are threatened by it.

At the beginning of the book of Revelation, John refers to his exile, "I … was on the island of Patmos because of the word of God and the testimony of Jesus."[14] Clearly, for him and for the other Christian witnesses he alludes to in his book, it was not only verbal witness to the reality of Jesus Christ that attracted persecution. Obedience to the commands of Christ to live a holy and devout life also spelled danger. The purity of the Christian life contrasted sharply with the idolatry and addictive immorality of pagan society. As one early text, the Wisdom of Solomon, expresses:

> Let us lay a trap for the just man … he is living condemnation of all our ideas. The very sight of him is an affliction, because his life is not like other people's, and his ways are different.... Outrage and torment are the means to try him with … let us condemn him to a shameful death.[15]

The message of Jesus represented an attack on idolatrous desires; his own death and resurrection was no less than a victory over the powers that lay behind the idols, and a promise of freedom to people living addictive lives. The apostle Paul wrote in this vein to the Thessalonians: "You turned to God from idols to serve the living and true God, and to wait for his Son from heaven, whom he raised from the dead—Jesus, who rescues us from the coming wrath." For the apostle this brought him comfort in his own sufferings: "In all our distress and persecution we were encouraged about you because of your faith. For now we really live, since you are standing firm in the Lord. "[16]

When our desire for God turns into idolatry and is defiled, we are perverted from our true nature: Our minds are darkened, and we disfigure creation. This false consciousness has widespread effects on our society. As one writer has put it, nonworship of God becomes the worship of the non-God. This means that being a witness to Jesus Christ, who is "the true and faithful Witness," demands drastic measures that the world rebels from accepting.

To witness to reality is dangerous, like a surgical operation, costly to doctor and patient alike. Its compassion appears cruel, yet the surgery has to be performed if health and life are sought.

Relying on Jesus Christ as Our Witness

It is a mark of true witness that one does not rely upon one's own subjective feelings, rather as navigators sail not by instinct but with reference to detailed maps and charts. There has to be some objective reality amid our confusion and the heat of our emotions. So at the heart of the Christian faith there is the final and absolute aliveness of Jesus Christ after his death. There is the certainty that the resurrection did take place, and that the tomb was really empty.

This has been a source of division for contemporary theologians. On the one hand there are those who in their hearts can believe only that Jesus died; for them the resurrection is merely an idea, albeit a very powerful one, that possessed the hearts of the disciples. They might add that the disciples were deceived in a way that modern thinkers are not! Then there are those who can attest, from the experience of Christ living within them, that Jesus literally rose again, in a bodily form untouched by the corruption of death; that his life continues for all time in the lives of believers, transforming them. It was not only Jesus' followers who witnessed his appearances, during the forty days that he ministered to them. Saul of Tarsus saw him for himself in a unique appearance on the road to Damascus years later, and there have been many witnesses to the reality of Christ throughout the history of the church. Indeed, it is a mark of all true Christians still, that they experience the transforming presence of Christ in their lives.

This truth is expressed in a simple hymn:

> I serve a risen Savior, he's in the world today ...
> He lives! He lives! Christ Jesus lives today! ...
> You ask me how I know He lives?
> He lives within my heart![17]

John's gospel focuses on the idea of Jesus Christ as a witness. Yet it also emphasizes Jesus' dependence on God, his Father. As Jesus says: "If I testify about myself, my testimony is not valid. There is another who testifies in my favor, and I know that his testimony about me is valid ... the Father who sent me has himself testified concerning me."[18]

Jesus himself depended upon others to confirm his testimony: There was John the Baptist who preceded him, the disciples who accompanied him, and you and I who follow him.[19] But behind all these human witnesses lies Jesus' own claim, which is founded on God's own character as the divine Trinity of Father, Son, and Holy Spirit, present and active in the world. The validity of Christ's witness is to be found deep within the heart of the Trinity.

Our validity as witnesses depends on that same reality: the Son who mediates for us with the Father, and the Holy Spirit who makes available both Christ's saving action and the Father's love for us to live by. And just as that Spirit brooded over the chaos at the beginning of creation, and all creation was brought into existence through Christ, the Word of God, by the action of the Father, so we need to experience Christ entering into the darkness of the desires and addictive chaos of our lives, to create us anew.

The purpose of John's Gospel is to help us build up our belief as a source of life within us. "These [things] are written," John wrote, "that you may believe that Jesus is the Christ, the Son of God, and that by believing you may have life in his name."[20] This is no vague mysticism: John was talking about the real life of a unique being, God-man, who died and rose again within real history and therefore within the real world, in a once-for-all event.

This reality can be communicated through symbolism, and it is such symbols that we shall explore in the rest of this book. Symbolism adds clarity to our speech, allowing truth and mystery to shine forth. Living with mere rationalism or with an orthodoxy that is purely theoretical and therefore lifeless condemns us to a constricting "landscape of the heart." Our intellect must be loving, and our feelings must be intelligent, to experience the deep mysteries of God. Our lives need to be symbolic lives, if they are to point beyond ourselves as a witness to Jesus.

SYMBOLS OF WITNESS

John's gospel has been called "The Book of Signs," because he used symbols to draw attention to the nature of Christ's witness. The symbolism that he used to communicate his gospel bridges the two worlds of Jewish and Greek thought.

In the prologue, Jesus is revealed as the *Logos*, or Word. Interpreted against a Greek background this could mean "reason," intellect. But this is not merely the rational mind-set that we discussed earlier; rather it is the mind of God personally present in his world, as at creation. For the Jew, "the Word" was an echo of the law given by Moses. At the time of Jesus, the interpretation of the law of Moses had become so influenced by the word-loving Greeks that it attracted almost as much reverence as God himself. Jesus himself was not seen as the law-maker, but rather a law-breaker, condemned to death as a common criminal.

The symbol of light was associated for the Greeks with the mystical illumination and understanding promised by the mystery religions, which Neoplatonism was later to emphasize so much. But for the Jews, the light was a judgment on blindness of heart. For some, it led only into greater darkness, as they failed to recognize Jesus as the Lord of Glory in their midst. Throughout his gospel John used symbolic language to convey the confrontation between light and darkness, good and evil.

John also took up the symbol of the vine as the people of Israel. Jesus gave this old symbol new meaning by saying, "I am the true vine and my Father is the Gardener." His people are the "branches" who bear fruit in their testimony as they "abide in the Vine," Christ himself.

In the course of John's gospel, Jesus is also described as the Bread of Life, the Lamb of God, the Water of Life, the real Wine at the wedding at Cana, the Resurrection and the Life, the True Shepherd and the Friend, as well as the more familiar figures of Master, Lord, and Savior.[21]

The Christian life, then, is a richly symbolic life, offering us many windows into the mysteries beyond our commonplace lives. We live truly when we live "poetic lives":

> Since all our keys are lost or broken,
>
> Shall it be thought absurd
>
> If for an art of words I turn
>
> Discreetly to the Word?
>
> Drawn inward by his love, we treasure
>
> Art to its secret springs:
>
> What, are we master in Israel
>
> And do not know these things?

Lord Christ from out his treasury
Brings forth things new and old:
We have those treasures in earthen vessels,
In parables he told,

And in the single images,
Of seed, and fish, and stone,
Or shaped in deed and miracle,
To living poems grown.[22]

COMMUNITIES OF WITNESS

In experiencing the truth of the gospel, we are linked with rich associations of human experiences and memories that echo throughout human history. Symbols light up the meaning of our past. But at the same time, to be strengthened as true witnesses, you and I also need community. Whittaker Chambers concludes his moving story with the occasion when Alger Hiss had been found guilty of perjury, and the voice of an elderly man called Chambers over the telephone saying: "God bless you! God bless you! Oh, God bless you!" and then hung up.[23] It was all he needed, that another human being did not believe he was mentally certifiable, that others too believed his testimony.

Jesus' appearances to the disciples after his resurrection were in the nature of pastoral visits. Each time, someone felt a new sense of receiving forgiveness. It was a liberation from a dead past that would no longer go on haunting them in shame and in guilt. It was the gift of a new start—a new life in Christ. Now he would never leave them, for the disciples received the presence of his Holy Spirit to accompany them always. The word *paraclete*, which is one title for the Spirit, means a constant daily companion, like the family tutor in a wealthy classical home, teaching pupils everything about life and relationships.

As a result, the disciples were conscious of living forgiven lives, not only healed of their brokenness but receiving a new way of "being" in all their relationships. It was much more than being acquitted on a criminal charge, though the forgiveness for past sin was real and vital. From now on all their relationships were transformed—they were living in a whole new world. The disciples saw people around them in a new light: no longer threats to self-interest, but opportunities for friendship and self-giving.

By the gift of God's Spirit, the disciples had the power to forgive other people and to care for them, to heal the sick, to liberate the imprisoned. Communities sprang up spontaneously and the changes that took place are recorded by Luke in the book of Acts:

> They devoted themselves to the apostles' teaching and to the fellowship, to the breaking of bread and to prayer. Everyone was filled with awe, and many wonders and miraculous signs were done by the apostles. All the believers were together and had everything in common.... Every day they continued to meet together in the temple courts. They broke bread in their homes and ate together with glad and sincere hearts, praising God and enjoying the favor of all the people. And the Lord added to their number daily those who were being saved.[24]

This new community life was wonderful—precisely because they believed and lived out the reality of the life, death, and resurrection of their living Lord. Today, many people feel nostalgic for such a vital community life. We are paying the consequences of our psychological self-absorption, of the Me generation, and experiencing the failures inevitable in a generation without the risen Christ. Personal experience of Jesus Christ who rose from the dead and is alive now is the original cell for the organic growth of true community.

We need to judge and forgive the failures of church structures in the past if vitality is to return to the contemporary church. That is why we may speak of the need for another

Reformation of the church in the twenty-first century. *The Habits of the Heart*,[25] as a well-known book refers to American memory, does not give us much present hope. But the return of community life is badly needed by modern society, and the Christian desire for God is the one hope we have for its renewal; the ultimate basis for human expressions of "community" is the Trinity of Father, Son, and Holy Spirit.

THE WITNESS OF THE SPIRIT

In the early church Christians were inspired to witness to God by the power of the Spirit. The Spirit opens our mouths when we are afraid, dumb, and confused within ourselves, making us bold. As the Greek word *parrhesia* implies, we are given a new assurance and affirmation deep within our hearts. It was the word first used in Athenian democracy to qualify the freedom to speak openly and to vote openly for city leaders.[26] It was also the word used by Socrates to express his bold assurance against his enemies: "They may be able to kill me, but they cannot harm me." But it was given a unique emphasis by Luke when eyewitnesses of the resurrection were given this boldness to preach of the things witnessed by them.

It is also the boldness of worship in the new covenant emphasized by the writer to the Hebrews; and it is the word used of the Christian martyrs, as stated by Cyprian: "If a man, keeping the Lord's precepts, and bravely adhering to Christ, stands against him [the Devil], he needs be conquered, because Christ, whom that man confesses, is unconquered!"[27]

This is indeed, as John says, "the victory that has overcome the world, even our faith. Who is it that overcomes the world? Only he who believes that Jesus is the Son of God."[28]

It is no accident that the word *martyros*, from which we get our word martyr, originally meant simply a witness. It combined the ideas of being present at the occurrence of some event, using all one's faculties to register it, and of having the insight to understand its significance. From these, one is then in a position to make known to others both its occurrence and its significance. This, according to the theologian Karl Barth, is what it means to be a witness.[29]

When the servants of the early church were called upon to die for their faith, the meaning of the word began to shift. They were not martyrs because they died—they died because they were witnesses of Christ. As the true object of their witness was the crucified Christ, his followers were also willing to die for their faith in him. Perhaps Protestants have made too much of martyrdom since the publication of Foxe's *Book of Martyrs* after the Reformation.[30] Catholics, on the other hand, have exaggerated the cult of sainthood. Both distort the New Testament understanding of what it is to be a committed follower of Christ.

Even in the early church there were fewer martyrs than is popularly believed, although there were some periods of more universal persecution in the late third and early fourth centuries. Individual stories about martyrs such as Polycarp, Perpetua, and Felicitas are inspiring indeed. But were they any more the Christian norm then than martyrs are now? Certainly, numerically there have been far more martyrs in the twentieth century than at any time in human history.[31] And Christian martyrdom requires a more critical appreciation of the meaning of the word than simply that someone dies for his or her faith, however important that may be.

Perpetua was a young married woman in Carthage at the turn of the second century; we still have an account of her arrest and imprisonment. She was nursing her baby at the time of her arrest, and her slave Felicitas was pregnant, giving birth prematurely so that she too could share in martyrdom. The jailer mocked Felicitas for crying out in pain during her delivery, knowing of her forthcoming torment in the arena, but she answered that this was her own pain, but when she was martyred, it would be Christ who bore her suffering. This revelation was also given to Saul of Tarsus, traveling on the road to

Damascus in order to persecute Christians: "Saul, Saul, why do you persecute me?"[32] Julia Beausobre had a similar experience as she prepared a food parcel for her husband in prison while awaiting her own arrest. She felt a blow on the neck, as "the unspoken words of Another" came to her:

> Of course it's no earthly use to any one of you. It can only cripple your bodies and twist your spirits. But I will share in every last one of your burdens as they cripple and twist you. In the blinding heat of compassion I will know the full horror of your deliberate destruction by men of your own race. I will know the weight of your load through carrying it alongside of you, but with an understanding greater than yours can be. I want to carry it. I need to know it. Because of my Incarnation and your Baptism there is no other way—if you agree.[33]

It is dedication to Christ that is martyrdom, not the consequences of this commitment. We "take up our cross" to follow Jesus voluntarily; only "if you agree."

The second mark of martyrdom is sharing with Christ in his death, so that we share also in his resurrection. "I share in every last one of your burdens," Christ assured Julia. It is a solidarity that is also shared by Christ's body, the church: "And if one part suffers, every part suffers with it."[34] The power of the weak is shown in Christ's grace and sufficiency.

We all, without exception, suffer. Each of us is called to bear disappointment, frustrations, the pain of suffering at different levels—from the loss of loved ones to the upheavals of a sinful world. And all Christians are called to accept their sufferings in the presence of God, and in the power of his presence; in other words, we are all called to be martyrs.

The causes of suffering may differ from age to age, and from culture to culture, but when we witness for Christ's sake of our own free will, and allow Christ to identify with us and with our pain, we do so with transformed feelings—with love, joy, peace, the hallmark of Christ's presence within us. Just as Paul saluted the friends to whom his letters are addressed in this manner, so we too can reveal the transformation that the resurrection brings into our lives.

There are, of course, other forms of suffering. Often suffering stems from our own foolishness, lust, or other selfish desires. If we do wrong things as a result of these desires, clearly we will bear the penalty; wrong choices and wrong ways that we follow bring their own consequences. Being a true witness of Jesus Christ is the opposite of this, for it means saying to God with Jesus, "Not my will, but thine be done," and acting that decision out in our lives. This is the transformation of desire from what is natural to what is spiritual, from what is my idea to what is God's plan for my life.

What our hearts truly desire, when God has set us free to fulfill the goal of our creation, is to live more "authentically"—which means in fuller humanity. For, as it has been beautifully summed up, God does not want our lives to be merely spiritual; he wants our spirituality to be truly human.

The twentieth century has understood Christian theologians to be people who explain an objective "truth-out-there," which is understood and explained by systematic analysis. This is the perspective of rationalism, the thought of the Enlightenment. In fact, true theology is what we may call "narrative theology" or "theology-in-life." It is a living theology because it is both spiritual and intellectual, illumined by the Holy Spirit and lived out in our hearts and minds. The story of such a life radiates the presence of Jesus Christ, risen and living in our midst.

The history of the church is a reminder that until the rise of the academic theology called scholasticism in the thirteenth century, all the great theologians, the witnesses to the truth of God, were also great saints. They lived lives of great holiness and used their intelligence in the service of God. They experienced a *lived theology*. This is even more significant than whether they gave their bodies in martyrdom—although some of them did. As a contemporary theologian has observed:

> They were pillars of the church, by vocation channels of her life: their lives produced the fullness of the Church's teaching, and their teaching the fullness of the Church's life. This is the reason for their enduring influence: the faithful saw in their lives an immediate expression of their teaching and a testimony to its values, and were so made fully confident in the rightness of teaching and action. It also gave the teachers themselves the full assurance that they were not deviating from the canon of revealed truth; for the complete concept of truth, which the Gospel offers us, consists precisely in this living exposition of theory in practice and of knowledge carried into action.[35]

One must cross the desert and dwell in it to receive the grace of God. It is here that one drives out everything that is not God. The soul needs to enter into this silence ... It is in solitude, in that lonely life alone with God ... that God gives himself to the soul that thus gives itself whole and entire to Him.

—Charles de Foucauld, *Letter*[1]

9

THE HEART'S DESERT JOURNEY

In the transforming life that Jesus offers there are stages which can be symbolized by different landscapes. Two of these, considered in the next two chapters, are the desert and the garden.

Until he was thirty years old, Charles de Foucauld lived the life of a wealthy playboy—dissolute, gallant, sensuous, and well-connected in fashionable Paris. It was on a geographical expedition to Morocco that he was first struck by the sight of the Arabs at daily prayer; clearly they possessed spiritual values he lacked. Years later, after his conversion to Christianity, Charles de Foucauld returned to the Sahara and was eventually killed by the nomad Tuareg people to whom he came to minister. Foucauld is an example of the simplicity of life that the "desert" can bring to the humble in heart, when someone is stripped of all desires, save one—Jesus Christ.

When he became aware that God was calling him,

Foucauld wrote: "As soon as I believed that God existed, I understood that I had no choice than to live for Him alone."[2] He then gave up everything he had and never returned to his former life of affluence.

Many people before Foucauld have done the same thing. In the fourth century AD, when the Roman persecution of the Christians came to an end with the death of the emperor Diocletian in 311, the "red" martyrdom of dying for Christ was replaced by the "white" martyrdom of the self-denying ascetic life. Thousands of men flocked into the deserts of Egypt to set up new experiments in Christian living. In solitude, or in small or larger communities, they sought to learn the ways of God. It was a movement that was more "caught" by example than deliberately "taught."

The Desert Fathers, or "Abbas," were great examples of devotion to God in the wilderness of the desert. From our historical distance it is easy to distort their values and see them as champions in the self-discipline of asceticism, reveling in extreme practices. Some of the Syrian fathers give this impression, as the legend of Simon Stylites living on top of his pillar of rock demonstrates. But in Egypt and Asia Minor the ascetic life was milder and more balanced. We, too, must not think of the deserts in our lives as an opportunity to outdo others in our spiritual radicalism, but as a way of hearing the voice of God more clearly.

The Orthodox leader Metropolitan Bloom has wisely observed: "Man can derive his life either from God or from the earth, and one way in which the lives of the desert saints can convey to us how much they depended on God, is to show us how little they depended upon the earth."[3] The desert Christian had his citizenship "in heaven,"[4] not in the worldliness of the compulsory Christianity declared by the Roman emperor Constantine. The flight to the desert of the heart is a quest for freedom from the bondage of "churchianity" and all the addictions of toxic "religious" life.

One of the disciples of Charles de Foucauld, Carlo Carletto, has said, "All the great religions were born between the desert and the steppe."[5] The Buddha left the forests of his home to spend time in the wastes of north India. Mohammed spent time on Mount Hira in the Arabian desert. Israel's faith was dominated by the Exodus and the wilderness motif when the people were later exiled in Babylon.

The cult of the "holy man," as Violet MacDermot has ably shown,[6] is rooted in the ascetic practices of the Near East, long before the beginnings of Christianity. The rise of asceticism and the spread of the great religions has been attributed to the vast expanses of desert to be found in the Near East and Central Asia, where frugal living is a necessity. It is undeniable that this was an incentive to focus upon "spiritual" rather than "material" desires. But each faith has interpreted what this "spirituality" actually means in very different ways.

That is why we introduced earlier the contrast between the "historical consciousness" of the biblical faith—its reliance on personal encounter and historical events—over against the "cosmological consciousness" of other ancient peoples in the Middle East and China, which does not find ultimate reality in the world or in human beings. This boils down to the complete contrast between living in the presence of the covenant God, Yahweh, revealed in the person of Jesus Christ, and worshipping impersonal deities, where ascetic practices—not divine love—control human existence. The desert environment itself is neutral.

In the Bible the idea of the desert is bound up with the personal nature of God. It is human pride and rebellion that banished Adam "from the presence of the Lord" in the Garden of Eden. Abraham made a fresh start by leaving "the city" to dwell and wander in the wilderness, and reached the Negev desert in obedient faith toward God. He becomes the "father" of all those faithful to the promises of God.

The story of Moses and Israel in the Exodus is preceded by that of Moses' own experience in the desert and his encounter with God there in "the burning bush." Moses was called by God to lead his people out of civilization in Egypt, the equivalent of "technological society" today, to spend time with God in the wilderness, to learn to become his people, and to be given a new identity—those "who were not a people" became "the children of Israel," God's own people. This motif recurs throughout the Old Testament; God trains and nurtures his people in the desert so that they become truly his!

The term *midbar* is used some 267 times in the Old Testament. It refers to the geographical desert, but is also a symbol of the periods in our lives when we need to be tested and learn the ways of the Lord.[7] The "wildness" of the place is symbolic of the "wildness" of our emotions that need to be curbed and redirected, as the Ten Commandments directed the Israelites to "walk in the way of the Lord." Otherwise we continue to have a "wilderness" within our hearts.

The great "love manual" of the Old Testament, the book of Deuteronomy, describes how Yahweh found and adopted Israel to be his people:

> In a desert land he found him,
> in a barren and howling waste.
> He shielded him and cared for him;
> he guarded him as the apple of his eye,
> like an eagle that stirs up its nest
> and hovers over its young,
> that spreads its wings to catch them
> and carries them on its pinions.
> The LORD alone led him;
> no foreign god was with him.[8]

The writer speaks of how Yahweh provided "fruit of the fields," nourishing the people with "honey from the rock" and "oil from the flinty crag." Yet in their rebellion Israel once more "abandoned the God who made him and rejected the Rock his Savior.... You deserted the Rock, who fathered you; you forgot the God who gave you birth."[9] Instead, they followed and worshipped foreign idols.

Likewise in the Psalms, the basic theme of relationship with Yahweh is always traced back to the exodus through the desert. "He brought out his people with rejoicing, his chosen ones with shouts of joy."[10] Israel is God's "possession," so deliverance from a rebellious spirit, or from the worship of false gods and their addictive practices, is cause for much joy. "Exodus" is a symbol of this divine deliverance of the human spirit from false desires. It gives God's people a completely new consciousness of their existence and identity. In "Zion" or the "presence of the Lord," they have become God's sanctuary:

> When Israel came out of Egypt,
> the house of Jacob from a people of foreign tongue,
> Judah became God's sanctuary,
> Israel his dominion.[11]

Just as the sanctuary is an exceptional territory, "holy unto the Lord," so the hearts of God's people are his dwelling place. It requires the "desert," however, to cleanse and purify our desires, so that we can become his worshippers "in spirit and in truth."

The exile in Babylon, suffered by the people of Israel centuries after the original exodus, signifies that whenever we stray again from "the Way of the Lord" we find ourselves in "a trackless waste" where all our willful paths end up in the sand! The prophets speak clearly about this retraining of the heart that is necessary from time to time, to control and reclaim "our inner wilderness" or "wilderness of desire." Once again "He will teach us his Way":

> A voice of one calling:
> "In the desert
> Prepare the way for the LORD;
> make straight in the wilderness
> a highway for our God."[12]

Everything that has been redirected into a "straight path," no longer lost in a trackless chaos, will become spiritually fruitful, to an extent previously unknown in the dryness of the desert:

> The desert and the parched land will be glad;
>
> the wilderness will rejoice and blossom.
>
> Like the crocus, it will burst into bloom;
>
> it will rejoice greatly and shout for joy.

Even the great forests of Lebanon, "the glory of Lebanon," will become symbolic of the "splendor of our God."[13]

The prophet depicts the vast transformation that spiritual renewal can bring into our lives. The eyes of the blind are opened, the mute tongue shouts for joy and water gushes forth to create streams in the desert so that the thirsty ground bubbles with springs and the burning sand becomes a pool. This is the wonderful prospect that lies before those who no longer live willfully in their own trackless desert, but who in obedience and humility return to the highway of life called the "Way of Holiness." This is where the unclean cannot go, only those who "walk in that Way."[14]

In the Gospels, we are introduced into that "Way" by the voice of John the Baptist:

> "Repent, for the kingdom of heaven is near." This is he who was spoken of through the prophet Isaiah: "A voice of one calling in the desert, 'Prepare the way for the Lord, make straight paths for him.'"[15]

The desert is a place to prepare our wasted emotions and trackless lives to receive God in Christ Jesus into our hearts. This we can do only by repentance, a radical change of heart and mind. Dwelling in the wilderness, John was equipped to "prepare the way of the Lord," as the forerunner of Christ.

The traveler knows that in the desert you do not look around at the scenery, for it is desolate. Rather "you find the earth the less important part of the landscape; you find yourself constantly raising your eyes to look at the sky. In the arid landscape the sky is the final arbiter."[16] As a Charles M. Schulz Peanuts cartoon expresses it: "When you live in the desert, there's nothing more exciting than watching the sun go down." And what is the result of this experience? Wilfred Thesiger, the explorer of Arabia, observed: "No man can live in the desert and emerge unchanged. He will carry, however faint, the imprint of the desert, the brand that will mark him a nomad."[17]

However, there is ambiguity in the desert, for while it allows room for the spiritual, it is "space" for the demonic as well as the divine. Matthew in his Gospel places the desert call of John the Baptist, the baptism of Jesus, and his temptations in the wilderness in the same part of the story.

Hearing John's call to repentance, Jesus was baptized. In order to experience the worthlessness of our fleshly nature and "die" to it, he identified with us in his baptism, though he had done nothing wrong. Jesus understands well the snakelike selfishness that rears its head to poison us. He knows the scorpionlike subtlety of hidden sin within us, because he too has dwelt in the desert and knows its inhabitants, good and evil.

I understood something of the force of Jesus' temptation in the wilderness as I sat by an evening fire with Kitty Muggeridge and my wife, Rita, and listened to Malcolm Muggeridge's draft of his week's writing:

> Reconstructing Jesus' encounter with the Devil, for the purpose of filming it, presented difficulties. The location was easy enough—anywhere in the stretch of desert between Jerusalem and the Dead Sea. The time, too—at that dramatic moment, when the shadows are longest and the jackal cries shrillest: just before the sun sinks below the horizon, to go out like a light, leaving the burning sand suddenly cold and dead. The difficulty was the Devil's appearance. How should we show him? ...

> Finally, it was decided that the Devil's presence should
> be conveyed only by a long dark shadow falling across
> the sand, and lengthening as the colloquy with Jesus
> proceeded. It may even have been Jesus's own shadow;
> dialogues with the Devil have a way of turning out to be
> soliloquies.[18]

We all know the evil of our "shadow self" more intimately than Carl Jung would have us believe, and we are certainly much more susceptible to temptation than secular psychology admits.

THE DESERT AND THE MONASTIC IDEAL

The monastic way of life has been with us for some sixteen hundred years; in other religions like Buddhism, longer still. So perhaps the religious search for godly desires is deeply part of human nature.

A rather different view is that of Paul Evdokimov, who interprets the spiritual foundations of monasticism as living out the responses of Jesus to the three temptations of the Devil. "One goes into the desert," he says, "to vomit up the interior phantom, the doubter, the double." The desert experience is an encounter with one's false self, the persona that we create to face the world. Our "inner phantom" is a betrayal of the true self, a betrayal of God's image and likeness that it is intended to be. But Christ, through his birth, baptism, and temptations, prepares our "way through the desert." Our new life in Christ is a voluntary devotion to him; it is in Christ's desert experience that the monastic vows of poverty, chastity, and obedience have their foundation.

Jesus' response to the first temptation, to turn stones into bread, is interpreted as the vow of poverty: "Blessed are the poor in spirit, for theirs is the Kingdom of Heaven." It seeks the fulfillment of God's will before that of human needs. The second temptation, to cast oneself from the pinnacle of the temple, causes Jesus to declare his loyalty to God, whose love does not need to be tested. This leads to the vow of chastity. It is the blessedness of the "pure in heart," who reject all love of self in favor of the love of God. For some this may mean celibacy, for others, that no love of anyone or anything can come before the claims of the Creator. It is therefore the antidote to an addictive life. Finally, there is the refusal of Jesus to bow down and worship in slavery to the Devil. This indicates the vow of obedience, which sets us free to serve God in the liberation of our new desires.

Blessed then are the meek, those who are wholly aligned to the will of God. Their humility keeps them from the illusory existence of the modern world that is so tempting and potentially so idolatrous. A threefold cord, we are told, is not easily broken. A life devoted to poverty, chastity, and obedience is likewise kept safe in the arms of God.

Monasticism, as we have seen, is not exclusively Christian. What most distinguished Christian monks from those of other great religions, however, was that they embraced poverty and renounced possessions, family, titles, and honors, indeed all the ways of the world, for the sake of Christ. As Jesus said to the rich young ruler: "If you want to be perfect, go, sell your possessions and give to the poor, and you will have treasure in heaven. Then come, follow me."[19]

This is the "apostolic life"—a life that literally takes the disciples in the Gospels as our examples. If we forget for *whom* such asceticism is practiced, monasticism becomes merely an institution that might be found in any religion.

The Desert Fathers were familiar with two great examples of the monastic life from the Egyptian desert: the life of Antony in lower Egypt and that of Pachomias in upper Egypt. Antony (251–236) lived over twenty-five years as a hermit before he rejoined Christian community, and his *Life*, written by Bishop Athanasius of Alexandria, idealizes the conflicts he had with demonic warfare and the temptations of the flesh.[20] A chaotic inner life tends to give rise to lust, and Antony expresses that tendency forcibly. His influence has perhaps been stronger in the Eastern church, although Western leaders like Augustine also were inspired by him personally, even when they did not follow the tradition of solitary Christian life.

Pachomias (286-346) was converted while in prison, through the visitation of a Christian community. Eventually he had over five thousand followers living in two or more communities. This tradition of loosely knit desert communities became more the norm in the Western church later.[21]

It is significant that monasticism was not originally inspired by the church hierarchy, and was therefore often regarded with suspicion by both clergy and bishops. It has been the case ever since that radical expressions of discipleship and of the spiritual life have represented an unspoken threat to the institutions of church life.

The Desert Fathers have left us their *Apothegmata* or "sayings," which are as simple as the life they led, yet highly practical.[22] Based on the practical advice which came from observing human nature at close range over a long period of desert life, the sayings represent a form of spirituality which is "caught" rather than merely "taught." There is, for example, the advice that the Abba or leader of a community is not just to be an authority figure but should be life-giving to the community. There is the rule of life that the former Roman senator, Arsenius, passed on to his disciples: "Be solitary, be silent, and be at peace." Abba Antony summarized his life by saying: "Whatever you find in your heart to do in following God, that do, and remain within yourself in him." Again, speaking of prayer as the way of life, he added: "Unless a man can say, 'I alone and God are here,' he will not find the prayer of quiet."[23]

The Way of the Desert was characterized by four qualities of life. The first was *humility,* described as "the tree of life which reaches up to the heights." Humility begins when we recognize the vast chasm that lies between us in our false desires and addictions and God's promises for newness of life. A humble person is one who turns away from the tyranny of the sinful self, to love God for God's own sake. Humility was sometimes symbolized by moving progressively further into the depths of the desert at different stages of one's life, as Antony actually did.

The second aspect of desert spirituality was to live an *obedient life*. One Abba, Thalassios, equated obedience with our part in the resurrection of Christ, after our old nature has died. It expressed self-abandonment to the will of God, being alive "to the praise of the glory of his grace." Thalassios also observed that: "obedient disciples are numbered among the confessors of faith."[24]

The third quality of desert spirituality was a life of *repentance*. This was seen as a return to the Garden of Eden, where human beings lived wholly in the presence of God, and therefore a return to the nature God intended for people when he made them in his own image. It is much more than contrition for one's past misdeeds and sins, rather the result of transformed desires, leading to a life lived wholly for God. The whole being of those who experience such transformed lives is marked by love. It is seen in *philia* or hospitality to others, giving space for their needs; and it is seen in *philoxenia*, serving others selflessly. That leads to the vision of God, for, observed Palladius, "If you have seen your brother, you have seen God." The result of such a life is to begin to feel a strong revulsion against one's former carnal, worldly desires. The more our desires are directed toward God, the more he transforms them, so that we desire him ever more ardently; we are changed in the very process of desiring, to desire in an ever more godly way.

Lastly, monastic desert spirituality is characterized by a radical self-disclosure and *honesty*. One of the most discerning masters of this "heart-reading" was Evagrius Ponticus (345–394), who wrote much to guide us about our *logismoi*, or disturbing inner thoughts.[25] These thoughts were said to be caused by demons, demonic prompting that arises from bodily needs, lust, fantasies, and obsessions.

When we collaborate with these inappropriate images and desires, then they develop a dynamism that can both destroy our lives and harden our hearts. The heart, as Peter Brown has wisely observed, "is a place where momentous, faceless options are mercifully condensed in the form of conscious trains of thought—*logismoi*. Little wonder then, that the wise Solomon said, 'Keep your heart with all diligence.' For to consent to such logismoi is to enter into partnership with demons. It is to give oneself over, on many more levels of the self than the conscious person, to an alternative identity: to lose oneself to the powers of numbness that still lurk in the hidden reaches of the universe, and to take on the character of chill demonic spirits who have been content to exist without the ardent search for God."

The confidence of a disciple in his Abba enabled him to exercise radical honesty by exposing all such inner thoughts to his spiritual father, for the great insight of the desert spirituality is that we are not safe to be on our own. Spiritual struggles against temptation and the accompanying *logismoi* are best dealt with by disclosure, either directly to God in prayer, or with the help of a soul friend, someone to whom you can reveal your inner nature without fear of condemnation. So Antony in prayer could say, "Lord, I am beset by much *accidie* [spiritual boredom or depression] and sinful thoughts. I want to be saved, but these thoughts do not leave me alone. What shall I do in my affliction?" A short time afterwards Antony had a vision of a man sitting nearby, plaiting rope ... it was an angel.

John of Climacus (who lived in the late sixth to early seventh centuries) vividly compares such *logismoi* to maggot eggs placed in the warm dung of our sinful nature. Only exposure can eradicate them, and for this we need a soul friend to help us. In the words of a sixth-century Abba, Dorotheos of Gaza, "Nothing is more burdensome, than directing oneself; nothing is more fatal";[26] because the fatal flaw of our inner lives is our tendency to self-deception. Outside help is therefore essential.

The eight types of *logismoi*, or vices, as forms of temptation, are discussed in the writings of the Desert Fathers. They are: gluttony, avarice, fornication, anger, grief, *accidie* or listlessness, vainglory, and pride. These are not to be confused with the later medieval "seven deadly sins," which are sinful actions; rather, they are tendencies to temptation, which may in fact be viewed as hindrances to prayer. As Andrew Louth has helpfully observed:

> These hindrances take, roughly, three forms: they can distract, they can occlude, and they can turn the ascetic in on himself in a way that destroys the very nature of prayer.[27]

There are plenty of distractions for us in our busy culture, even when we pray for just a brief period; but for the Desert Fathers, who spent long hours or days alone before God, *logismoi* could do violent damage to the life of prayer. Distractions were viewed much more severely than they are now, as remnants of an old way of life that had been renounced—allowing ourselves to become distracted from prayer in this way could strengthen the powers of the *logismoi* to tempt us.

What the teaching of the *logismoi* shows us is that there are desires not only false in themselves, but which, when they possess us, also falsify our true identity and meaning in life. Indeed, the three temptations faced by Jesus contain in essence all eight *logismoi*.

Greed or *gluttony* was called "belly-madness" or "madness of the throat" by Clement of Alexandria, an early Christian thinker. Remembering that the word for "soul," which is the appropriate organ and faculty of desire, is originally derived from the breath of the throat, we see that such "throat" madness distorts and corrupts all our valid needs and desires.

Fornication, avarice, and *anger* are expressions of these corrupt desires. They express respectively the false desire for lust instead of love; the false desire for money that trusts in material things instead of God's providence; and the false desire for our own way which boils up in anger, ultimately approaching demonic powers.

These desires lead to spiritual depression, *accidie,* for people are being falsely fed and sustained in unreality, and long to be alone within their own moodiness. *Grief* can be selfish and self-absorbing in the same way.

Vainglory is the essence of the second temptation of Christ, to show off your own virtues. Like *pride,* it is ultimately forgetful of God, for it is really love of self and, as Aristotle noted, "This great friendship for oneself becomes for each the cause of all missteps."[28] Indeed, one moves from self-love to all the false desires, and therefore vices, characterized by self-will.

Dorotheos of Gaza was a great psychologist of self-will and perceived its association with self-conceit, self-bondage, and living instinctually rather than spiritually. In short, self-will tries in vain to justify a life of addiction.

Casting Off Habit in the Desert

Dorotheos put it simply when he observed: "It is one thing to uproot a blade of grass and another to uproot a great tree." He also said: "For we can cut off unruly desires when they are newly born and we don't think about it; we allow them to grow up and harden against us so that we make the last evil greater than the first."[29] Although they lacked our modern knowledge about addiction, the Desert Fathers nevertheless had a very shrewd awareness of addictive emotions. They saw clearly what happens when we yield to instinctive desires and bad habits. Repeated and ingrained bad thoughts and actions bring their own punishment.

So Dorotheos warned: "Believe me, brothers, a man with a single passion set into a habit is destined to punishment. Maybe he will do ten good actions for every one resulting from bad habit, but the latter will prevail over the ten good actions."[30]

In the book of Hosea, God speaks of the idolatrous Israel as an adulterous lover:

> Therefore I am now going to allure her; I will lead her
> into the desert and speak tenderly to her.

It is like a seduction—but a legitimate one, for God wants to woo back and remarry the faithless partner in the marriage, "forever; I will betroth you in righteousness and justice, in love and compassion." Then the wayward lover will "acknowledge the LORD."[31] So, too, we are led into the deserts of our hearts to be redeemed, liberated from our seductive but addictive desires, to become recommitted to God at a deeper level of surrender in love. There is not just one kind of desert experience, but as many as there are differing personalities and personal stories, yours and mine.

For the "perfectionist" there is the desert of imperfection, where we have to face up to our own weaknesses and let God alone give us humility to face and work through them. For the "giver" there is the desert of inadequacy, where we face the flight from our own sinfulness. We too are in need of help from others and, above all, from our God. The "doer" is lured into the desert of uselessness, where we seem to get nowhere and where we face up to the need to become a powerless "child" of God. The "idealist" who has assumed romantically that life will be interpreted and identity given merely by artistic creativity is placed in the desert of ordinariness. The "observer" or "scholar" is placed in the desert of solitude, until the inner loneliness that substituted "ideas" for relationships has been confronted.

The "rigid" or "loyal" maintainer of the status quo, afraid of change, is placed in a desert of flux that appears as disorienting as sand flying in the desert winds. The "fun lover" who fears suffering and pain will wander in the desert of desolation, where for a time life is dominated by pain. Similarly, the "controller" ends up in the desert of weakness, and is made vulnerable to the threat of the chaotic in a wholly new way. The "pleaser" or "peacemaker" needs freedom in the desert storms, where survival requires confrontation with reality and refuge lies only in God—learning to speak the truth becomes a terrible risk that has to be taken.

Many personal stories, our stories, can and must be told in these differing desert contexts. I was recently told by one rigid "loyalist" that he was forced to take employment in the desert of Saudi Arabia. "There," he confessed, "I saw myself mirrored in the intransigence and dogmatism of Arabs who fiercely believed the only true God was Allah, and I found my own dogmatism hopelessly outmaneuvered by the same traits of Islamic inflexibility. But now I saw only too clearly that they mirrored my own alter ego." My friend had to spend several years in that desert before he was freed from his addiction. I think of my own addiction to an idealized self, seeking identity in my dreams of creativity. I have spent at least some ten years in my desert of loneliness and silence, in order to be freed and find refuge only in Christ.

For each of us, living the desert experience is a necessary preparation for walking more closely with God, and for being set free from false desires to love God more intimately. It is spiritually essential in order to gain more self-knowledge in silence and solitude, so that God's Word can penetrate through the different levels of our life's story. Prayer becomes a richer reality, as we begin to experience a greater desire to know God. Patience and gentleness begin to mark our lives more convincingly. The acceptance of suffering is more obvious; it is no longer resentful but even joyous, as our spirits rise above the circumstances that constrain us.

It is as if the imprisonment of the desert is essential if we are to win new freedom over all circumstances. Trust and dependence upon God are deepened, as we become the Lord's well-diggers, to provide others with streams in the desert. This is echoed by the psalmist: "As they pass through the Valley of Baca [i.e., weeping], they make it a place of springs."[32]

We can find a spirit of detachment that expresses self-emptying and purified desires, that is undiscouraged by the blows of life, the disappointments and even the sense of helplessness over forces beyond our control.[33] We too can say with Paul: "I can do everything through [Christ] who me strength."[34]

If it is accepted and used creatively, the spiritual experience of the desert can become the instrument of transformation. Our inner, as well as our outer lives, become expanded, deepened, and richly freed, to enjoy peace, love, and joy. Peace, because we no longer live with the stress of inner conflicts surrounding our desires and their frustrations. Love, because God has become so much more real, and the buried images of our negative feelings about him have been gradually removed, one by one. Holy feelings of appreciation of God's character and intimate experiences of his presence give us gratitude for his patience and grace toward us. Love begins to flood our being, in all-round gratitude for our existence. Joy comes spontaneously, because we are uniquely recognized, and we come to realize gradually that the whole of our desert experiences have been "tailor-made" for us, after all.

In retrospect, we begin to understand that it was a necessary part of God's divine plan and purpose for us, though we could not see this at the time. Then we can be grateful for the Way of the Lord through the desert, in which we have been sustained, guarded, and guided. The lessons of the desert are never finished, so we can expect to go back again. But we now see that self-surrender and commitment to God is an ongoing process, sometimes in desperation, at other times in more trustful recommitment.

The desert is a "place of disaffection," "emptying the sensual with deprivation, cleansing affection from the temporal." It is necessary sometimes to experience the "desiccation of the world of sense" as well as the "evacuation of the world of fancy," to realize more fully that "the Word in the desert is most attacked by voices of temptation." But if we endure these strippings, the shedding of our phantom past, under the gracious hand of God, then we may reach what T. S. Eliot has called the "condition of complete simplicity (costing not less than everything)."[35]

Now the LORD God had planted a garden in the east, in Eden; and there he put the man he had formed. And the LORD God made all kinds of trees grow out of the ground—trees that were pleasing to the eye and good.... A river watering the garden flowed from Eden.[1]

10

THE GARDEN OF
LOVE'S DESIRE

We have seen in the last chapter how it is not the desert we choose, but the desert that is chosen for us, that can prepare and change us most effectively.[2] What we can choose, though, is our garden, the garden of the Lord, where we are reminded we are made "in the image and likeness of God," to desire his love alone. The biblical image of the garden is that which is fertilized by the presence of the Lord, where he is loved and desired above all else. The garden is the sphere where God rules in the sovereignty of his divine love.

The symbol of the garden was well known in the ancient Near East.[3] It was the place of security and refreshment; of exotic desires and their fulfillment, because its plants and spices were rare and precious things from faraway places that excited the senses with their perfumes and beauty. "Eden" means delight and embodies luxury, joy, and erotic rapture.

The garden was also a royal retreat where the king could

enjoy whatever his wealth and power could offer. It provided the setting for royal banquets and for national celebration. Planted with vineyards, fruit trees, and flowers, the garden was watered with elaborate displays of fountains and aqueducts. It symbolized the extravagance of royal desires and realized the most lavish of human dreams.

Religious passion also used the symbol of the garden. In pagan religion it was the setting for cultic eroticism, dancing, drunkenness, and the orgies associated with temple prostitution. These were the "abominable things" that the Old Testament prophets denounced as unworthy of Yahweh, for "they go into the gardens, following one in the midst [the cultic leader], to then practice things that are an abomination." We hear of one such wicked king, Manasseh, who was "buried in his palace garden."[4] He got what he deserved for his perverted desires.

What this tells us is that religion and eroticism were much more related in the ancient world than perhaps we are prepared to recognize today. Yet can our sexuality really be so separate from our spirituality? Too much religion has been associated with unnatural asceticism and the repression of our emotions, as if it were all a matter of starving ourselves of our physical nature. Reason, not desire, has been the motivation of many religious people. The fear of passion and intimacy has kept them from finding fulfillment in their religious life, and the Song of Solomon seems to be an embarrassing misfit of Scripture. Love is not always seen as a godly desire.

Clearly, the symbol of the garden of love is ambiguous, just as human desires are also a cause of much ambiguity. Some people are more attracted to the wildness of nature, where the physical contact with the "wild" connects them with the unbridled psychic realm within, in fierce independence of spirit, living as loners. Perhaps this matches the pantheistic approach to life of being part of the evolutionary chain of being, of "belonging" to the land rather than to the God who created it all. There is also a fluidity in nature, which allows one to remain undefined, romantic, and with no set limits. The vast wheeling skyline allows room for delusions of being "divine." Expansion of spirit gives free rein to an imagination that can remain wild in a wilderness.[5]

For others, however, the wilderness within is too painful to allow such reinforcement from outside. As I meet bewildered young people who have been emotionally or sexually abused, their cry is something like: "When will I leave behind me the emotional confusion of the inner wasteland?" For them, the security, the intimacy, and permanence of "the interior garden" seems so much more attractive. Those too, who have mistakenly sought intimacy in sexual promiscuity long for an "enclosed garden" that is no longer exposed to every passing encounter and affair.

THE PRIMACY OF LOVE

There are many indications around us today that force us to recognize that love is more important for human well-being than knowledge. Bernard Häring, one of the foremost spokesmen for the *aggiornamento* of the Roman Catholic Church—bringing it up to date—in the Second Vatican Council of the 1960s, speaks of the personal struggles he himself had to convince his fellow leaders in the Church "that Christian morality must be permeated by Christ's love, and it must be understood as receiving Christ, who is the manifestation of the heavenly Father's love."[6]

The theologian von Balthasar goes further, saying that Christianity itself is destroyed, "if it lets itself be reduced to transcendental presuppositions of a man's self-understanding whether in thought or in life, in knowledge or in action." He adds: "It is obvious that Christianity—if we acknowledge it to be a genuine revelation—is not primarily, but secondarily a communication of knowledge, a 'doctrine.'" Primarily it can only be God's action, continuing the drama between God and man begun in the old covenant.[7] "God's covenant is the struggle of His love with sinful man."[8]

Of course, this recovery of the centrality of love in the encounter between the human and the divine affects the institutional character of church ministry. The Jesuit Wilkie Au has spoken out boldly: "In the past, the prominent mode of ministry required that ministers communicate their knowledge (what they knew). Today, effective ministry requires them to share themselves (who they are).... The shift in ministerial emphasis from giving what one knows to sharing who one is requires that ministers today go beyond being impersonal dispensers of 'the truth' or distant suppliers of 'the answers' to share the problems people face."[9] Unfortunately, there is as yet no equivalent of Vatican II in the Protestant world, and there is a great need for doctrinal *glasnost* to bring a change in direction to its rationalistic approach.

The early leaders of the church recognized very clearly the primacy of love. According to the epistle of Barnabas, we were created to love, because we are "the children of love." In his argument against the Gnostics, a sect which taught that salvation depended on secret knowledge, an early bishop, Irenaeus, said: "Apart from the love of God, neither knowledge, nor the understanding of mysteries, nor faith, nor prophecy avails anything—without love all are hollow and vain." Eusebius of Alexandria wrote: "Man cannot do anything good without love."

John Chrysostom and Simeon the New Theologian both spoke of love as the summit of the spiritual life.[10] And, as we shall see, the medieval monk Bernard of Clairvaux was the great theologian of love.

It is, of course, the persistence of the classical influence in Western thought, reinforced by the Enlightenment, that blinds us to the awareness that love is the key to life. In classical philosophy, God neither loves the world nor humanity, but is indifferent. Even so, it is reasoned, people tend toward God and desire him through their natural need for love. However, happiness does not depend on love; it lies in self-sufficiency. This is the antithesis of Christian teaching, for love is of God, as the apostle John testified.[11]

The "secret" of Christianity is the recognition that Jesus Christ expresses the love of God, and therefore that love expresses the very nature of God. Human beings are powerless to attain divine love without the aid of God, but happiness lies in receiving this gift of love from the Father, made available to us through Jesus, by the Spirit.

THE NEED FOR TRUE CHASTITY

Today, the alarming warfare between the sexes, the obsession with lust, and the confusion of sex with love all point to the need for a major change of attitude and outlook if our civilization is to be sustained. It is all symptomatic of the disease that has arisen when knowledge is put before love in our culture and religion.

A morality of knowledge, based on thought, judgments, and laws governing conduct, argues John MacMurray, is a morality based on will, which goes back to the Greek Stoic philosophers and was also influenced by Roman law. "To live rightly was to dominate the emotional life by reason, and so to act by will; that is to say, in the way that you have rationally decided to act, whether you want or not. Now that opposition between will and impulse has gone deeply into our European moral tradition."[12] The church's emphasis upon celibacy is pure stoicism, and the church itself has a poor record of recognizing the supremacy of love. It boils down to the fatal mistake that intellect, rather than emotion, is the governing principle of good conduct. This is an intellectual morality and deserves the same condemnation that Jesus gave the moralistic Pharisees in his day. It is a telling admission that much of our so-called "Christian morality" is really not Christian at all!

If love were our motive in all we do, then the virtue of chastity would rank as high as honesty. Chastity is emotional sincerity, by which we express our emotions openly, not dishonestly. It involves saying how we feel. Many patients are relieved to be able to express their feelings for the first time with an understanding therapist. But when the mind dominates and censors the emotions, untold damage to the psyche takes place, in repression, suppression, and all the mechanisms we impose on our memories to distort our inner lives. Eventually, emotional pretense can lead only to the death of the soul. As MacMurray puts it bluntly: "To tamper with the sincerity of your emotional life is to destroy your inner integrity, to become unreal to yourself and to others, to lose the capacity of knowing what you feel. There is nothing more destructive of all that is valuable in human life."[13]

Chastity is not to be confused with sexual celibacy. Since it is emotional reality, it does not repress sexuality, but accepts it realistically. Unchastity can and does operate as much in marriage as in singleness; if two people marry simply because they want the gratification of legalized sex, then neither really loves the other; they are only loving themselves in each other's passion. True chastity is selfless, loving for the sake of the other. Yet who is selfless all the time?

Since our expulsion from the Garden of Eden, the ideal of chastity has been too high for human beings. We are all sinners, all egoists and full of selfish desires in our natural condition. It is in the sexual life that we find that self-giving is actually most difficult to sustain. To single out sex as the most special experience of all is to unleash a terrible weapon that destroys the selflessness of true love—we cannot live up to this impossible ideal, so we give up any hope of selfless love and settle for loveless sex. How crazy we are, then, to build the vast organization of modern society upon the exploitation of sex, directly or indirectly.

Chastity is the area of life in which we most need God. For if God is love, and we hunger for love, then ultimately nothing less than God will do to satisfy our hunger. George MacDonald describes this need:

We are all lonely, Maker—each a soul

Shut in by itself, a sundered atom of Thee.

No two yet loved themselves into a whole;

Even when we weep together we are two.

Of two to make one, which yet two shall be,

Is Thy creation's problem, deep and true,

To which Thou only hold'st the happy, hurting clue.

No less than Thou, O Father, do we need

A God to friend each lonely one of us.

As touch not in the sack two grains of seed,

Touch no two hearts in great world's populous.

Outside the making God we cannot meet him

he has made our Brother: homeward, thus,

To find our kin we first must turn our wandering feet.[14]

God is needed for love to change a lonely "I" to a glorious "we." In that case, the love of God must hold first place in our hearts if we are to benefit from this liberating, selfless love. "I am not I until that morning breaks, not I until my consciousness eternal wakes." Chastity is the recognition that without receiving the love of God, I cannot love anyone or anything authentically. For God, not humanity, is the source of love. That is the secret of all human desiring—it is God who loves in and through us.

Gregory the Great, often called "Doctor of Desire," clearly understood the falseness of the fulfillment we experience when we seek love in the wrong places, in contrast to the way our desires are transformed when we seek them in God's love alone:

... the delights of the body, when we do not possess

them, awaken in us a great desire for them; but when we

possess them and enjoy them to the full they immedi-

ately awaken in us a feeling of aversion. [But] ... spiritual

delights work in the opposite way. While we do not pos-

sess them we regard them with dislike and aversion; but

> once we partake of them we begin to desire them, and
> the more we partake of them, the more we hunger for
> them.[15]

Loving God is not an attraction to the world; so if we are to seek God's love it means forfeiting the love of the world. But once we have tasted and seen that the Lord is good,[16] our desires are transformed by his chaste love. That is the spirit so beautifully expressed in the hymn associated with Bernard of Clairvaux and his school of love:

> Jesus, Thou joy of loving hearts,
> Thou fount of life, Thou light of men,
> From the best bliss that earth imparts
> We turn unfilled to Thee again.[17]

THE GARDEN OF THE LORD

At the heart of the biblical motif of the garden is that it is God who creates the garden of divine love, seeking friendship with us, as once with Adam and Eve. Paradise is the divine presence, and to exclude God from our lives and loves is to be expelled from the garden. This disaster comes through pride, doubting the wisdom of God's love, and listening to the serpent's innuendo, "Did God really say that?"[18]

The prophet Ezekiel likened the powerful king of Tyre to a giant cedar in the garden, great and wise:

> You were the model of perfection,
> full of wisdom and perfect in beauty.
> You were in Eden, the garden of God.[19]

But when his "heart became proud" and shut God out, even the powerful king was cut down and excluded from the garden. We can enter the garden of the Lord to live a resurrected life only as we die to ourselves and to our false desires.

THE DESIRE

I remember vividly showing a great forest magnate of British Columbia a new painting of a giant pine falling in the forest. As an old man, aware of his mortality, he cried out in anger, "Take it away! It's awful." "But," I gently pointed out, "don't you see the fresh green on the cut hillside? There is also resurrection after the fall of the tree!" "I don't believe in resurrection," he said, despairingly. He died soon after.

> The LORD will surely comfort Zion
> and will look with compassion on her all ruins;
> he will make her deserts like Eden,
> her wastelands like the garden of the LORD.
> Joy and gladness will be found in her,
> thanksgiving and the sound of singing.[20]

If the desert represents our constant need for repentance and freedom from our addictions, the garden symbolizes our restored communion with God and the celebration of his presence in our lives.

The monks of the Middle Ages clearly recognized that they were cultivating the garden of the Lord. They originally led an enclosed life, vowing to remain within the monastery walls for the rest of their lives. The great monastic founders, first Benedict and then Bernard, gave this life a vital spirituality. They both taught that desires for God grow and become chaste, above all, through the exercise of humility. This means knowing myself, learning to see myself as I am seen and known by God. It is seeing the tension between God's purpose for me, made in God's image and likeness, and my own falling into sin and alienation from myself and society.[21]

The great gulf between the believer's earthly state and his or her heavenly destiny means there is a constant fluctuation between fear and hope, desolation and consolation, periods of dryness and of spiritual refreshment. Yet God's love is patient and gentle in these alternations, and the process of conversion continues throughout. Knowledge of God and of self both progress, and the fruits of humility begin to mature, in modesty, innocence, patience, and gentleness, as well as meekness. There is a growing conviction that the human being lives with a great void that only God can fill, for we are made to be lovers of God. To be truly human is to desire God above all things. Yet we continue to oscillate between a fearful emptiness and a delighted love and experience of God.

THE VOCABULARY OF DESIRE

The Eastern church experienced a central awareness of need prompting the desire for God, which they called *penthos*.[22] It was the spirit of mourning for what is lost, just as expulsion from Eden was a loss. Their sorrow was the sorrow of the repentant, seeking to return to the way of salvation, and to restore broken friendship with God.

In the West, the word used was "compunction," which signified a stinging or piercing sensation, as if the heart itself was pierced.[23] Its primary function was not a negative pain as of guilt for wrongdoing, but a positive stimulation, to arouse us from moral stupor and complacency, by intensifying our desires for God. We are drawn to God more by gratitude than by guilt, more by God's kindness than by his wrath. Yet our ingrained habits and addictive emotions need to be pierced through; we need to be inspired by new prospects and higher standards of what a holy and godly life entails. We become then far more deeply and richly motivated to follow such a lifestyle.

Compunction is a gift of God, for we certainly could never imagine it possible by ourselves, nor could we make ourselves feel it artificially. What the contemporary Christian needs to discover is that the initial experience of conversion requires an ongoing experience of compunction. Our daily faults are cause for sorrow, as is our lack of zeal to desire God more ardently. False confidence, moral apathy, cynicism, and bitterness can all contribute to a lack of sensitivity in expressing the desires of the heart in God's presence.

If compunction hollows us out to allow greater capacity for God's loving presence, then "waiting upon the Lord" is our exercise of patience, to allow God to continue his work within us. For clearly, God has much more to do *in* us than even *through* us. It is significant, as Marcus Bockmuehl has observed, that Paul seems to interpret "waiting upon the Lord" as an expression of loving God.[24] In Isaiah 64:4 we read:

> Since ancient times no one has heard,
>
> no ear has perceived,
>
> no eye has seen any God besides you,
>
> who acts on behalf of those who wait for him.[25]

In quoting this passage Paul speaks of this revelation being given to those who *love* God. This love looks forward, trusting in God's own character. So we also love God when we trust his future actions, a hope for the future that is based on the love we have already experienced. This desire for God grows over time; it is patient and peaceful in waiting. So Bernard of Clairvaux could say: "Holy desires grow through delay."[26]

Another word in the vocabulary of desire that requires explanation is the word *affectus,* which implies much more than our word "affection." It is a word indicating spiritual maturity—the next stage after compunction.

It implies first of all that spiritual desire comes from the human heart, from the very core of our being. This desire is acted on by God's Spirit to bring the adoring soul into personal contact with God, to experience his loving presence. This produces a knowledge of God through love, made possible only by experiencing God in the most intimately personal way.[27] We see this knowledge illustrated in the closeness of a married couple, where each knows intuitively what the other thinks and so communicates it to those outside. *Affectus* is that loving intuition and feeling-with-God which leads to a sensitivity to God, even to his own mind—a higher knowledge than that merely reached by reason. As Bernard said: "The reasoning of faith should not be the object of petty human rationalization."[28] Knowledge by love is to will what God wills, and to adhere to it unchangeably; *affectus* is an unwavering attachment of heart and will to God.

This conjunction of our will with God's will makes it possible to have "the mind of Christ." It is the "renewal of our mind" which can take place when we offer him our very personalities.[29] It is the opposite of natural knowledge, even when we call it "theology," for it does not "objectify" knowledge as "out there," but recognizes that God's nature is to reveal himself personally to them who love him.

Modern liberal theology often assumes that God's revelation is really a human reaction to what we interpret as an external event. This allows no place for God's presence in our hearts. At best, some theologians are prepared to distinguish dogmatic from mystical theology, where the former is public knowledge and the latter is the private knowledge of the "mystic"—someone whom others recognize as having had a "mystical experience," whatever that means. But the fathers of the monastic school of love, such as Bernard of Clairvaux, William of St. Thierry, Aelred of Rievaulx, and their communities, were simply taking into their daily lives the personal experience of salvation—the love of Jesus Christ, given by the Father and sustained by his Holy Spirit within our hearts. As believers, we can all do this.

Affectus is not a mysterious experience that is fully independent of the normal procedure of thought and reason. Experience, insight, and intelligence are all part of it, but they are also deepened. Unlike the purely rational approach to knowledge, where the knower and the known may continue to have no connection whatever after the disclosure of a fact, it is rooted in the "likeness" that the knower—the believer—seeks to have with the known—God.[30] There is bonding in this sympathy of love for each other.

This is the essence of what is called "monastic theology," where the contemplative or reflective monk sought to experience and become like God through *affectus*. Instead of being a theology of speculation, it is one of admiration and prayer, where prayer is the means of admiring and sharing the mind of God.[31]

THE STAGES OF LOVE

Monastic or spiritual theology reached its culmination in the Song of Solomon. Although this book of the Bible is viewed with some embarrassment by contemporary preachers, in the Middle Ages it was the subject of over 800 commentaries, which contained the highest thought of such theologians as Origen, Gregory the Great, and Bernard of Clairvaux.[32] To them it expressed the noblest aspect of chaste love, the love of God in Christ for the soul.

It describes such love as mutual: As the woman's eagerness is matched by the man's delight, so the soul's pursuit of God is matched by God's response to the soul. It is expressed with one's whole being—body, soul, and spirit. Nothing is held back, no reservations are made. Indeed the main melody of the love song is that it is an exclusive love, tested, yearned for, boasted in, and therefore truly a covenant love.[33]

Such love between God and the soul is total commitment, like two flames that become one, indeed like two bodies that become "one flesh in the Lord." The theologian Nygren, whom we discussed earlier, never really understood how it could be so intensely erotic and yet so perfectly chaste.[34] Such love is beautiful; its song is supremely lyrical, and its language utterly lovely. The soul radiates beauty in the presence of the divine love of the Lord himself, a love which stimulates all the senses to the ecstatic joy of worshipping God, the Beloved.

Where there is the daily practice of chaste love, loving God with God's own love, and loving others likewise, as Bernard describes in his beautiful treatise on the love of God, then the Song of S;p,pm can become a daily meditation, inspiring the heart to follow Christ through all the trials of daily life. Bernard of Clairvaux used these passages as weekly lessons for worldly Christians, to help them become more spiritual and godly in their ways.

A favorite theme of the twelfth-century commentators was that of the threefold kiss with which the believer loves God: the kiss of the feet; the kiss of the hand; and the kiss of the lips.

Using the example of Mary, who wept in repentance, kissing the feet of Jesus and wiping them with her hair as a sign that her woman's glory was now devoted to Christ, these writers remind us that the kiss of the foot is the first or penitential stage of love. Smashing the alabaster box of ointment that she carried between her breasts as the stock-in-trade of a prostitute, Mary also indicated that she was renouncing forever her adulterous life. Her total devotion was now to her Lord. Simon, the Pharisee, in whose house she performed this penitential act of devotion, could not understand this. As a religious leader, he remained coldly and distantly intact from the presence of the Lord, wrapped up in his own self-righteousness.

A friend of mine has written a poem about this event:

Ask me nothing. Only let me unlatch
your sad sandals. Let those Pharisees watch
and spit like men too poor to have me! No
man told me to come. None can make me go.

But you could tell me with a look to leave.
Here, it breaks, take my all, Jesus, grieve
with me, I wash you with my broken—all
my tears were in that bottle, now they fall
through my foolish hair, your feet, my shame
rises, all the room is roaring ...

I must leave—all these eyes!—I will be killed
before the next cockcrow no doubt. But I
have held the Lord. I am not afraid to die.
—Margaret D. Smith

The Song of Solomon must be understood by the purifying, chaste kiss of repentance, without which the soul cannot serve the Lord in gratitude. In the same way, our desire to love God must increase gradually.

Bernard's interpretation continues with the kiss of the hand, the helping hand of Jesus, who helps us to serve him in our weakness. In our love for God and our neighbor, theory must be followed by practice, but we cannot achieve anything without Jesus' help.

These two "kisses" prepare the soul for that ultimate gift of spiritual grace, to kiss Jesus with "the kiss of the mouth." Only the purification of chastity with the first "kiss" and the helping hand of the second, which "will steady our trembling knees" can enable us to enter into the intimacy of the third "kiss." This most intimate of all gestures reminds us, says Bernard, that in Jesus' humility he became a human being so that we should become like him, and be united forever with him.[35]

Cleverly, Bernard breaks off his explanation at this point, for guests have just arrived at the door, and the matter of love that he has been so ecstatic about will now be actually practiced for their sake, in the duties of hospitality. Perhaps you too, reader, have to break off here to attend to the chores.[36] Such is desire for God—a fragmented affair. However, the structure of the Song of Solomon is also fragmented. Its sequence is as follows:

1:2—2:7	Longing and discovery of the beloved
2:8—3:5	The lover's approach, followed by suspense, and invitation to renewed intimacy
3:6—5:1	The wedding ceremony, consummation, and satisfaction
5:2—8:4	The frustration of losing the beloved, then finding him again
8:5—14	Passionate affirmation and further commitment

These contrasts of coming and going, finding and losing, joy and sadness, mark our lives as well. They simply intensify the progress of desire. Bernard and other commentators saw that such alternation is a human and yet a deeply spiritual experience, which is part of our love for God, as well as our experience of his love for us. It is due to a variety of reasons:

1. The ways of God are unpredictable; the Spirit blows like the wind, says Jesus.
2. Human nature is fickle and changeable.
3. Each of us has a unique character, each having our own "story" of our Beloved to tell, different from any other.
4. Our spiritual growth is interwoven with a diversity of thoughts, desires, and actions, making our development uneven.
5. Each season of life has its distinctive moods, emotions, and values, creating a variety of subjective experiences of God.[37]

Our desires for God change therefore, mellowing and ripening slowly. We must not forget, however, that the Holy Spirit is actively present in a diversity of ways and times. In spite of this fluctuation between darkness and light, desolation and consolation, God is always present with the soul, intensifying our desires for him. There is, therefore, a great variety in the development of both our intellectual and emotional life before God, whom we love ever more dearly and passionately, for the heart does not seek an easy stability, but feels intuitively that it is designed to be satisfied by God alone.

Indeed, "it is fitting that the taste of divine presence vary," notes Bernard, "according to the various desires of the soul. In this way, the infusion of the taste of the heavenly sweetness is adapted one way and another to suit the different longings of the soul that seeks him."[38]

Suffering also intensifies the heart's desires for God. Moreover, the presumption that God will act in our time rather than his is eliminated if we are as content to wait for God in the "dark night of the soul" as in the broad daylight of God's embrace. It will only be after death that this interplay of absence and presence will finally be over. In this world, human beings require the changing movements of desire to continue throughout life.

Speaking of Mary's search for her beloved Jesus, after she had seen him dead and laid in the tomb, Bernard evokes this beautiful search that we must all pursue, who truly desire him as our love:

> Never despair of finding Him ... Seek Him by desire, follow Him through action, and in faith you will find Him.[39]

Of course our conscious motives for seeking and finding him will all be different, yet he will be found by all who love him—as Jesus promised, all who seek will find. My friend sings once more:

SONG OF MARY MAGDALENE

And have you gone to the valley?
Have you flown far away, Lord of mine?
Oh, I love you more than I ever did
When your body was here and we drank wine.

I stand among the flowers
That brighten the stone by your grave.
Now you've gone away like a mortal man,
When you promised to seek and to save?

O woman, why do you cry?
Are you looking for someone like Me?
Sir, if you have carried my Lord away,
Tell me where, and I'll take His body ...

Scarce had I passed those watchmen,
When I found the one whom my soul knows.
He had died, but there He was standing,
And I held Him and would not let Him go.

—MARGARET D. SMITH

The ultimate demand of desire, however, is that we must let Jesus go. We must die as he did, alone, if we wish to rise and live with him. His constant coming and going is a measure of our constant need to die to the old way of life in order to live more consistently in the new way of loving him. Without this constant correction of our desires, we would settle down all too easily to a degenerate and sentimental self-sufficiency, convinced that we had achieved perfection.

INTIMACY, REPOSE, AND HEAVENLY ANTICIPATION

Modern observers of love realize that it is a multidimensional reality, with three sides to the triangle: commitment, passion, and intimacy.[40] This may remind us of Augustine's triangle of mind, will, and memory.

Robert J. Sternberg, a professor of psychology at Yale University, has noted that commitment is the rational and reflective side of love; we stick with someone we know. Even then, as we have seen, our "knowledge" is emotional as well as rational, for if it is purely rational there is no basis for loyalty.

Passion is what motivates love, leading to physiological arousal but also to addictive tendencies. Like a weather change, it can happen quickly and die down quickly, and by itself it is fickle and unreliable for sustained relationships. It can become an addiction, with one or both partners depending to an unhealthy extent on the other, manipulating and being manipulated, either sexually or otherwise.

Intimacy is the more emotional component of love, including such aspects as closeness, deep sharing of one's own inner feelings and thoughts, and expressing personal support for the other.

Distortions of love arise when the sides of the triangle are unequal. Romantic love is intimacy with passion, but has no deep commitment; fatuous love is passion with commitment, but has no intimacy; companionate love may be commitment and intimacy, without passion. Lesser substitutes for love such as "liking" may have only intimacy, "infatuation" may have only passion, and "reverie love" only commitment. The emptiness and scarring which many people carry from childhood can lead them to distort subsequent relationships in an attempt to compensate for their earlier experiences. For instance, people hungry for intimacy may seek to love God passionately—as one writer has described in *Mystical Passion: A Spirituality for a Bored Society.*[41] Yet we need to guard against such "compensatory emotions," for the original wounds can remain unredeemed and unhealed.

Mature love for God will have deep intimacy, because Christ has entered deeply within the heart, to give it healing and freedom from all blockages within. Christ comes also with passion, not to make us religious addicts, but to bring the emotional freedom we need. Christ inspires us to commitment, because he reveals the truth of God; like Peter we can admit: "Lord, to whom can we go? You have the words of eternal life."

Just as the Song of Solomon is replete with the experiences of intimacy, passion, and commitment, so the lover of God can rest in the garden of love, the presence of the Beloved. In the Psalms, the symbol of "Zion" is the place where God is present with his people. From Zion, God "blesses" his own:

> For the LORD has chosen Zion,
> he has desired it for his dwelling:
> "This is my resting place for ever and ever;
> here I will sit enthroned, for I have desired it."[42]

It is a beautiful image—God having a greater desire to be intimate with his own people than they can ever have of being with him. Our repose in God's love can be just that. God knows and wants intimacy with us, much more than we can ever imagine possible. Why then hide anything from him—our sexual problems, our emotional tensions and addictions, our intellectual concerns, our struggles of the will? They are all known to him, so we can safely surrender them all into his keeping. Then we can repose in his bosom, as his beloved disciple did at the Last Supper. John reports Jesus' words in the upper room before his passion:

> Do not let your hearts be troubled. Trust in God; trust also in me. In my Father's house are many rooms; if it were not so, I would have told you. I am going there to prepare a place for you. And if I go and prepare a place for you, I will come back and take you to be with me that you also may be where I am.[43]

Perhaps the "many rooms" or "dwelling places" are, in fact, the infinite quality of the intimacy we can have with our Lord. Each one of us has a special place in his heart that only we can fill. Heaven, then, expresses an infinity of such loving relationships between God and human beings. The greatest theologians of love, such as Augustine of Hippo, Gregory the Great, and Bernard of Clairvaux, have highlighted specific areas of our earthly life where aspects of the heavenly future can be anticipated.

One lies in what Bernard calls "the paradise of good conscience." The practice of a holy, virtuous life in God's presence is the spiritual outcome of desiring God. This desire implies diligence, discipline, and devotion. It is what the Old Testament calls "standing before the Lord." Or, as Bernard puts it, "To meditate on and desire what is above is uprightness."[44] There is a role for self-awareness in the need for spiritual growth that leads to our cultivating a good conscience. This expresses itself in the repose of a happy life, one that walks close to God. Indeed, Bernard interpreted the conscience as God's dwelling place, where God comes into contact with humanity. So a good conscience is a foretaste of heaven.

Renouncing the standards and motivations of this world has its counterpart in experiencing the paradisal life of "dwelling in Zion." It is, as Paul puts it, to "set your minds on things above, not on earthly things. For you died, and your life is now hidden with Christ in God. When Christ, who is your life, appears, then you also will appear with him in glory."[45] This does not mean despising human existence and seeking "an angelic life" instead. It means living a truly human life, life as God has planned for us.

At times, this may include so-called "mystical experiences," which Paul describes as taking him "into the third heaven." Whenever we love God so much that self is set aside, we are being taken out of ourselves in the true ecstasy of divine love. Loving God, we will forget ourselves. Then a deep repose, a quieting of soul takes place, and a deepening stillness, calm, and quietness of communion overtakes us.

Heavenly-mindedness is also very practical, however. Our family and friends are always the first beneficiaries of these glimpses of heaven. Our own serenity of countenance quiets others' fears; the saints of God generally radiate love and light. Perhaps the symbol of the halo should not be so despised as it has been in the past. The promise from this far-off paradise that we shall have "glory" is enough to make our faces shine in anticipation.

Malcolm Muggeridge discovered after his conversion that he had new eyes to recognize "God's light-people," whom he learned to spot in a crowd. People noticed by God are indeed "glorious," and much beloved by many others. We conclude this glimpse of paradise with the insights of C. S. Lewis:

> The promises of Scripture may very roughly be reduced to five heads. It is promised, firstly, that we shall be with Christ; secondly, that we shall be like Him; thirdly, with an enormous wealth of imagery, that we shall have "glory"; fourthly, that we shall, in some sense, be fed or feasted or entertained; and finally, that we shall have some sort of official position in the universe-ruling cities, judging angels, being pillars of God's temple.[46]

My words and thoughts do both express this notion,
That Life hath with the sun a double motion.
The first Is straight, and our diurnal friend,
The other Hid, and doth obliquely bend.
One life is wrapt In flesh, and tends to earth.
The other winds toward Him, whose happy birth
Taught me to live here so, That still one eye
Should aim and shoot at that which Is on high:
Quitting with daily labour all My pleasure,
To gain at harvest an eternal Treasure.

—George Herbert[1]

11

THE CHRISTIAN AS
PILGRIM

O ne of the most compelling images of the Christian life is that of the pilgrim, traveling through life toward God. Herbert's "double motion" of Christian pilgrimage is a reflection on Paul's words in Colossians 3: "Your life is now hidden with Christ in God." Like the words of the poem, read in the normal manner, our life takes a horizontal, conventional course as we move through our daily tasks. In the eyes of other people this is our *curriculum vitae*, on which they judge our merits. But at the same time we are undertaking another journey that is invisible to the world. This is the journey of the heart, which is being shaped and directed by the desire for Christ, our Lord, and its movement is an upward one.

This ascent, however, is like that of a helicopter or a jump jet, which remains horizontal while it ascends. Our life can move toward God while giving the appearance that we are merely moving along the journey of our days; though if we start to feel that there is no upward movement corresponding to the horizontal one, we get impatient with our spiritual journey. Yet as long as Christ is our "Treasure," we are going in the right direction. In another poem, Herbert speaks of this dimension of things, the horizontal path of life, as "my crooked winding ways, wherein I live." But, he corrects himself, "wherein I die, not live: for life is straight, straight as a line, and ever tends to thee."[2] Like the contradictory movements of desire in the human heart, the horizontal life of the pilgrim is indeed a zigzag, as George Herbert well knew.

He was Public Orator at Cambridge University, a post that had led to important political posts for his two predecessors. As a friend of the young Charles I, Herbert could also have expected high office. Yet between 1619 and 1630, when he was serving as a priest in a small country parish, he had no offers of any post at all. It was in this harsh period of his personal pilgrimage that he composed the group of his poems that we know as *The Temple,* expressing the switchback motions of the Christian life, with all its questions about the meaning of pilgrimage. Among the things that hinder Christian pilgrimage listed by Herbert in his poems are lust, drink, vain talk about God, lying, idleness, and gambling, all common in the society of his time, especially at court.

There are many people today who have become interested in spirituality and who read the writings of the saints in order to make spiritual benefits somehow rub off on themselves. They want to learn the techniques of meditation and contemplation, without necessarily accepting the doctrinal truths that the mystical pilgrims have held dear. Herbert is speaking against exactly this sentiment, for he sees very clearly that spiritual theology is grounded in the life and death of Jesus Christ.[3]

It is the reality of Christ that throws all our motives and attitudes into question. All our desires and passions must be subject to Christ's desires and the passion of his death. In Herbert's poem "The Church's Porch," where to enter the porch of the church is to be sprinkled with holy water, to be set apart by ritual cleansing from the ways of the world, he describes the true path of the pilgrim: "Thy bounteous Lord allows thee choice of paths: take no byways." Practical advice for the true pilgrim follows, with a simple conclusion:

> In brief, acquit thee bravely; play the man.
> Look not on pleasures as they come, but go.
> Defer not the least virtue: life's poor span
> Make not an ell, by trifling in thy woe.
> If thou do ill; the joy fades, not the pains:
> If well; the pain doth fade, the joy remains.[4]

Though pilgrimage is a basic feature of many religions, the Christian faith sees it as a metaphor for the whole of life. It is not merely a journey, geographical or spiritual, to some place that is viewed as "sacred." It is the symbol of life lived in the tension between our "home" with God and our mortal state of exile in the world. So the psalmist speaks in Psalm 119:54 of "the house of my pilgrimage" (NASB), referring to the immortal aspirations of our mortal bodies.[5] As Augustine of Hippo observed:

> As long as [the citizen of the heavenly city] is in this
> mortal body, he is a pilgrim in a foreign land, away from
> God; therefore he walks by faith and not by sight ...
> While this Heavenly City is on pilgrimage in this world,
> and he calls out citizens from all nations and so collects
> a society of aliens, speaking all languages.[6]

If we "seek first the Kingdom of heaven,"[7] argued Jonathan Edwards in a sermon on Christ the pilgrim, then we have become pilgrims. "He that is on a journey, seeks the place he is journeying to. We ought above all things to desire a heavenly happiness: to go to be ... with God, and dwell with Jesus Christ."[8] What the pilgrim passes *en route* must be viewed as transient, "so we should enjoy heaven then rather than earthly things." We should travel in a state of self-denial, free from the burdens and temptations of life. "'All other concerns of life ought to be entirely subordinate to this," he adds.[9] And clearly, if Christians are pilgrims, part of our Christian duty is to help one another on this journey toward God.

THE NATURE OF PILGRIMAGE

The earliest record we have of a Christian pilgrim is Melito of Sardis (about AD 160), who is supposed to have identified the holy sepulchre. He traveled from Rome "to the place where these things were done" (referring to Christ's earthly life). Many of the great fathers of the church, such as Origen, Jerome, and Eusebius, visited and stayed in the Holy Land, and Helena, the mother of the Roman Emperor Constantine, became the most famous of the early pilgrims, restoring the traditional sites of Jesus' ministry. The historical and geographical realities of the incarnation thus prompted people to travel to the Holy Land.

Even so, there has always been a tension between the outer physical journey and the inner journey of the heart toward God, as Antony of Egypt in the fourth century sensed. Bishop Athanasius recorded his words:

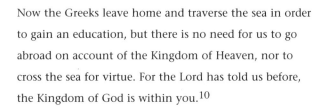

> Now the Greeks leave home and traverse the sea in order to gain an education, but there is no need for us to go abroad on account of the Kingdom of Heaven, nor to cross the sea for virtue. For the Lord has told us before, the Kingdom of God is within you.[10]

Pilgrimage developed throughout the Middle Ages and reached its peak in the fifteenth century. By then it had become corrupted in many respects, having become a way to earn oneself merit in heaven, and so the Reformation laid less stress on it. But pilgrimage as a metaphor for the Christian life was given new emphasis later by such classics as Bunyan's *Pilgrim's Progress*. "Your cell is Jerusalem," Bernard of Clairvaux reminded his monks in the Middle Ages. For them, the Christian life was to be an inward, spiritual journey. Many great Christians, from Augustine onwards,[11] have been acutely aware of being travelers through life.[12] The Bible also uses this symbol—"walking in the way of the Lord," as it is described in the Old Testament— indeed, the writer to the Hebrews describes the whole Christian faith as this "way." There are a number of essential elements that can usefully be identified in this type of pilgrimage.[13]

First of all, pilgrimage entails separation from home; a departure as radical as the rites of passage from adolescence to maturity which are seen in every culture. It symbolizes a new beginning in discipleship. But unlike the pagan physical rites of passage, Christian pilgrimage is a "passage" from one condition of the heart to another, a spiritual journey which is open to every Christian, not just the religious professionals. It offers that liberation from oppressive social structures that is often associated with renewal movements within the life of the church. Pilgrimage thus offers freedom, and yet it also deepens loyalty to one's faith.[14]

Pilgrimage is made to a fixed place. It is not tourism, nor does it tolerate idle curiosity. It is not mere wandering, and is often motivated by a search for forgiveness or for holiness of life. It is true that the pilgrim will return to living in the secular world, yet, it is hoped, with increased spiritual maturity.

Spiritual pilgrimage is the development of our inner potential: not just what certainly will be, but also what may be, if the heart is properly directed now in its desire for God. It is a choice, made of our own free will, as to which direction our lives should follow: a choice for godliness, the decision of the lover of God to follow the desire above all other desires, that "I might know him."

The symbol of pilgrimage brings together the different threads of one's life and weaves them all together in the awareness of life as a journey, with a clear direction and a certain destination. Its model is the way of the cross and resurrection; this directs our behavior, and what we do is interpreted in its light.

Pilgrimage involves hardships and personal sacrifices, maybe giving up all that we hold dear. Physical dangers and trials on a geographical pilgrimage are obvious, but the religious trials of the journey inward are subtler and no less dangerous spiritually.

Geographical pilgrims to the holy places could easily be distracted by curiosity, looking at classical remains in southern Italy or Greece, forgetting the biblical world for the respectability of the classical world. The church too in its scholarship has been waylaid precisely by such temptation; we can see this more clearly as it at last breaks free from the seductions of Enlightenment thought. It is all too easy to become religious tourists, as Chaucer scathingly reveals in the motley dispositions of his pilgrims in *The Canterbury Tales*.

In literature, the dream of William Langland's *Piers Plowman* and John Bunyan's *Pilgrim's Progress* also give us plenty of opportunity to understand the devices of our own hearts, and the difficulties of keeping "on course" as spiritual pilgrims. Perhaps the *Journal* of André Gide, written in 1890, may shed light on this journey. Gide gives five principles:

- We all need a Rule of Conduct in our lives.
- Morals consist in establishing a hierarchy among things and in using the lesser to obtain the greater. This is the ideal strategy.
- Never lose sight of the goal; never prefer the means to the end itself.
- Regard yourself as the means; thus never favor yourself at the expense of the chosen end, the work.
- If all pilgrims, medieval and modern, kept to these principles of pilgrim conduct, there would perhaps have been fewer wasted lives.[15]

MYSTICS AS PILGRIMS

The fourteenth century was a period of terrible confusion; it was the time of famine, the Black Death, and earthquakes, while in the church there was division and false teaching. Yet it was also the time when the spirituality of Christian mystics reached the heights of insight and fervor. Perhaps we, too, may be waiting for similar spiritual renewal after the horrendous cruelties of the twentieth century.

Pilgrimage was still very popular at this time, but not everyone saw merit in it. Berthold of Ratisbon wrote: "What is the point of going all the way to Compostela to see some bones, for the real St. James is not there, but in heaven. Also, all you have to do to enter the presence of God is to go to the parish church."[16] Life as a spiritual and inward journey became a more authentic message. "Works in themselves are nothing," wrote Thomas à Kempis, in his classic *The Imitation of Christ,* "communion with God is everything."[17] Richard Rolle (1300–49) said something similar: "Contemplation cannot be achieved unless a man leave the tumult of the world and give his heart entirely to God; so that he finds his delight in desiring God in solitude."[18] Clearly, the journey of the heart begins with a desire to love God.

Rolle continues: "If you desire to arrive at the love of God and to be set on fire with desire for celestial joys, and to be made resistant to the contempt of earthly men, do not be negligent in reading and meditating on the Sacred Scripture … for Scripture helps us much to advance in goodness."[19] Rolle's concern to help ordinary people enjoy the contemplative life makes his works *The Mending of Life* and *The Fire of Love* very readable today. The slow, prayerful reading known to the monks as *lectio divina* was a way of reflection he wanted everyone to share, to fulfill the desire for God. "For remember," he wrote, "nothing less than God can fill the human soul, which has a capacity for God alone, and thus the lovers of earthly things will never be satisfied."[20]

Book 15 of *The Fire of Love* recounts how one day, praying in chapel by himself, Rolle entered into a mystical experience of divine music, sweetness, fire, and the intense awareness of the love of God. Thereafter his life poured out in lyricism and love for Christ. His love for Christ was "in longing ever more for Him."

Walter of Hilton (who died in 1396) was a more mature contemplative who took the trouble to discuss the variety of options open to ordinary Christians in following the Christian life. To those with a modest faith who were sincere and yet preoccupied with their secular living, he recommended following "the active life"—helping others in a life of Christian service.

Those exclusively dedicated to the life of the "religious," in other words, monks and nuns, were pursuing "the contemplative life"—a life of prayer lived close to God, and holding other people in God's presence. The middle way that he advocated for his correspondent was "the mixed life," both prayer and activity. Perhaps he was trying to reduce some of the ecstatic excesses of Rolle's followers by recommending that "godly desire needs to be ruled by discretion" in the avoidance of "simplistic extremes." Keeping a balanced life, by living in the world, yet still not being part of it, was best, he argued. Thinking of the gospel story of Jesus and the two sisters, we have to be both "Marthas," active in the disciplines of virtue, and "Marys," enraptured by the life of contemplation.

Hilton quoted from Augustine: "The life of each Christian is a continual desire toward God." This was not to be seen as an ecstatic experience, but translated into the continual practice of "loathing of all worldly pleasures and fleshly delight in your heart, and a fulsome longing for the endless bliss of God's presence. This, in my view, may be thought of as the true character of desire for God. For as long as we are in this body we are pilgrims from the Lord."[21] Since this desire for God becomes a habit through practice, it is effective whether it is felt consciously or unconsciously.

> This desire for God is the root of all effective service.
> Know then, without doubting, that whatever good work
> you undertake for God, whether it is bodily or spiritual, is

THE DESIRE

> an employment of this desire. Therefore, when you per-
> form a good service, or pray, or think on God, do not be
> doubting inwardly whether you really have a "feeling" of
> spiritual desire or not. Your action exhibits your desire.[22]

In Hilton's short treatise *Of Angel's Song,* he took up the issue of the emotional and physical phenomena called "mystical experiences," which he considered greatly overrated.

The true mystical life of the Christian lies in the maturing of his or her love for God and in God's union with the soul, not in having hyperemotional states. Self-induced visions are delusions, which if unchecked can cause great harm. "It is enough for me to live principally in faith, not in feeling," Hilton declared.[23] He recognized that the great danger of mysticism lies in its inclination toward individualism and peculiar emotional states, and he must have been deeply troubled by the Free Spirits and other movements of the times. In his mature work *Coming to Perfection,* or *The Scale of Perfection,* as it is more popularly known, he sees the mature Christian growing as a "Spiritual Pilgrim," who "would up to Jerusalem," that is, to enter into the contemplative life, with the goal of union with God.

This particular pilgrimage demands that we travel in meekness and in love. "Meekness says: 'I am nothing and I have nothing.' Love says: 'I desire only one thing, and that is Jesus' ... The less you feel you are or have in your own strength, by virtue of meekness, the more you will covet Jesus in the desire of love."[24] In this "desire for Jesus" you will have a stronger, more mature life, for it implies the reform of both faith *and* feelings in the transformation of your emotional life. This is God's work, in which we can cooperate during our earthly lives, but it is also part of the wholeness we shall enjoy fully in heaven. It is this grace that actually fuels effective prayer, not some technique we may think we can master. Thus, "progress toward Jerusalem is growth in desire for Jesus."[25]

Hilton warned in this context that we should not confuse

mere emotions with true spiritual experience; reform of faith must be joined to reform of feelings, a lesson that has often been forgotten in the history of the church. He offered two guidelines for this inner journey. First, we should never seek bodily feelings as evidence of spiritual growth. Our emotional state is no sound guide for our spiritual condition. But, secondly, when we do experience a change in our feelings, they will reflect our deepest convictions and desire for God, which will lead us forward in our pilgrimage.[26]

Julian of Norwich (1342–1416) took this a stage further forward. She meets head-on the spiritual depression which faithful Christians may face when their own emotions become entangled with such issues as the origin and effects of sin, and the participation of the believer in the cross of Christ and his sufferings. Human experiences of despondency, of desolation in prayer, even of God's apparent absence from us, are explored deeply and with great theological insight in her work *The Revelations of Divine Love*. Julian gave hope to every pilgrim when she said:

> And so I understand that any man or woman who voluntarily chooses God in his lifetime for love, he may be sure that he is endlessly loved with an endless love which makes that grace in him. For He wants us to pay true heed to this, that we are as certain in our hope to have the bliss of heaven while we are here, as we shall be certain of it when we are there.[27]

Her conviction was that God is love, and that ultimately love will triumph.

But Julian desired to know more. She longed to enter into the thoughts of the women of the New Testament, especially of Mary, mother of Jesus, and to find out what they experienced when they stood at the foot of the cross and watched the sufferings of their beloved Lord. At the age of thirty, Julian's wish was granted in sixteen visions, her *Showings*, reinterpreted later by her theological reflection. She wanted to endure in herself three wounds, not physical but spiritual: sorrow for her own sinfulness; human compassion for her suffering Lord; and a "sincere longing for God."[28] Meanwhile, she experienced a mysterious sickness that took her to the verge of death.

When she recovered, her prayer life developed considerably. She discovered that God is the source of her prayers, since he wills us to pray in accord with what he is working out in our lives.

Julian also learned, following the apostle Paul, that we cannot know our true selves unless we see ourselves as "in Christ," for there is no genuine humanity without Christ in our midst. God sustains all created things, as we have already seen in Julian's beautiful parable of the hazelnut, created, sustained, and loved by God.[29] "Yet," she warned, "don't get lost only in what *is*, but turn to see what was intended and you will know what you will be." For salvation was for Julian the fulfillment of a divinely intended and created humanity; we are saved by the fulfillment of God's desire for us. She concluded her deep reflections, in deepest commitment to the God who loves us, "Know it well. Love was His meaning."[30]

While Julian described our longing for God as a continuous experience, albeit a desire that is alternately satisfied and frustrated, Hilton focused on "the desire for Jesus" that carries us through the dark night of the soul—that time of spiritual dryness when God seems completely absent.

The unknown author of *The Cloud of Unknowing* also stressed the power of desire for God as central to the Christian pilgrimage. But at this point, the most advanced expression of medieval mystical life, we no longer rely on the fluctuations of desire for God.

The writer was in an age of transition (writing for the first time in common English rather than in Latin), and there is a new stress on the individual soul, and a conviction that God is vitally needed at the center of our life. Instead of tracing the "affirmative way of love" that Rolle, Hilton, and Julian showed, the author took "the negative way," focusing on the impossibility of understanding God, "the Wholly Other." Once desire for God has been unleashed, the contemplatives to whom *The Cloud* is addressed must "stand in desire" all the rest of their lives.[31] Love, purely and wholly directed to God, becomes now "a naked intent unto God," that reduces all one's intentions in life to the simple aim of living for God alone. Yet this single-minded desire for God actually costs enormous effort—certainly much pain and sacrifice of self, and the wholehearted pursuit of interior silence, for it is God who speaks and human beings who listen.[32]

The first part of *The Cloud* describes this unceasing desire for God, while the rest of the book deals with various objections and offers help with anticipated difficulties. The thrust of its argument is that our intellect will never be able to "grasp and comprehend God." But we are fitted by being "made in the image and likeness of God" to desire and live in God's love, though without intellectual understanding of what we do. "Your whole life now must be one of longing if you are to reach spiritual maturity" is the message of the book.

THE NEOPLATONIC PILGRIM

Since the Middle Ages Christians have been faced with the problem of how to distinguish between the true Christian way of the mystics—a simple love of God—and other expressions of spirituality influenced by pagan Platonic thought. One example of the latter can be found in the Neoplatonic symbolism of "the Ladder of Ascent." John Climacus or "John of the Ladder" (about 579–649) was a Syrian monk in the Sinai Desert who wrote a treatise entitled *The Ladder of Divine Ascent,* where the image of Jacob's ladder is used to describe thirty steps, compared to the "thirty years of hidden life that Jesus had before his public ministry."[33]

Steps 1–3 are renunciation, detachment, and exile.

Steps 4–7 are the practice of vital virtues.

Steps 8–13 deal with the expulsion of negative passions.

Steps 14–23 concern struggles against other passions.

Steps 24–26 describe the active virtues.

Steps 27–30 are the enjoyment of the contemplative life itself, reaching a climax in the love of God.

The imagery *of The Ladder of Divine Ascent* does not, however, have the same meaning as when Jesus told his disciple Nathanael: "You shall see heaven open, and the angels of God ascending and descending on the Son of Man."[34]

When Jesus became human it was God who took the initiative in his relationship with us. Human beings do not have to struggle to gain the favor of a remote God who, according to Greek philosophy, feels nothing for us. Human religion assumes that it is human beings who have to climb up the "ladder of ascent" to reach the perfection which is God. This is where Neoplatonism differs from true Christianity.[35]

Neoplatonism takes heed of the injunction of John of Climacus and of the pseudo-Dionysian tradition later, "I entreat you, let us climb with zeal and faith up this spiritual and heaven-scaling ladder."[36] Similarly, Benedict of Nursia (about 480–547) urged: "If we wish to attain the pinnacle of the highest humility and quickly come to that heavenly exaltation to which the ascent is made … by our upward-striving works, erect the ladder which was revealed to Jacob in his dream."[37] This is attractive to human beings, because it is a practical method, and in our technological society, we long for sure-fix spiritual techniques to gain our ends.

However, the initiative of God's grace seen in Jesus Christ is perhaps where the Platonic *eros* that reflects an unfeeling God is furthest removed from the Christian *agape*. And the hiddenness of God in the "negative" theology of *The Cloud of Unknowing* can satisfy the human need to reach out in union to God, though there is no "knowledge" or technique that enables us to control the situation.

The tradition of the ladder of divine ascent developed later with the circulation of many devotional manuals using this symbolism. It was promoted by Hugh of St. Victor in the West in the late twelfth century, and the anonymous author of *A Mirror for Simple Souls* in the thirteenth century, as well as through the Franciscan monk Bonaventure (1221–1274). It reflected the medieval mind-set that assumed life was governed by a hierarchy of being, the Great Chain–of–Being that all social arrangements were assumed to follow. It reinforced the hierarchical government of the Church, and tended to interpret Christian life in the context of "power," rather than in terms of human relationships. It interpreted God's helping power as being influenced "according to merit"—how far up the ladder you were.

The very notion of "rungs" that one climbs emphasized a concentration on particular devotional practices, just as today spiritual disciplines are still interpreted by some "activist" Christians as developing athletic prowess for the spiritual journey. It is a Platonic idea, and a dangerous one, to detach oneself so much from the world around us as to despise it, and leads only to irresponsibility and lack of care for the created world. It also suggests that everyone needs to follow the same regimented route to God, and leaves us indifferent to those who fall off the ladder by imperfection.

The underlying assumption of the Neoplatonic pilgrim is that like is attracted to like. If God has made us in his image and likeness, then we shall inevitably be attracted to climb the ladder of perfection and seek to do good deeds for him. This becomes more of an instinctual religion than the humbling realization that we have all fallen away from God; as Paul says: "For all have sinned and fall short of the glory of God."[38] The Reformation corrected this Neoplatonic tendency to see the religious life as somehow "natural" to humanity, even though there was hard climbing involved.

It could also be observed that the symbol of the "ladder of ascent" does not provide enough flexibility to understand the human psyche, and it cannot provide enough insights to face the changes and chances we encounter on the journey of life. Its stages represent the achievements of the spiritual athlete in following ascetic disciplines, but there is more to life than being athletic; it is more deeply concerned with relationships than that.

Certainly Martin Luther with his naturally depressive nature came to that conclusion as he climbed the Scala Santa in Rome, said to be the staircase that Jesus walked down after the Last Supper, on his knees, in order to try to please God. It left him more frustrated than ever, and later it reinforced his determination to correct the doctrine of "merit," earning God's love, that had brought so much corruption into the church.

SOLDIER PILGRIMS OF THE WORD

With the Reformation came the growing awareness that the Scriptures were alive and relevant to the Christian's daily walk through life. Like Luther and Calvin before him, Bishop Jewel of England argued that the Bible, not the authority vested in the pope, was the key to the kingdom of God: "We have searched the Holy Bible, which we are sure cannot deceive, one sure form of religion, and have returned again unto the primitive church of the ancient fathers and apostles."[39] The availability of the Scriptures in the ordinary language of the people, with the Geneva Bible of 1560 and the Authorized Version of 1611, enabled Christians to develop a habit of daily reading the Bible and of living by its teachings. One of the earliest works on this theme of the guidance and protection given by the Scriptures in daily life was John Downame's (died 1652) *The Christian Warfare* (1608), which commented on Ephesians 6:10–18 in four volumes of sermons:

Finally, be strong in the Lord and ... [p]ut on the full armor of God so that you can take your stand against the devil's schemes. For our struggle is not against flesh and blood, but ... against the powers of this dark world and against the spiritual forces of evil in the heavenly realms. Therefore put on the full armor of God, so that when the day of evil comes, you may be able to stand your ground, and after you have done everything, to stand. Stand firm then, with the belt of truth buckled around your waist, with the breastplate of righteousness in place, and with your feet fitted with the readiness that comes from the gospel of peace. In addition to all this, take up the shield of faith, with which you can extinguish all the flaming arrows of the evil one. Take the helmet of salvation and the sword of the Spirit, which is the word of God. And pray in the Spirit on all occasions with all kinds of prayers and requests. With this in mind, be alert and always keep on praying for all the saints.

William Gurnall's *The Soldier in Complete Armour* (1656) continues this symbol of the Soldier-Pilgrim being guided and protected by the Word of God.

However, it is John Bunyan's (1628–1688) *Pilgrim's Progress,* written in 1678, that has been and remains the masterpiece of the "pilgrimage" genre of writing. For it was Bunyan's own experience of the Word of God in his own troubled and often depressive moods that rescued him to complete his pilgrimage. He lived with the conflict between the fearful terror of the justice of God and the deep assurance of the love of God in his life. He demonstrated scriptural authority in daily living, even though it was often treated metaphorically rather than literally. Bunyan's plan in *Pilgrim's Progress* was to use the experiences of the Israelites in their exodus from Egypt, and apply them to himself and other fellow Christians. He did not speak any less "truly" for doing so metaphorically.

The story begins with Bunyan's own despair, "What shall I do?" The Evangelist meets him and gives him instruction, which is relevant at two levels. First, the way is for all Christians, "From This World to That Which Is to Come," like the Old Testament instructions of "the Way of Israel." Yet it is also the inner way of faith for the individual believer, which Bunyan experienced himself. Compared with the writings of the solitary mystics of the fourteenth century, however, the pilgrimage is much more sociable, in that there are meetings with those who either hinder or who help in the inner journey of the soul going toward God; as well as a chart of experience, it has become a teaching aid.

The complex nature of faith is heightened by the nature of the faith of each individual pilgrim. "How far the way is," whether it is "safe" or "dangerous," "hard" or "gentle," all depend on the inner state of the pilgrim, as the Shepherds tell Christian and Hopeful in the Delectable Mountains. Our response to people who want to have precise instructions about the way to go needs to be rather like the Cheshire Cat's enigmatic replies to Alice:

> "Would you tell me, please, which way I ought to go from here?"
>
> "That depends a great deal on where you want to go," said the Cat.
>
> "I don't care where," said Alice.
>
> "Then it doesn't matter which way you go," said the Cat.
>
> "—so long as I get somewhere," Alice added as an explanation.
>
> "Oh, you're sure to do that," said the Cat, "if you only walk long enough."[40]

If our faith is about to collapse at any moment, then we won't get very far, wherever we are going. So built into our journey there has to be personal perseverance as well as an understanding of where it is we want to go.

The genius of Bunyan's allegorical framework is that we get both at the same time. First he gives us the whole Reformed understanding of covenant theology, that we go through several stages in our Christian life: from effectual calling, to justification, sanctification, and glorification; all one reality, yet experienced in stages, too. The pilgrimage is in fact one long process of conversion—or of sanctification—that continues throughout the whole of one's life. The more violent and dramatic conflicts occur early in one's Christian experiences, such as that of the encounter with Apollyon. The hostile society of Vanity Fair comes later. But even late in Christian experience we may still find ourselves in despair, as Christian found himself, in Doubting Castle. Indeed Christian finds himself subject to doubt throughout his pilgrimage. For Bunyan never felt that Christians are completely secure in their faith as long as they are in this world. And even after experiencing so many deliverances, crossing the dark river of death is still a terrifying passage.

In contrast to her brooding, naturally depressed husband, Bunyan's wife, Christina, is depicted as having a very different journey. She has a clearer, less-obstructed pilgrimage, and finds herself much more willing to trust the various guides who lead and protect her way. Christina also has the motivation of her husband having gone ahead of her into the King's presence. Being "heavenly minded" is so much easier for us when our loved ones are there ahead of us. Having Great-Heart as a guide is a great asset for the pilgrimage. It reminds us of how Solomon himself asked in his wisdom that he might have "a heart for God."

It is unlikely that Bunyan knew of Gregory the Great's opinion that our relationship with God is initially undesirable and the things of the world much more desirable, yet he realized this as well. The initial landscapes of Bunyan's *Pilgrim* are spiritually unpleasant, so that it is tempting to linger in the outwardly pleasing Vanity Fair. But the later landscapes of the spiritual journey become increasingly attractive, such as the

Delectable Mountains, and Beulah appears as a whole new country for the pilgrim. Once the pilgrim is filled with the Spirit of God, these spiritual environments appear vast and rich indeed. The River of Life, vineyards, and all the sensuous imagery we touched upon in the Song of Solomon are now appreciated in the loving chastity of the divine Presence, for this new Eden is where Immanuel, God with us, dwells.

The great triumph of the meditative life of Bunyan and the true Puritans is that heaven is depicted and dwelt upon as that which provides our humanity with its superlatives; not as an escape from the body, but integrating body, soul, and spirit. All that was at odds within the personality, all that was wavering, and all that was paradoxical, is now harmonized, unified, redeemed, and also glorified. And for both Bunyan and Herbert the guide on this journey is the Word of God, both at the beginning and end of our pilgrimage:

> The Bible is the looking-glass of souls, wherein
> All men may see
> Whether they be
> Still as by nature are, deformed with sin;
> Or in a better case
> As new adorned with grace.
>
> —GEORGE HERBERT, *SYNAGOGUE*

> The Bible! That's the book, the book indeed,
> The book of books!
> On which who looks,
> As he should do aright, shall never need
> Wish for another light
> To guide him in the night.
>
> —GREAT-HEART, IN BUNYAN'S *PILGRIM'S PROGRESS*[41]

Being born, in the sense of constantly experiencing change, does not come about as the result of external initiative, as is the case with the birth of the body,... Such a birth occurs by choice. We are in some manner our own parents, giving birth to ourselves by our own free choice in accordance with whatever we wish to be, whether male or female.... We can most certainly enter upon a better birth into the realm of light.

—Gregory of Nyssa, *The Life of Moses*[1]

12

CHILDREN OF GOD: A SYMBOL FOR TODAY

Up to now we have been considering symbols of the Christian life from the history of spirituality. But what of today? Is there a symbol to express the spiritual struggles of our own time?

No symbol can get to the heart of the mysteries of the Christian life more radically than that of the child—the child of God. Why? Because God revealed himself in a child, the child Jesus. The "child" is symbolic of how personal our Christian lives are, because personal relationship is so deeply part of God's nature. As the apostle John said, "God is love."

Today, when so many of us are bogged down in the despair and misery acquired in our childhood, we may feel that there can be no escape from the past. The rapid expansion of the counseling profession in our society speaks for itself; we have acquired new insights into the emotional deprivation and suffering that result from childhood experience.

Just as social conscience awoke to the evil of slavery in the early nineteenth century, so today there is a new universal awakening to child abuse. Society in the southern United States was shattered to its roots, both economically and socially, when the Civil War confronted the problem of slavery and swept it away as the basis of the plantation economy. Something equally drastic may happen to us in the West in the twenty-first century, once we become more universally aware of the fragility of childhood. Already, even a president of the United States, Ronald Reagan, has seen his daughter "go public" about the emotional denial and blindness of her own parents.

Gregory of Nyssa (about 332–395) recognized long ago that to grow up is to take responsibility for our own childhood. "Reparenting" is the new edge to therapy, yet the Christian faith has said since its beginning, "You must be born again." We need a second chance, we need a second childhood. Our first birth was not our choice, nor should we carry the "family conspiracy" of the neuroses of the generations before us. In Christ, Gregory argued, new birth can be our choice; in a spiritual way "we are … our own parents." For the spiritual life, or *epektasis,* is a continual growth, a process of remembering the past to live forgiven lives, more fully ourselves, in the future.

As we have seen, this has nothing to do with the so-called "Aquarian Conspiracy" that would promise us new life through reincarnation. Any with a penchant for Chinese art could be deluded into thinking that they were once a courtier in the Ming dynasty; or if a man was unfaithful to his wife, that he had been Henry VIII. No, it is much more realistic to examine the emotional threads of our childhood, and see them rewoven into a different tapestry: not a tapestry of human failings, but one of God's love, where we are part of his divine family.

We face a crucial choice: Are we to live in an impersonal world, where we have to fend for ourselves alone, or are we to live under the shelter of a God whose being is love and who is the source of all personal being? These two worldviews clash irreconcilably. The Egyptians sought to kill all the male children of Israel, although secretly Moses was hidden in the bulrushes by his mother. Gregory commented in his *Life of Moses* that all the firstborn of Egypt were killed, "for it is necessary to destroy the first born of evil."[2] In the time of Jesus' infancy Herod was to order the slaughter of the innocents, to ensure that the divine child was also destroyed.

Secularism today operates on the principle that we live in an impersonal world; and psychology also assumes that individual health can be attained without reference to a personal God. The Neoplatonism of Gregory's day has much in common with humanism today: "For truly barren is profane education, which is always in labor but never gives birth."[3] A friend of mine despaired that the more he knew about himself psychologically, the deeper he dug his pit of self-containment and isolation that could not bring healing to his relationships. Abortion, truly the "slaughter of the innocents" for a self-absorbed society, also symbolizes the clash of values between those who live in an impersonal universe and those who value the human dignity of every person, including the unborn child.

The Radical Symbol of Childhood

Curiously, the significance of childhood has been little regarded and understood in human history. In medieval art, the child was portrayed simply as a dwarfed adult. It is only in the seventeenth century that we have the first evidence of toys and clothes designed appropriately for children. Certainly the Puritans and Pietists of that time were strong on family values, and the term "domestic economy" was first used of the religious upbringing of the family, only later gaining a secular meaning as the economic management of nations. Behind family worship and the care of children lies the attitude of Jesus toward children:

> I tell you the truth, unless you change and become like lit-
> tle children, you will never enter the kingdom of heaven.[4]

When Jesus set a child before the disciples they wanted to get rid of it, not realizing that in one sense, Jesus *is* the child.[5] To transform our natural desires, he places a child before us as the symbol and indeed the reality of the new life he offers us.

When he challenged the religious expert Nicodemus, that unless a man is born again, he cannot see the kingdom of God, Nicodemus could not grasp the idea: "Surely he cannot enter a second time into his mother's womb to be born!" Pure thought still struggles with the concept of "newness" as God's gift of spiritual life. The notion of receiving a new childhood was too much for Nicodemus, and is still too much for many of us today. The desires of our heart do not go that far.

Much of our living today, even our religious faith, is distorted by the fact that we view life either as a system of thought that needs explaining and arguing about, or else as the agenda for a full timetable of organized activities. This creates a personality driven by the values of the market, that knows little of soul friendship, or of the personal nature of God. It is not aware of the child Jesus.

How then is true childhood so radical? Thérése de Lisieux (1873–1897) spoke of it as her "little way": to desire one thing only—to love Jesus. Six weeks before her death, at the age of twenty-four, she explained what it meant:

> It is to recognize one's own nothingness, to expect
> everything from God as a child expects everything
> from its father. It is to be concerned about nothing,
> not even making one's fortune ... Thus I remain a
> child with no other occupation than gathering flowers,
> the flowers of love and sacrifice, and offering them to
> the good God for His pleasure. Being a child means
> not attributing to yourself the virtues you practice or
> believing yourself capable of anything at all; it means

recognizing that the good God places the treasure of virtue in the hands of His child to be used when there is need of it—but it is still God's treasure. Finally, it means never being discouraged by your faults, because children fall frequently but are too small to hurt themselves much.[6]

We must stay little, says Thérèse, so that we are being carried in the arms of God. Thus it is essentially a life in relationship we seek, to be the "children of God."

We see this reflected in several ways in our lives. First, we may observe that we *never lose our childhood.* We speak of "the child as father to the man." Psychiatrists say that some 85 percent of a person's personality has been determined by the age of six.[7] The tyranny of an abused childhood will haunt someone in adulthood, but the memory of a loving childhood can bless that person throughout life.

Consequently, *our childhood retains the past and directs our future.* Human existence is not pushed through time, like toothpaste through a tube, as if past is only past and future is only future. Our past can paralyze our future, and our future can liberate our past; the present is the meeting point of both past and future.[8] We do not need to remain "stuck" into a painful past; we can allow ourselves to have a second childhood, as persons who are transformed.

Furthermore, *the child is the person before God,* as Thérèse showed in her short but holy life. Does any small child not have a real awareness of God, I wonder? A friend working among children has been amazed at how they can express a religious faith, even when they come from secular homes without any teaching about God. Long before another friend became a Christian, she learned as a child to draw crosses, which represented to her how much Jesus loved her in a loveless home. The psalmist too sees how childhood is directed by God, even when the infant is still unborn:

My frame was not hidden from you

when I was made in the secret place.

When I was woven together in the depths of the earth,

your eyes saw my unformed body.

All the days ordained for me

were written in your book

before one of them came to be.[9]

The apostle Paul likewise speaks of God's call coming to him from birth.[10] This suggests that the way our parents treated us in childhood is not, after all, the final statement about our lives. God was with us even before birth, ordaining our future potential.

Thus *childhood is the promise of new beginnings,* when it is God alone that we desire. What we have lacked in our natural life and identity, God's love can redeem and remake in us. Only God knows all about us, and only God can give us the unique desires of our hearts, because we were made for relationship with him. Sadly, human parents can lead us away from Jesus, who is our true destiny. We need more models like Hannah, who saw her child Samuel as a gift from God, and gave him back to the giver of the gift.

Moreover, *childhood allows us to be transformed by an openness to God.* Christ the child, the Son of God, wants to take many children "unto glory"; he wants us to be adopted into the divine family of the Holy Trinity. His mission on earth was to "translate us out of darkness into the Kingdom of [God's] dear Son." Thus Jesus held a child in his arms not only to glorify the state of childhood, but to reveal the way God lives in relationship, a relationship into which he desires to adopt us. For only a personal God can have children, adopted by his own choice.

And *the fullness of human life consists of being a child of God.* Being a human child is only the beginning of life; but being the child of God is the full maturity of our human destiny. It is our ultimate bliss, the fulfillment of all our desires. Today, beyond the awareness of the primal scream of infancy, beyond the silence of childhood abuse, and beyond the adult abuse of our sexuality, indeed, beyond the woundedness of all our relationships, God is gently redirecting our hearts, to help us see his divine intention that we should be his children.

This new relationship gives us such assurance in our hearts, such healing in our lives, such freedom from emotional bondage, that we no longer live the lives of addicts, lives of despair. Instead we live in the love of God, the God and Father of our Lord Jesus Christ, who by his Spirit enables us to cry in the spirit of our adoption, "Abba, Father!"[11]

So it is that *our childhood before God is the only appropriate relationship to have before the Trinity.* The mystery of God being three and yet one, Father, Son, and Holy Spirit, has perplexed many who have attempted to rationalize it, since it is a unity of relationship that can only be known in love. It is inconceivable that we could ever have known God as our Father, had it not been for Christ coming to us as the Son of God, and it would still be beyond our experience, but for the working of the Holy Spirit in our hearts. Our new childhood reflects the reality of the Trinity. We are the choice of the Father, in relationship with the Son; and we know the presence and power of the Holy Spirit within us and for us.[12]

PRISONERS OF CHILDHOOD

In great contrast to this potential new state, our natural childhood is fragile and precarious. Miguel de Unamuno observed that the child is an infinite believer, and it is the very trust of a little child that leads to so many wounds that later in life can become explosive and hurtful to others. Our natural tendency is to wound others with our own wounds. The child in us may become enraged at the indignity of living in an impersonal world, and children's unmet needs can become so painful that they replay their childhood drama in all kinds of antisocial behavior later in life. For example, a boy might end up inflicting untold violence on women as a result of childhood neglect from his mother.

We do not lose our childhood, but it can destroy us; how often do I see this in daily counseling with the troubled and hurt of this world. Can a daughter who lived through her father's suicide ever be freed from a melancholic life? Can a son ever experience genuine desire when his disturbed mother has always manipulated his own feelings? Can the traumas of childhood that destroyed the experience of love, or of trust, or of inner significance, ever be redeemed, or the wounds of childhood, those deeply implanted scars of inadequate personal relationships, ever be removed? These questions are being asked more now than at any time in the past.

Such heightened understanding of our own consciousness may also give us insights that we can use to enrich our faith. We need to face up to them, because our first instinct is to run away from the pains of our own childhood. As the child psychologist Alice Miller has observed, "Experience has taught us that we have only one enduring weapon in our struggle against mental illness: the emotional discovery and emotional acceptance of the truth of the individual and unique history of our childhood."[13]

A child psychiatrist is able to spell out how a healthy, normal child can grow up into an addict or a criminal, schizophrenic or hysterical, an obsessive, anorexic, or obese person.[14] The tragedy is that often, as we have seen, the deprivation suffered by the child will be revenged upon others, thus perpetuating the trap.

A self-absorbed person has had an emotionally insecure parent who used the child to satisfy his or her own needs and longings, so that the child had to behave in a particular way to gain parental approval. The child therefore interpreted parental "love" as playing out this role. Such children in turn play out the same relationship with their offspring, and the cycle continues through the generations. The result is that they never have the freedom to express their own feelings and to become emotionally honest. If the problem is undetected, they will also introduce it into their religious life. Such people need always to be the center of attention, and often defend their hidden emotions by an intellectual faith.

The "grandiose" person must always be admired, even in false saintliness, while the depressed person is more honestly coping with much buried material in his or her background. But both states are really inner prisons of the "self." Neither is free to know the whole story of their true life, so a false "self" is projected restlessly and with much denial of reality. Anger, discontentment, envy, insecurity, aggression, and a tendency to feel shame or guilt are the consequences.

Bonding with their own children may become a problem, and their children may rebel against the faith they purport to have—Christians themselves can all too easily drive others away from Christ. Contempt for the Christian faith often arises as an emotional defense against the feelings of guilt and shame imposed on a sensitive child. Edmund Gosse's *Father and Son* is a classic of this kind. Hermann Hesse's book *A Child's Heart* and his novel *Damian* are similar. The humiliation of a sensitive, explorative child, a sense of being walled in by strength that is insensitive to the child's feelings, on the part of people who may be inwardly insecure themselves with no way of admitting their own fear and helplessness, all go to make up contempt for the weak and sensitive later in life. Seeing God as in alliance with parental insensitivity is a sure way of destroying a child's faith, "all," added Hesse, "humiliating me under the damnable mask of kindness." He confessed:

> Like most parents, mine were no help with the new problems of puberty, to which no reference was ever made. All they did was to take endless trouble in supporting my hopeless attempts to deny reality and to continue dwelling in a childhood world that was becoming more and more unreal. I have no idea whether

> parents can be of help, and I do not blame mine. It was
> my own affair to come to terms with myself and to find
> my own way, and like most well-brought-up children, I
> managed it badly.[15]

Hesse also writes: "The adults acted as if the world were perfect and as if they themselves were demigods, we children were
nothing but scum."[16] "If I were to reduce all my feelings and
their painful conflicts to a single name, I can think of no other
word but dread. It was dread, dread, and uncertainty, that I felt
in all those hours of shattered childhood felicity: dread of punishment, dread of my own conscience, dread of stirrings in my
soul which I considered forbidden and criminal."[17] Meanwhile
his parents were idealizing a picture of family life that did not
actually exist, in the name of their faith, and for the sake of
appearances.

In turn, Hermann Hesse later poured out all his reactions to
a reading audience of young people who were ready for revolt
and revolution. It was the same with the film director Ingmar
Bergman, who has described his childhood as one long humiliation. He has projected this through his films as one long, cold
winter of secularism, in revolt against a destructive religiosity.

One of the most terrible examples of a mutilated childhood
is that of Friedrich Nietzsche (1844–1900). When he was only
four, his beloved father died of a brain disease, and soon afterwards his little brother also died. Emotional bewilderment
dominated the child's mind after that, for the women with
whom he lived thereafter—his grandmother, two aunts, mother,
and younger sister—could do nothing to restore the lost men in
his life. He suppressed his genuine feelings, becoming a model
child and pupil. He kept all his observations to himself, and only
later did he turn all his suppressed rage and questioning upon
the world of scholarship, rather than on his family. He turned
away from the death of his father and the unbearable contradiction between the morality preached at him and the cold and

manipulative behavior directed against him by his family,[18] preaching instead against Christianity itself.

For a time Friedrich attached himself to Richard Wagner, as to a father, but when this relationship fell through in disillusionment, the grandiosity of Nietzsche, and his despair behind it, intensified to the point of madness during the last eleven years of his tragic life. The truth about Nietzsche was that he was a mistreated child, unable to understand his own wounded and suppressed childhood, and so unable to cry out or defend himself where his weaknesses really were. His writing misled Hitler and the whole Nazi perversion about the Superman into thinking he described the German Reich as noble. Instead, it led to one of the bloodiest genocides in human history.

Reading the childhood stories of Stalin and Hitler[19] only completes this diabolical history of the twentieth century. In the twenty-first century will we learn from these stories of the potential for evil that can be released when the feelings of children are suppressed? No wonder the poet Robert Frost asked:

> A voice said, Look in me oh stars
> And tell me truly, men of earth,
> If all the soul and body scars
> were not too much to pay for birth.
> —ROBERT FROST, *A QUESTION*

BECOMING A CHILD OF GOD

Our natural reactions to the pains of our childhood are as varied as our own stories. Some people disengage completely by getting as far away from home as possible, whether rebelliously or quietly. Modern mobility makes this relatively easy to do. Some people enmesh themselves in despair, like the elder son in the parable of the prodigal son who "worked dutifully at home," but was secretly bitter because of an inadequate relationship with his father. They reflect a codependency, a conspiracy of silence within the family that is neither healthy nor liberating. Still others "triangle" by playing politics, setting one member of the family against the other in order to gain an illusory sense of control and power. In our divorcing culture it is not surprising that some people are advocating another false solution—to "divorce your parents."[20] All these ways are cul-de-sacs of futility.

Again we come up against the realization that only God can redeem our childhood. A new way of living requires of us "new birth," and indeed "new parenting." On our own we can only try to make up for the wounds we received in childhood by behavior that expresses compensatory attitudes and actions. I may try to "please" others, or I may be defensive, or aggressive, or boastful. I may indeed learn a form of compensatory behavior, reacting against my perceived hurts, which may make me so successful in my career or profession that I receive accolades of "success." But in reality, such behavior never gives "life" to others.[21]

If I craved attention as a child, I may now be a political leader, or if I fled from self-knowledge, I may be a public communicator. If I was manipulated emotionally, I may now not really know when I am a good administrator and when I am really a manipulator. If I was lonely, yet afraid to realize it, I may be a scholar, living always in the realm of ideas, but with no intimacy with other people.

In a world that rejects the reality of a personal God who can give us deep and lasting healing, these consequences are understandable, but it is sad indeed to see how so many Christians genuinely accept the need of "new birth" but never go beyond that, seeing conversion as an event, not as a lifelong process. They never expect that their personalities, sick as they are, will change significantly. Indeed they may regard their compensatory behavior as God-given talents, viewing their behavioral addictions as "gifts." Thus the neglected child grows up to be grandiose, or the child denying emotional damage grows up to dramatize the faith in ecstatic ways. The angry child may interpret life as the world persecuting him for his faith, and become a pseudomartyr. Little wonder, then, that it is Christians themselves who tragically distort the reality of the faith and cause many who observe them to stumble.

We cannot hide our story of childhood suffering from the loving eyes of God, as we have seen in Psalm 139: God is "familiar with all my ways." The Lord has "searched me and you know me." "You perceive my thoughts from afar." "Before a word is on my tongue you know it completely."[22] Need we wonder at the intimacy of God's knowledge of us if he created us?

Perhaps, then, we need to be aware that the symbolic identity of the child before God implies more than the natural bond between parent and child. It expresses God's own nature, as the Father who loves us before we loved him, the gift of love given to us in Christ, and the sharing of love that is initiated by the Holy Spirit, which makes love real to us. It is only as a "child of God" that we can properly respond to the mystery of God as Trinity, though we do not yet see God clearly, unlike the angels of children, who, according to Jesus, "always see the face of my Father in heaven."

Violence in relationships with children causes confusion and distortion in God's relationships with them, causing them to sin.[23] And the damage done to the divine image in humanity has been so great that only the Child of God in Jesus Christ can restore the relationship between human beings and God. Coming alive spiritually requires me to face the shock of realizing that I am a sinner, wholly inadequate to be restored to relationship with God on my own merits. It requires a truly childlike spirit of trust and humility to repent and be converted. How different was the childhood of Jesus from our own; Jesus always identified with the Father, saying, "I always do what pleases Him."[24] This is the essential contrast between his divine sonship and our natural childhood.

Yet it has always been God's purpose that we should be "adopted" into the divine life of God. So when we repent and are baptized "in the name of the Father, and of the Son, and ofthe Holy Spirit,"[25] we can now exclaim "Abba, Father" from the depths of our new life, through the power of the Spirit. The dependence on God as Father for our new identity, our new obedience to the will of God, and our new intimacy with the divine love, are all privileges as well as responsibilities. We pursue holiness, because all our desires are now to please Christ and be like him. It then becomes our greatest desire to say, with the psalmist:

> One thing I ask of the LORD,
>
> this is what I seek:
>
> that I may dwell in the house of the LORD
>
> all the days of my life,
>
> to gaze upon the beauty of the LORD
>
> and to seek him in his temple.[26]

It is this "practice of the presence of God" that the medieval mystics recognized led to the "reform of faith and feelings."[27] It is not merely that we are given more intelligence and theological knowledge, but that we seek also a transformation of our emotional life, and hence of our behavior. A purely intellectual change of mind will never be sufficient, for our will and feelings have to be redirected and given new health. The general Protestant prejudice against the life of contemplation—being rather than doing for God—has left us with only limited spiritual resources for our Christian "persons" to be transformed.

THE SOURCE OF DESIRE

We come then to our conclusion, which is to state what has been implicit throughout this book. If we deny the true source of human desire we shall remain, as Augustine reminds us, "restless," or as we have recognized in chapter 2, "addicts," cheated by the shallowness of our solutions to the problems of life. Unless we identify the true source of human desire, our desires will remain unfulfilled. Humanly speaking, we can give only half an answer to the question, where does desire come from? Our sense of need, of incompleteness in human relationships, points the way. Certainly our modern realization that reason is not enough is also true; our emotions and feelings go much deeper than our thoughts about them. A sense of the inadequacy of parental care is also growing in our culture today.

Nowadays, as East and West are tending increasingly to come together within "the global village," we can perhaps distinguish two primal tendencies—the maternity of the East and the paternity of the West—as two opposing traditions. In Japanese culture, for example, a primary role is played by *amae,* the relationship between the mother and child. The child is now outside the womb, in its own "separateness," and yet it clings to the mother, afraid of becoming an individual. It has been suggested that the word *amae* is related to the childish word *uma-uma,* the first word all Japanese speak, indicating the child's need for nourishment. Japanese psychiatrist Takeo Doi has shown the importance in all Japanese personal and social behavior of this desire for *amae,* that is, the desire to be passively loved and the unwillingness to be taken out of the warm mother-child circle, damaging as this might be for the adults within Japanese culture.[28]

In the West we have a much stronger patriarchal heritage, rooted in the Western interpretation of the Judeo-Christian tradition. Significantly, Freud interpreted the root of Western neurosis as the desire to kill one's father, as shown in the Oedipus complex, while Nietzsche went further in declaring the "death of God." As early as 1919 the psychiatrist Paul Federn, a pupil of Freud, described this present age as "the Fatherless Society."[29] Other "fathers" have been set up in the vacuum left by the supposed absence of God, such as the communist father figure of Lenin, or even Freud himself who became the accepted "father of psychoanalysis." As Federn observed, in spite of the diminishing of the father-child motif in the West, a totally fatherless society is humanly impossible.

But the exaltation of modern human beings' independence and rebellion from parental control, and society's approval of self-sufficiency, has consequences which we must face as well. It has been a Western tendency to admit guilt, wrongdoing against God, perhaps absorbing self-destructive shame with it. In the East shame has always been more prominent than guilt, reflecting the situation of "the self" alone in an impersonal world. The maternal bias in the Eastern worldview has been its substitute for a lack of personal nature in the divine, and as shame results in the loss of *amae,* the Japanese fear "loss of face." Significantly, the secularized West, having lost the sense of a personal God, is now emphasizing the role of shame far more, with a vast gulf between the successes and the failures of society.

Bonhoeffer observed: "Shame is man's ineffaceable recollection of his estrangement from the origin; it is grief for the estrangement, and the powerless longing to return to unity with the origin.... Shame is more original than remorse."[30] Now shame is being given far more recognition by Western psychologists as an underlying cause of neurosis.[31] Indeed, we may interpret shame as the deprivation of the self in whom the desires of the heart are not recognized, nor fulfilled in authentic relationships.

However, our final question is to ask which is primary: the role of natural childhood under our parents, expressed as *amae,* or the spiritual childhood we may enter into with God, expressed as *Abba*? I believe that even the formative influence that our natural childhood has on us is secondary to this primary relatedness to God, our Creator-Redeemer. The promise of divine adoption is not just a figure of speech, but is fundamental to the fulfillment of our earthly childhood. It is in God that we find the source of our desires, and without God our human desires are doomed to remain frustrated and unfulfilled. This was the conclusion of the psalmist:

Whom have I in heaven but you?

And earth has nothing I desire besides you.

My flesh and my heart may fail,

but God is the strength of my heart

and my portion forever.[32]

NOTES

1. The Secrets of Our Existence

1. T. S. Eliot, *The Complete Poems and Plays* (London and Boston: Faber & Faber, 1990), 61.

2. Quoted by John Francis Kavanaugh, *Following Christ in a Consumer Society* (Maryknoll, NY: Orbis Books, 1983), 21.

3. Quoted by Joan Burbick, "Emily Dickinson and the Economics of Desire," *American Literature* 58, no. 3 (1986): 361–378.

4. Ibid., 377.

5. For an exhaustive study see John Pedersen, *Israel, Its Life and Culture* (Oxford: Oxford University Press, 1973), 99–181.

6. Lionel Trilling, *Prefaces to the Experience of Literature* (New York and London: Harcourt, Brace, Jovanovich, 1967), 22–27.

7. A good judgment of these issues is given by Dietrich von Hildebrand, *The Sacred Heart, Source of Christian Affectivity* (Baltimore: Pelican Press, 1965), 25–114.

8. Prov. 4:23.

9. Jan C. Bovenmars, *Biblical Spirituality of the Heart* (Staten Island, NY: Abba House, 1991). This is a useful biblical survey on this theme.

10. Prov. 16:9.

11. Quoted in lgumen Chariton of Valamo, *The Art of Prayer: An Orthodox Anthology* (London: Faber & Faber, 1966), 63.

12. Blaise Pascal, *Pensées*, trans. John Warrington (London: Everyman's Library, 1960), 60, no. 228.

13. For a profound study of this theme, see Eric Voegelin, *Order and History*, vol. 1, *Israel and Revelation* (Baton Rouge: Louisiana University Press, 1956).

14. *The Confessions of Saint Augustine*, trans. Edward Pusey (New York: Collier Books, 1961), 159.

15. Eliot, 61.

16. Quoted by Emile Male, *The Gothic Image*, trans. Dora Nussey (New York: Harper & Row, 1958), 390.

17. Ibid., 390–399.

18. Pascal, 203.

19. Psalm 100:3–5

20. Sebastian Moore, *Jesus, the Liberator of Desire* (New York: Crossroads, 1989), 60.

2. Our Desire for God

1. Ps. 115:4–8.

2. Quoted by Eric Voegelin, "Immortality: Experience and Symbol," *Harvard Theological Review* LX (1967): 235–279.

3. Deut. 26:5–10.

4. Ps. 136:1–4.

5. Isa. 50:4–5.

6. Isa. 53:1–3.

7. See Eric Voegelin's profound study on these changing forms of consciousness in antiquity in his *Order and History*, vols. 1, 11 (Baton Rouge: Louisiana State University Press, 1956, 1987).

8. Francis Bacon, *The Physical and Metaphysical Works of Francis Bacon*, ed. Joseph Devey (London: George Bell, 1898), 391.

9. Eric Voegelin, *Order and History*, vol. IV (Baton Rouge: Louisiana State University Press, 1956, 1987), 121.

10. C. S. Lewis, *A Study in Words* (Cambridge: Cambridge University Press, 1967), 41.

11. Blaise Pascal, *Pensées*, ed. Louis Lafuma, trans. John Warrington (New York: Everyman's Library, 1960), 82, no. 301.

12. Col. 2:8.

13. See interesting study in Walter Wink, *Unmasking the Powers: The*

Invisible Forces That Determine Human Existence (Philadelphia: Fortress Press, 1986), 119–120.

14. Ibid., 121.

15. Julian of Norwich, *Showings*, trans. E. Colledge and J. Walsh (New York: Paulist Press, 1978), 5.

16. Thomas Molnar, *The Pagan Temptation* (Grand Rapids: Eerdmans, 1987), 89–90.

17. Jean Houston, *The Search for the Beloved* (New York: St. Martin's Press, 1984). See also Christine Downing, *The Goddess: Mythological Images of the Feminine* (New York: Crossroad, 1989).

18. For example, Jean Shinoda Bolen, *Gods in Everyman* (New York: Harper & Row, 1989).

19. G. K. Chesterton, *The Everlasting Man* (Garden City, NY: Doubleday Books, 1955), iii.

20. Charles Williams, *Many Dimensions* (Harmondsworth, Middlesex: Penguin Books, 1952).

21. Isa. 44:9.

22. Ps. 95:3.

23. 1 Cor. 8:6.

24. Chesterton, 187.

25. Francis Bacon, *Novum Organum in the Physical and Metaphysical Works of Francis Bacon*, ed. Joseph Devey (London: George Bell, 1898), 390–391.

26. James Houston, *In Pursuit of Happiness* (Oxford: Lion Publishing, 1990).

3. Who Are the Addicts?

1. Quoted by Linda Schierse Leonard, *Witness to the Fire: Creativity and the Veil of Addiction* (Boston: Shambhala Publications, 1989), 14. I am indebted to her rich studies of literary archetypes of addictions in this chapter.

2. Quoted by John Burnaby, *Amor Dei* (Norwich: The Canterbury Press, 1991, 97).

3. Augustine, *Confessions*, trans. Edward B. Pusey (London: Collier Macmillan, 1975), 11.

4. Ibid., 12.

5. Ibid., 13.

6. Ibid., 13.

7. Linda Schierse Leonard, *On the Way to the Wedding: Transforming the Love Relationship* (Boston: Shambhala Publications, 1986).

8. Gerald May, *Addiction and Grace* (San Francisco: Harper, 1988), 42–90.
9. Thomas Wolfe, *The Autobiography of an American Novelist*, ed. Leslie Field (Cambridge: Harvard University Press, 1983), 35–36.
10. Leonard, *Witness to the Fire*, 3.
11. Fyodor Dostoyevsky, *The Gambler*, trans. Andrew R. MacAndrew (New York: W. W. Norton & Co., 1981).
12. Ibid., 28.
13. Ibid., 28.
14. Richard Wagner, *Tristan and Isolde*, trans. Andrew Porter (New York: Riverrun Press, 1981), 73.
15. Jack London, *John Barleycorn* (Santa Cruz, CA: Tanager Press, 1981), 6.
16. Ibid., 53.
17. Ibid., 60.
18. Ibid., 343.
19. Fyodor Dostoyevsky, *The Brothers Karamazov*, trans. Richard Pevear and Larissa Volokhonsky (New York: Vintage Books, Random House, 1990), 44.
20. Ibid., 108.
21. Ibid., 244.
22. Ibid., 322.
23. Dostoyevsky, *The Brothers Karamazov,* 774
24. Quoted by Hans Kung and Walter Jens, *Literature and Religion* (New York: Paragon House, 1991), 241.
25. Matt. 19:14.
26. Dostoyevsky, *The Brothers Karamazov,* 774.
27. Augustine, *Confessions*, trans. R. S. Pine-Coffin (Harmondsworth, UK: Penguin, 1961), 24.

4. The Quest for Love

1. Jane Lahr and Lena Tabori, *Love: A Celebration in Art and Literature* (New York: Stewart, Tabori & Chang Publishers, 1982), 1.
2. Erich Fromm, *The Art of Loving* (London: George Allen & Unwin, 1952), 83.
3. Rainer Maria Rilke, *Letters to a Young Poet* (14 May 1904, Rome).
4. Fromm, 132.
5. Nancy Qualls-Corbett, *The Sacred Prostitute: Eternal Aspects of the Feminine* (Toronto: Inner City Books, 1988).

6. Martin S. Bergmann, *The Anatomy of Loving: The Story of Man's Quest to Know What Love Is* (New York: Fawcett Columbine, 1987), 21–35.

7. Ibid., 36–56.

8. Ibid., 59.

9. Roger Scruton, *Sexual Desire* (London: Weidenfeld & Nicolson, 1986), 216–219.

10. Anders Nygren, *Eros and Agape* (London: S. P. C. K., 1953), 166–210.

11. Bernard McGinn, *The Foundations of Mysticism* (New York: Crossroad, 1991), 41–61.

12. The theme of romantic love is well treated by Denis de Rougemont, *Love in the Western World* (New York: Pantheon Books, 1956).

13. Bergmann, 96–97.

14. Quoted by F. Goldin, *The Mirror of Narcissus in Courtly Love* (New York: Cornell University Press, 1964), 95.

15. Bergmann, 130.

16. See Arthur Guirdham, *Christ and Freud* (London: George Allen & Unwin, 1959); and Hans Kung, *Freud and the Problem of God* (Yale: Yale University Press, 1990).

17. Scruton, 195–212.

18. Søren Kierkegaard, *Works of Love,* trans. Howard and Edna Hong (New York: Harper Torchbooks, 1962), 26.

19. G. A. Turner, "Love," *International Standard Bible Encyclopedia*, vol. 3, gen. ed. Geoffrey W. Bromiley (Grand Rapids: Eerdmans, 1986), 173–176.

20. On the nature of Christian love, in addition to Anders Nygren's work, see also M. C. D'Arcy, *The Mind and Heart of Love* (London: Faber & Faber, 1964); Daniel Williams, *The Spirit and the Forms of Love* (Lanham, MD: University Press of America, 1981); and Leon Morris, *Testaments of Love* (Grand Rapids: Eerdmans, 1981).

21. Rom. 13:8.

22. 1 Cor. 13:13.

23. Kierkegaard, 23–24.

24. John Burnaby, *Amor Dei: A Study in the Religion of Augustine* (Norwich: Canterbury Press, 1991).

25. M. C. D'Arcy, *The Mind and Heart of Love* (London: Faber & Faber, 1964).

26. Rom. 5:8.

27. Rom. 8:38–39.

28. C. Fitzsimons Allison, *Fear, Love and Worship* (New York: The Seabury Press, 1962), 117–131.

29. Jean Pierre de Caussade, *The Sacrament of Every Day*, trans. Kitty Muggeridge (San Francisco: Harper & Row, 1984).

5. The Sickness of Modern Desires

1. William Golding, *The Paper Men* (London: Faber & Faber, 1984), 7–16.

2. Quoted by Lionel Trilling, *Sincerity and Authenticity* (Oxford and New York: Oxford University Press, 1971), 11. See Hans Küng and Walter Jens, *Literature and Religion* (New York: Paragon House, 1991), 3–20.

3. Blaise Pascal, *Pensées*, trans. John Warrington (London: Everyman's Library, 1960), 30, no. 92.

4. Ibid., 59–60, no. 224.

5. Küng and Jens, 9, 13.

6. Søren Kierkegaard, *The Sickness Unto Death,* trans. Walter Lowrie (Princeton, NJ: Princeton University Press, 1954), 135.

7. Ibid.

8. Charles M. Shelton, *Morality of the Heart* (New York: Crossroad, 1990), 67–68.

9. Ibid., 98–116.

10. Christopher Lasch, *The Minimal Self* (London and New York: W. W. Norton, 1984).

11. Jonathan Edwards, *Treatise Concerning the Religious Affections*, ed. John E. Smith (New Haven: Yale University Press, 1959), 101.

12. Thomas Molnar, *The Pagan Temptation* (Grand Rapids: Eerdmans, 1987), 88.

13. Ibid., 132.

14. Christopher Milne, *The Path through the Trees* (Toronto: McClelland & Stewart, 1979), 252–253, 260.

15. William Golding, *Free Fall* (London: Faber & Faber, 1959), 160–161.

16. Ibid., 164–165.

17. Frank Gado, *First Person* (Syracuse: Syracuse University Press, 1973), 92.

18. Joseph Waidmeir, "It's the Going That's Important, Not the Getting There: Rabbit's Questing, Non Questing," *Modern Fiction Stories* 20 (Spring 1974), 13.

19. See Eccl. 1:14.

20. John Updike, *Self-Consciousness: Memoirs* (New York: Fawcett Crest Ballantyne Paperbacks, 1989), 242–243, 246.

21. Ibid., 264.

6. Despair: The Fate of the Desiring Soul

1. T. S. Eliot, *The Complete Poems and Plays* (London: Faber & Faber, 1990), 381.

2. Søren Kierkegaard, *The Concept of Anxiety,* ed. and trans. Reidar Thomte (Princeton, NJ: Princeton University Press, 1980), 22.

3. *The Cocktail Party*, from Eliot, 413.

4. Ibid., 414–416.

5. Quoted by Marion Woodman, *Addiction to Perfection* (Toronto: Inner City Books, 1982), 24.

6. Victor Hugo, *Les Misérables*, trans. Lee Fahnestock and Norman MacAfee (New York: Penguin Books, 1987), 1385.

7. See suggestive study of boredom in Thomas C. Oden, *The Structure of Awareness* (Nashville: Abingdon Press, 1969).

8. Virginia Woolf, *A Writer's Diary* (London: Hogarth, 1965), 140.

9. Conrad W. Baars, *Feeling and Healing Your Emotions* (Plainsfield, NJ: Logos International, 1979), 149–150.

10. Quoted by C. Stephen Evans, *Søren Kierkegaard's Christian Psychology* (Grand Rapids: Zondervan, 1990), 13.

11. Søren Kierkegaard, *The Sickness Unto Death,* trans. Walter Lowrie (Princeton: Princeton University Press, 1954).

12. Quoted in Evans, 81–82.

13. Kierkegaard, *Sickness*, 135.

14. Quoted by Eric Voegelin, *Order and History,* vol. 1 (Baton Rouge: Louisiana University Press, 1974), 111.

15. Claus Westermann, *Praise and Lament in the Psalms* (Atlanta: John Knox Press, 1981), 116ff.

16. Ps. 8:3–4.

17. Isa. 1:3.

18. Jer. 8:5, 7.

19. Kierkegaard, *Sickness*, 133–134.

7. Jesus Christ: The Heart's Resurrection

1. T. S. Eliot, *The Complete Poems and Plays* (London: Faber & Faber, 1969), 104.

2. See Johannes Baptist Metz, *Faith in History and Society* (London: Burns & Oates, 1980), for a chapter on Memory, 88–99.

3. Augustine, *The Confessions of Saint Augustine,* trans. Edward Pusey (New York: Collier Books, 1961), 159.

4. Eliot, 194–195.

5. Helen Gardner, ed., *The Faber Book of Religious Verse* (London: Faber & Faber, 1972), 329.

6. Quoted by Malcolm Muggeridge, *Jesus, the Man who Lives* (London: Collins, 1975), 25.

7. Isa. 53:3.

8. See the beautiful meditation of Hans Urs von Balthasar, *Does Jesus Know Us? Do We Know Him?*, trans. Graham Harrison (San Francisco: Ignatius Press, 1980). References that follow are: Luke 5:22; Matt. 12:22; Luke 9:48; John 2:24; 4:25–39; 16:30; 21:17.

9. 1 Cor. 4:5.

10. Heb. 4:15.

11. Heb. 2:18.

12. See the excellent translation by Richard Pevear and Larissa Volokhonsky, Fyodor Dostoyevsky, *The Brothers Karamazov* (New York: Vintage Books, Random House, 1990).

13. Bruce K. Ward, *Dostoyevsky's Critique of the West* (Waterloo, Ontario: Sir Wilfred Laurier University Press, 1986), is an excellent study of this subject.

14. Dostoyevsky, 250.

15. Ibid., 251.

16. Ibid., 252.

17. Ibid., 256.

18. Ibid., 257–258.

19. Quoted in Ward, 137.

20. Thomas F. Torrance, *Space, Time and Resurrection* (Edinburgh: The Hansel Press, 1976).

21. Rowan Williams, *Resurrection* (London: Darton, Longman & Todd, 1982), 29.

22. George Herbert, *The Country Parson, The Temple,* ed. John N. Wall, Jr. (New York: Paulist Press, 1981), 177.

23. Calcined: burned to ashes.

24. Herbert, 155.

8. Transformed Desires

1. Edwin Paxton Hood, *Christian Praise* (London: The Tyndale Press, 1957), 132.
2. Whittaker Chambers, *Witness* (New York: Random House, 1952), 4.
3. Ibid., 25.
4. Ibid., 21.
5. Matt. 27:16; Mark 15:7; Luke 23:19; John 18:40.
6. Pär Lagerkvist, *Barabbas*, trans. Alan Blair (New York: Random House, 1968), 138.
7. Ibid., 146.
8. Ibid., 149.
9. Practical advice on this topic is given by Joyce Nevelle, *How to Share Your Faith Without Being Offensive* (New York: The Seabury Press, 1981).
10. Alister McGrath, *Explaining Your Faith without Losing Your Friends* (Grand Rapids: Zondervan, 1989).
11. A strong indictment of this issue is the book by Stephen Arterburn and Jack Felton, *Toxic Faith: Understanding and Overcoming Religious Addiction* (Nashville: Thomas Nelson, 1991). See also Virginia Curran Hoffman, *The Co-dependent Church* (New York: Crossroad, 1991).
12. J. P. M. Sweet, "Maintaining the Testimony of Jesus" in *Suffering and Martyrdom in the New Testament*, ed. William Horbury and Brian McNeil (Cambridge: Cambridge University Press, 1981), 103.
13. John 18:37.
14. Rev. 1:9.
15. Sweet, 106.
16. 1 Thess. 1:9–10; 3:7–8.
17. Carol M. Giesbrecht, ed., *The Hymnal* (Baptist Federation of Canada, 1973), 463.
18. John 5:31–37.
19. See this theme elaborated by J. Earnst Devey, *The Jesus of John* (London: Lutterworth Press, 1958).
20. John 20:31.
21. John Painter, *John: Witness and Theologian* (London: S. P. C. K., 1975).
22. James McAuley, "An Art of Poetry" in *The New Oxford Book of Christian Verse*, ed. Donald Davie (Oxford: Oxford University Press, 1981), 260–261.

23. Chambers, 794.

24. Acts 2:42–47.

25. Robert Bellah and others, *The Habits of the Heart* (San Francisco: Harper & Row, 1985).

26. *Theological Dictionary of the New Testament,* vol. IV, ed. G. Kittel and G. Friedrich, trans. G. Bromiley (Grand Rapids: Eerdmans, 1974), 474–508.

27. Cyprian, *On the Glory of Martyrdom,* 249.

28. 1 John 5:4–5.

29. Karl Barth, *Church Dogmatics,* vols. 1, 2, ed. G. Bromiley and T. Torrance (Edinburgh: T&T Clark, 1976), 206ff., 227ff., 414ff., 440ff.

30. Carolyn Osiek, "Early Christian Theology of Martyrdom," *The Bible Today* (May 1990): 153–157.

31. Johannes Baptist Metz and Edward Schillebeecks, "Martyrdom Today," *Concilium* (Edinburgh: T&T Clark, 1983).

32. Acts 9:4.

33. Quoted by Kallistos of Diokleia, "What Is a Martyr?" *Sobernast* 5:1 (1983), 8.

34. 1 Cor. 12:26.

35. Hans Urs von Balthasar, *Word and Redemption* (Montreal: Palm Publishers, 1965), 50.

9. The Heart's Desert Journey

1. Charles de Foucauld, *Meditations of a Hermit,* trans. Charlotte Belfour (London: Burns & Oates, 1981), 137.

2. René Voillaume, *Follow Me,* trans. Allan Neame (London: Darton, Longman & Todd, 1978), 13.

3. Benedicta Ward, *The Wisdom of the Desert Fathers,* foreword by Anthony Bloom (Fairacres, Oxford: SLG Press, 1986), vii.

4. Phil. 3:20.

5. Andrew Louth, *The Wilderness of God* (London: Darton, Longman & Todd, 1991), 26.

6. Violet MacDermot, *The Cult of the Seer in the Ancient Middle East* (Los Angeles: University of California Press, 1971). See also Peter Brown, *The Cult of the Saints* (Chicago: University of Chicago Press, 1981).

7. Shermaryahu Talman, "The Desert Motif in the Bible and in Qumran Literature," Festschrift vol. in honor of Frank Moore Cross, 31–63.

8. Deut. 32:10–12.

9. Deut. 32:13, 15, 18.

10. Ps. 105:43.

11. Ps. 114:1–2.

12. Isa. 40:3.

13. Isa. 35:1–2.

14. Isa. 35:5–8.

15. Matt. 3:2–3.

16. Lance Morrow, "Trashing Mount Sinai," *Time* (19 March 1990), 76.

17. Quoted by David W. F. Wong, "Wilderness and Prayer," *Serve the Lord with Gladness*, ed. Howard Peskett and David W. F. Wong (Singapore: Biblical Graduate School of Theology, 1991), 17.

18. Malcolm Muggeridge, *Jesus, the Man Who Lives* (London: Collins, 1975), 25.

19. Matt. 19:21.

20. D. J. Chitty, *The Letters of St. Anthony* (Oxford: SLG Press, 1975).

21. D. J. Chitty, *The Desert a City* (Oxford: Oxford University Press, 1966).

22. Ward, 975.

23. Ibid.

24. Ibid.

25. Evagrius Ponticus, *The Praktikos and Chapters on Prayer,* trans. and ed. J. E. Bamberger (Kalamazoo, MI: Cistercian Publications, 1970), 64.

26. Quoted by Tomas Spidlik, *The Spirituality of the Christian East* (Kalamazoo, MI: Cistercian Publications, 1986), 249. See whole section on the *logismoi*, 248–256.

27. Louth, 29.

28. Aristotle, *Nichomachean Ethics,* IX. 8.

29. Dorotheos of Gaza, *Discourses and Sayings*, trans. Eric P. Wheeler (Kalamazoo, MI: Cistercian Publications, n.d.), 173, 179, 181.

30. Ibid., 181.

31. Hos. 2:14, 19–20.

32. Ps. 84:6.

33. See Susan Annette Muto, *A Practical Guide to Spiritual Reading* (Denville, NJ: Dimension Books, 1976), 58–95, for readings of Scripture on such desert blessings.

34. Phil. 4:13.

35. T. S. Eliot, *The Complete Poems and Plays* (London and Boston: Faber & Faber, 1990).

10. The Garden of Love's Desire

1. Gen. 2:8–10.
2. Charles Cummings, *Spirituality and the Desert Experience* (Denville, NJ: Dimension Books, 1978), 167.
3. G. Lloyd Carr, *The Song of Solomon,* Tyndale Old Testament Commentaries (Leicester, England, and Downers Grove, IL: InterVarsity Press, 1984), 55–60.
4. 2 Kings 21:18.
5. Jane Hollister Wheelwright and Lynda Wheelwright Schmidt, *The Long Shore: A Psychological Experience of the Wilderness* (San Francisco: The Sierra Club and Natural Philosophy Library, 1991).
6. Bernard Häring, *Toward a Christian Moral Theology* (Notre Dame, IN: Notre Dame Press, 1966), 57.
7. Hans Urs von Balthasar, *Love Alone: The Way of Revelation* (London and Dublin: Sheed and Ward and Veritas Publication, 1968), 43.
8. Ibid.
9. Wilkie Au, *By Way of the Heart* (New York/Mahwah: Paulist Press, 1989), 21.
10. Cited by Tomas Spidlik, *The Spirituality of the Christian East*, trans. Anthony P. Gythiel (Kalamazoo, MI: Cistercian Publications, 1986), 295–297.
11. 1 John 4:8, 16.
12. John MacMurray, *Reason and Emotion* (London: Faber & Faber, 1942), 123.
13. Ibid.
14. George MacDonald, *Diary of an Old Soul* (Minneapolis, MN: Augsburg Publishing House, 1975), 130.
15. Quoted by Bishop Chrysostomos and J. Thornton, *Love* (Brookline, MD: Hellenic College Press, 1988), 66–67.
16. Ps. 34:8.
17. *Children Praise* (London: Tyndale Press, 1957), 103.
18. Gen. 3:1.
19. Ezek. 28:11, 13, 17.
20. Isa. 51:3.
21. David N. Bell, *The Image and Likeness: The Augustinian Spirituality of William of St. Thierry* (Kalamazoo, MI: Cistercian Publications, 1984).

22. Irenee Hausherr, *Penthos: the Doctrine of Compunction in the Christian East* (Kalamazoo, MI: Cistercian Publications, 1982).

23. Michael Casey, *A Thirst for God, Spiritual Desire of Clairvaux's Sermons on the Song of Songs* (Kalamazoo, MI: Cistercian Publications, 1988), 120–129.

24. Marcus Bochmuehl, "To Love God Is to Wait for Him," in *Loving God and Keeping His Commandments*, ed. Marcus Bochmuehl and Helmut Burkhardt (Basel: Brunnen Verlong-Giessen, 1991), 39–48.

25. See also 2 Cor. 2:9.

26. Casey, 71.

27. Amedee Hallier, *The Monastic Theology of Aelred of Rievaulx* (Shannon, Ireland: Irish University Press, 1969), 29.

28. Quoted by Jean Leclercq, *The Love of Learning and the Desire for God* (New York: Fordham University Press, 1982), 214.

29. Rom. 12:1–2.

30. Odo Brooke, *Studies in Monastic Theology* (Kalamazoo, MI: Cistercian Publications, 1984), 234.

31. Quoted by Leclercq, 225–226.

32. E. Ann Matter, *The Voice of My Beloved. The Song of Songs in Western Medieval Christianity* (Philadelphia: University of Philadelphia Press, 1990), 203–210.

33. David A. Hubbard, *Ecclesiastes, Song of Solomon, The Communicators Commentary* (Dallas: Word Books, 1991), 261, 263.

34. Anders Nygren, *Eros and Agape* (London: S. P. C. K., 1953).

35. Bernard of Clairvaux, *Sermons on the Song of Songs*, vol. 1. (Kalamazoo, MI: Cistercian Publications, n.d.).

36. Ibid.

37. Casey, 254.

38. Bernard of Clairvaux, 49.

39. Casey, 276.

40. Robert J. Trotter, "The Three Faces of Love," *Psychology Today*, September 1986, 47–54.

41. William McNamara, *Mystical Passion: A Spirituality for a Bored Society* (New York and Toronto: Paulist Press, 1977).

42. Ps. 132:13–14.

43. John 14:1–3.

44. Casey, 283, 285.

45. Col. 3:2–4.

46. C. S. Lewis, *The Weight of Glory and Other Addresses* (Grand Rapids: Eerdmans, 1972), 7.

11. The Christian as Pilgrim

1. George Herbert, *The Country Parson, The Temple,* ed. John N. Wall (New York, Toronto: Paulist Press, 1981), 203.
2. Ibid., 312.
3. Diogenes Allen, "The Christian Pilgrimage in George Herbert's *The Temple, Modern Christian Spirituality,* no. 62, ed. Bradley C. Hanson (Atlanta: Scholars Press, American Academy of Religion, 1990), 65–84.
4. An ell is a mere forty-five inches. Herbert, 137.
5. "Pilgrimage," *The Illustrated Bible Dictionary,* part 3 (Leicester, England: InterVarsity Press, 1990), 1231.
6. Augustine, *City of God,* ed. David Knowles (Middlesex, UK: Penguin Books, 1972).
7. Matt. 6:33.
8. Jonathan Edwards, "The True Christian's Life, A Journey Toward Heaven," *The Works of President Edwards,* vol. IV (New York: Leavitt & Allen, 1852), 573–584.
9. Ibid., 573–584.
10. Quoted by Jill Haak Adels, *The Wisdom of the Saints* (Oxford: Oxford University Press, 1987), 119.
11. Gerhardt Ladner, "Homo Viator: Medieval Ideas on Alienation and Order," *Speculum* XLII (1967), 233–259.
12. John C. Olin, "The Idea of Pilgrimage in the Experience of Ignatius of Loyola," *Church History* 48 (1979): 387–392.
13. William G. Johnson, "The Pilgrimage Motif in the Book of Hebrews," *Journal of Biblical Literature* 97, 2 (1978): 239–251.
14. Victor and Edith Turner, *Images of Pilgrimage in Christian Culture* (New York: Columbia University Press, 1978), 2–20.
15. Quoted by Neville Coghill, *Visions from Piers Plowman* (London, New York: Oxford University Press, 1970), 5.
16. Quoted by Vera and Helmut Hell, *The Great Pilgrimage of the Middle Ages: The Road to St. James Compostela* (New York: Clerkson N. Potterline, 1966), 27.
17. Thomas à Kempis, *The Imitation of Christ.*
18. Richard Rolle, *The Fire of Love and the Mending of Life* (Garden City, NY: Doubleday, Image, 1982), 70.

19. Ibid., 74.

20. Ibid., 129.

21. Quoted by Margaret R. Miles, *Practicing Christianity* (New York: Crossroads, 1988), 60.

22. Rolle, 24.

23. Walter of Hilton, *Eight Chapters on Perfection and Of Angel's Song,* trans. Rosemary Dorward (Fairacres, Oxford: SLG Press, 1983), 20.

24. Walter of Hilton, *Toward the Perfection of Love,* trans. David Jefferys (Portland, OR: Multnomah Press, 1988), 107.

25. Ibid., 108.

26. Julia Gatta, *Three Spiritual Directors for Our Time* (Cambridge, MA: Cowley Press, 1986), 32–47.

27. Julian of Norwich, *Showings,* trans. Edmund Colledge and James Walsh (New York, Toronto: Paulist Press, 1978), 214.

28. Ibid., 214.

29. Ibid., 30.

30. Ibid., 342.

31. *The Cloud of Unknowing and Other Works,* trans. Clifton Walters (Harmondsworth, Middlesex: Penguin Books, 1978), 60.

32. Julia Gatta, *Three Spiritual Directors for Our Time* (Cambridge, MA: Cowley Press, 1986), 91–123.

33. John of Climacus, *The Ladder of Divine Ascent* (New York, Toronto: Paulist Press, 1982).

34. John 1:51.

35. See my article, "Reflections on Mysticism," in Bochmuehl and Burkhardt, 163–181.

36. Quoted by Margaret R. Miles, *Practicing Christianity* (New York: Crossroads, 1988), 63.

37. Ibid., 65.

38. Rom. 3:23.

39. Quoted by John R. Knott, Jr., *The Sword of the Spirit: Puritan Responses to the Bible* (Chicago and London: Chicago University Press, 1980), 14.

40. Ibid., 141.

41. Quoted by George Offor, *The Whole Works of John Bunyan,* vol. 3 (Grand Rapids: Baker Book House, 1977), 74.

12. Children of God: A Symbol for Today

1. Gregory of Nyssa, *The Life of Moses,* trans. Abraham J. Malherbe and

Everett Ferguson (New York and Toronto: Paulist Press, 1978), 55–56.

2. Ibid., 113.

3. Ibid., 57.

4. Matt. 18:3.

5. John 3:3–4.

6. Quoted by Peter Thomas Rohrback, *The Search for Saint Therese* (Garden City, NY: Hanover House, 1961), 167.

7. Paul D. Meier, *Christian Child-Rearing and Personality Development* (Grand Rapids: Baker Book House, 1978), 49.

8. Karl Rahner, *Theological Investigations*, vol. IV, trans. David Bourke (New York: Crossroad, Seabury Press, 1977), 33–50.

9. Ps. 139:15–16.

10. Gal. 1:15.

11. Rom. 8:15.

12. See the excellent meditations of Hans Urs von Balthasar, *Unless You Become Like This Child,* trans. Erasmo Leiva-Merikakis (San Francisco: Ignatius Press, 1991).

13. Alice Miller, *The Drama of the Gifted Child*, trans. Ruth Ward (New York: Basic Books, 1981), 3.

14. Meier, 49–79.

15. Miller, 93.

16. Ibid., 94.

17. Ibid., 96.

18. See the psychoanalytical study of Nietzsche in Alice Miller, *The Untouched Key* (New York: Doubleday, Anchor Books, 1990), 71–134.

19. Alice Miller, *For Your Own Good: Hidden Cruelty in Child-Rearing and the Roots of Violence*, trans. Hildegarde and Hunter Hannum (New York: Farrar, Straus, & Giroux, 1984), 162–197.

20. John Bowlby, *Child Care and the Growth of Love* (Harmondsworth, UK: Penguin Books, 1963), 182.

21. Nicholas Lehmann, "The Vogue of Childhood Misery," *The Atlantic* vol. 269, no. 3 (March 1992), 119–124; Dennis B. Guernsey, *The Family Covenant* (Elgin, IL: David C. Cook, 1984), 34–43; James Houston, *In Pursuit of Happiness* (Oxford: Lion, 1990), 85–92.

22. Ps. 139:1–4.

23. Matt. 18:10, 6.

24. John 5:19, 8:29.

25. Matt. 28:19.

26. Ps. 27:4.

27. Walter of Hilton, *Toward the Perfection of Love,* trans. David Jeffreys (Portland, OR: Multnomah Press, 1988).

28. Takeo Doi, *The Anatomy of Dependence*, trans. John Bester (Tokyo, New York and San Francisco: Kodansha International, 1973).

29. Ibid., 152.

30. Dietrich Bonhoeffer, *Ethics* (New York: Macmillan, 1964).

31. See survey of literature on shame in Robert Karen, "Shame," *The Atlantic Monthly* vol. 269, no. 2 (February 1992): 40–70.

32. Ps. 73:25–26.